The Bible According to Tintoretto

A biblical and theological guide to Jacopo Tintoretto's paintings at the Scuola Grande di San Rocco

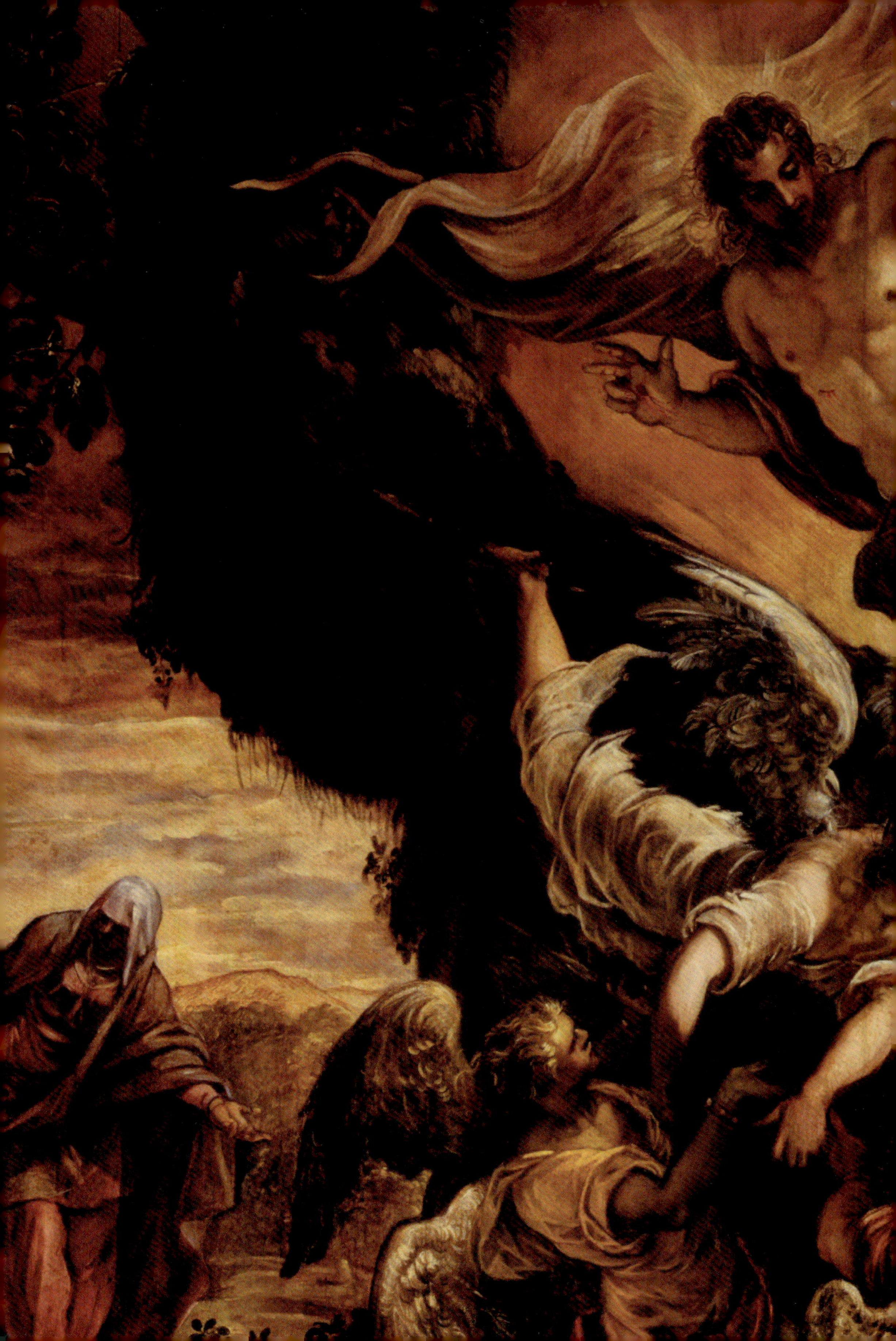

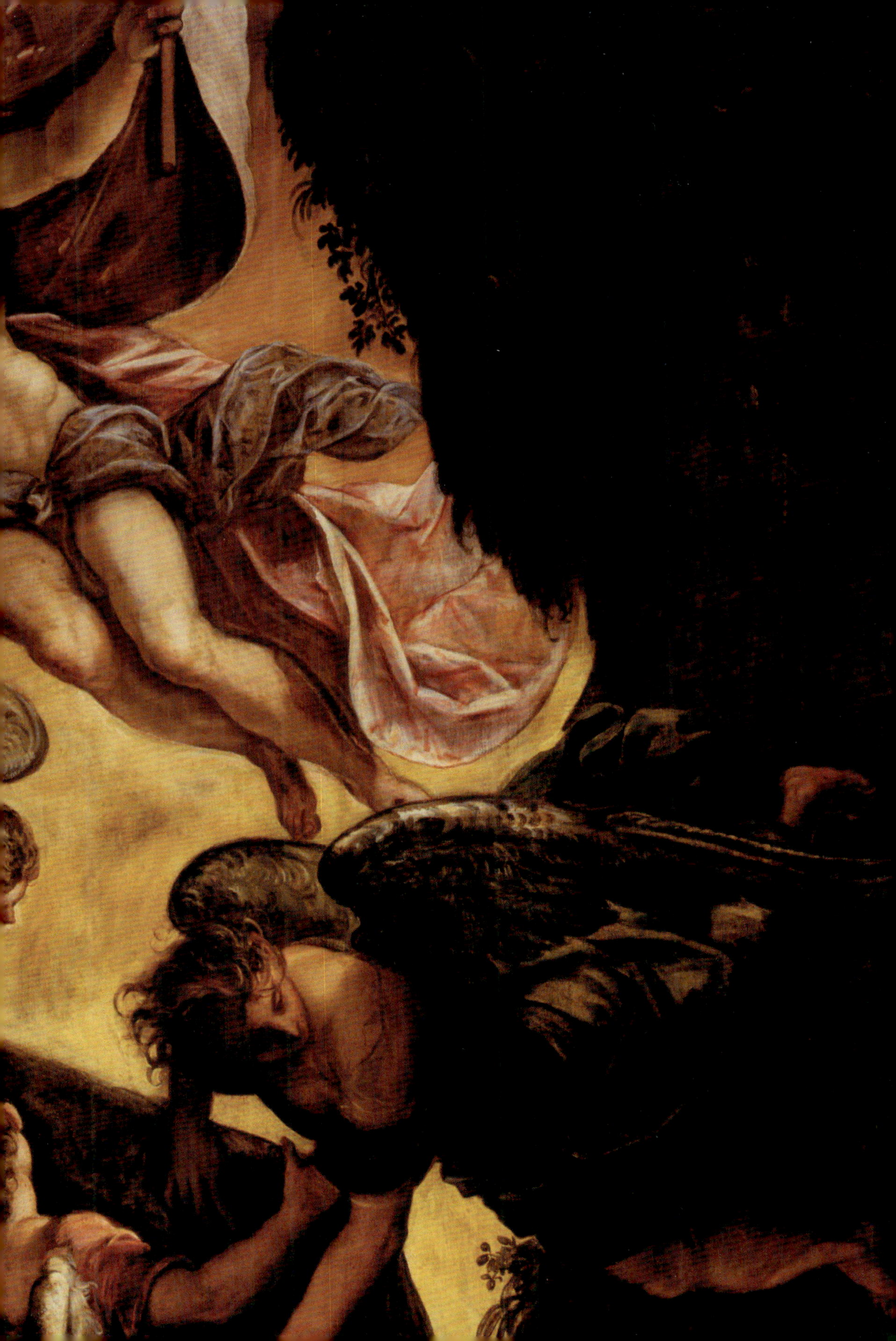

Ester Brunet

The Bible According to Tintoretto

A biblical and theological guide to Jacopo Tintoretto's paintings at the Scuola Grande di San Rocco

STUDIUM GENERALE MARCIANUM VENETIIS

MARCIANUM PRESS

This volume was produced with the contribution
of the "Lorenzo Biasin" grant and the
Scuola Grande di San Rocco

On the cover:
Jacopo Tintoretto, *Agony in the Garden,*
Scuola Grande di San Rocco, Venezia

On the back cover:
Jacopo Tintoretto, *Ecce Homo*,
Scuola Grande di San Rocco, Venezia

The photographs of Tintoretto's canvases were taken by Cameraphoto Arte di Venezia and published with the kind permission of the Scuola Grande di San Rocco.

Paging and graphics:
Anna Maria Mendola

Translated from the Italian by
Sergei Tseytlin

ISBN 978-88-6512-139-9

Index

Presentation

The work of Jacopo Tintoretto, one of the giants of Venetian painting, has always been the object of attention, study and in-depth examination, as well as of dispute and mockery. A series of writings – starting with quotations from Giorgio Vasari and Carlo Ridolfi and ending with the recent studies produced by Francesco Valcanover and Astrid Zenkert – allow us to grasp the quality and the message in his vast collection of oil paintings. The innovations in the fields of composition, perspective, light, color, movement and technique do not only indicate the mutation of figurative expression, which matured through his art in Late Renaissance Venice, but also bear witness to the new and dramatic representation of the human being that would go on to distinguish the Baroque era.

This maturation of Tintoretto's style, as a sign of existential anxiety, can especially be seen in the narrative cycle that covers the walls and ceilings of the Scuola Grande di San Rocco, where dozens of ***"teleri"*** (canvases) created in what seems to have been a period of solitude and compulsive work lasting more than twenty years (1564-1587), depict the episodes of the Old and New Testaments. It is a thorough illustration of biblical events, unique in its completeness, stateliness and systematic nature, rendered opportune by the regulations promulgated earlier by the Council of Trent with the aim of giving a unitary structure to the theological foundations of the Roman Catholic Church.

These are the causes and reasons that determined the cycle's composition and that gave it homogeneity and coherence. The exegetic depth and the symbolic precision of the paintings, arranged in cinematic sequence on the walls of the Scuola, imply that the artist may have been assisted by a ***"consultant"***.

Though Benedetto Croce's methodology in the field of art criticism, which throughout the 1900s stressed the aesthetic approach, ended in eclipsing the content and nexus of an artwork, especially the religious ones, in the case of the San Rocco cycle it was precisely the content and nexus that were fundamental for both the client, a charity confraternity, and the painter, a profound believer. In fact, to understand the dramatic sequence of the biblical episodes depicted by Jacopo Tintoretto's feverish brushstroke at the Scuola Grande di San Rocco, it was considered sufficient to allude to the tempestuous political climate of the second half of the 16th century in Venice, Italy and Europe in general, which were ravaged by plagues, famines, interdicts, wars (with the Protestants, the Ottomans and other kingdoms and

empires), as well as to the economic and social decadence of the Venetian Republic.
The relationship between form and content, an old dilemma, was crucial in the history of figurative expression in the great monotheistic religions, which feared idolatry and therefore tended to prohibit figuration, confining it to calligraphy, geometry, decoration, or even limiting its typological development, as in the case of the Byzantine icons after the iconoclastic interdiction had been overcome.
It is the Catholic Church, instead, that turns to the language of images with the intention of promoting the integration of story and figure, aware that the word, limited by linguistic babel and alphabetic diversity, can find its universal complement only in form, which is comprehensible directly, even without any particular cultural mediation.
From the fresco narration, such as the "Biblia pauperum (Pauper's Bible)", which has existed for many centuries on the walls of sacred buildings, we move on, through the Renaissance, to a greater complexity in the representation, which, after the Council of Trent, was given the task to evoke sentiments, to involve the spectator, to reproduce the reality of the moment.
This is the revolution, in its religious and figurative implications, that was created by the artists of the 16th century.
Although Tintoretto often contextualizes the biblical story in historical events, it does not mean that his great compositions will not dedicate a main scene to Moses, the Prophets or Christ himself. For they are key figures of the salvation. They are the ultimate protagonists.
The current volume wishes to fill the gap between form and content, that is, to reconstruct, even if only through mere divulgation, the meaning of the single paintings and to reestablish their relationship, emphasizing the pictures' message and reproducing, if possible, the original texts that inspired them.
The Renaissance city that Tintoretto evokes becomes a home for the entire biblical itinerary, from Genesis to the Resurrection. The Mysteries and the Prophecies, just as the Truth and the Dogmas, thus constitute the essence of the pictorial representation, even within the context of the contemporary ***"Babel".***
This approach, largely unusual and innovative, engendered unexpected discoveries and unthought-of interpretations, which were made possible not only through textual research in the theological field, but also by reinterpreting the epoch's cultural crises,

such as the rise of Protestantism, the conflict with the Islamic world, the relationship with Judaism, as well as the problematic acceptance of classicism as a cultural and formal model.
Furthermore, the theme of reality, or rather the ***"truth"*** in the depiction, emerges as an ethical and figurative force, since it helps to recompose the mannerist laceration that had separated form from content.
This work, made possible through the ***"Lorenzo Biasin"*** grant awarded to Ester Brunet and the collaboration between the ***Studium Generale Marcianum*** and the ***Scuola Grande di San Rocco***, presents a more complete, captivating and astonishing Tintoretto, not only as an illustrious painter but also as a man of his time, with all the anxieties, doubts and anguish that his epoch experienced.
His interpretation of biblical events, though rigorous from the orthodox perspective, appears dramatic and unsettling. In a way it is relevant also to our time, if it is possible to say that the present is characterized by doubt, suffering and endless searching for the meaning of existence.
These pages can help interpret the great "teleri" in a new light, in one of literal content, one that will offer the contemplation of the pictorial masterpieces the intelligence of their spiritual intention.
Jacopo Tintoretto deserved this interpretation.

Scuola Grande di San Rocco
Architect Franco Posocco
Guardian Grando

Studium Generale Marcianum
Professor Brian E. Ferme
Rector

Venice, January 2012

Introduction

Tintoretto in San Rocco: general inspirational themes

The Scuola di San Rocco, founded in 1478, was erected with the aim of helping the needy, particularly the sick during epidemics. The Confraternity was therefore a center of assistance and devotion that managed extensive patrimonies destined to supporting the poor. Jacopo Tintoretto, who soon became a brother, worked there for an exceptionally long period of time: almost 25 years. Although the painter did not dedicate the entire cycle to the history of the patron saint, but only a few paintings, what happened to Roch of Montpellier, whose remains the church possesses, is an essential starting point for understanding the comprehensive meaning of the decoration. According to pious devotion, this medieval saint was born with a vermilion cross impressed on his chest; having become a Franciscan tertiary at the death of his rich parents, after having given all his belongings to the poor, he moved to Rome and helped and miraculously healed many plague victims with the sign of the cross. It is precisely the cross, as a way to salvation and origin of the sacraments, that is the main theme in the two halls of the first floor: the Sala dell'Albergo, which is decorated with a cycle dedicated to the *Passion* of Christ, culminating in the giant **Crucifixion** that covers the entire front wall of the entrance; and of the Sala Superiore, whose ceiling's main *telero,* dominating the room's decorative pattern, shows the biblical episode of the **Brazen Serpent**, which prefigures the crucifixion.

The liberation from death, which occurs thanks to the redeeming sacrifice of Christ, is attainable for man through the sacraments and the cross, or rather by means of a life consecrated to the emulation of Christ, just like that of St. Roch, who, on the central oval of the Sala dell'Albergo's ceiling, experiences the beatific vision of God.

A complex and stratified view of the salvational meaning of the *sacraments*, Eucharistic and Baptismal, in relation to the Easter of Christ, is presented by Tintoretto on the walls and ceiling of the Sala Superiore, in observance of the decrees passed by the Council of Trent (1545-1563), which clarified the Catholic doctrine on the sacraments after it was challenged by the Protestant Reformation Churches. Here the painter shows the impressive *History of Salvation* according to a time that is no longer the historically linear one: the events of the Old and New Testaments that the cycle connects, the first being prefigurations of the second, are not arranged chronologically, but rather reflect the di-

mension of the sacrament as an efficacious and always present salvational sign.
Tintoretto returns to the story in order to show the mystery of the incarnation, of the human and earthly body of the Son of God: in fact, a cycle dedicated to the Lord's infancy decorates the walls of the Sala Terrena and shows a prelude to the public mission of Jesus, who is the protagonist of the halls on the upper floor. The key role of *Mary* as interpreter and custodian of the mysteries related to Christ's infancy unveils the real meaning of this prelude, which should actually be considered as an interlude, continuously suspended between prophecy, fulfillment and prefiguration of future events, especially Easter. The fantastical and poetic atmosphere, which above all envelops the **Flight into Egypt** and the two vertical panels to the sides of the altar, emphasizes this suspended and contemplative dimension.

The guide's characteristics and specifics

More than one scholar has considered Tintoretto's production at the Scuola Grande di San Rocco, and not without reason, not only one of the richest pictorial cycles of the 16th century and of all time, but also one of the best organized and most complex depicted theological "discourses".
However, apart from some special cases, there have not been many scholars who approached Tintoretto's work from a historical-theological point of view. Therefore, first and foremost the present book offers a close examination of the studies carried out from this perspective, aimed at collecting, organizing and completing the most successful results. The reader will not find a formal method of looking into the paintings, nor any profound stylistic analysis – aspects that have already been dealt with in other visitor guides, such as Francesco Valcanover's book, which has been reprinted many times. The present work intends to be a deft, and yet accurate, text explaining the elements of faith and devotion found in the *teleri* to a large public.
The guide follows the paintings' chronological order: it begins with the Sala dell'Albergo, the farthest from the entrance (to reach it the visitor must pass through the Sala Terrena and the Sala Superiore) but the first to be painted by Tintoretto (1564-1567); it continues with the Sala Superiore (1576-1581; with an altarpiece from 1588), for which it offers various itineraries; and it ends with the Sala Terrena, which Tintoretto decorated, with

the help of his workshop, between 1581 and 1584. The visitor will then have to proceed along a backward itinerary, one that is contrary to the direction determined by the Scuola's architecture, but one that is indispensable in order to better understand the decoration's internal meaning and the expression on the whole.
After a brief introduction of each section, which contextualizes the cycles and highlights the general themes, some specific notes are dedicated to the paintings. Each note is composed of a citation in the actual language of the biblical passage inspiring the painting, followed by a comment. As can be seen from the plans placed at the beginning of each section, if we also count the monochromes on the Sala Superiore's ceiling (repainted in the 18th century on the original Tintoretto ones), there are about seventy Tintoretto paintings. Since the selection process was inevitable, the paintings with the least biblical and theological importance were partially included in the notes explaining the most prominent paintings. Some choices, such as the one to explain, at the expense of the more famous works, *teleri* like the **Circumcision** in the Sala Terrena or the **Probatic Pool** in the Sala Superiore, both seldom taken into account by artistic historiography (the first, because it was definitely painted by Jacopo's son, Domenico; the second, due to heavy reworking done as a result of floods), were based on the priority to have the decoration's theological meaning stand out. Therefore, paintings that are formally less remarkable or more unfortunate than others offer some significant and original solutions.

INDICATIONS:

The black numbers in square parentheses – e.g. **[5]** – refer to the plans located in the introductive part of each section.

The caption in bold italics "note" followed by a number – e.g. ***(note 5)*** – refers to the numbered notes.

The caption in bold blue italics "fig." followed by a number – e.g. ***(fig. 5)*** – refers to the images published in the text.

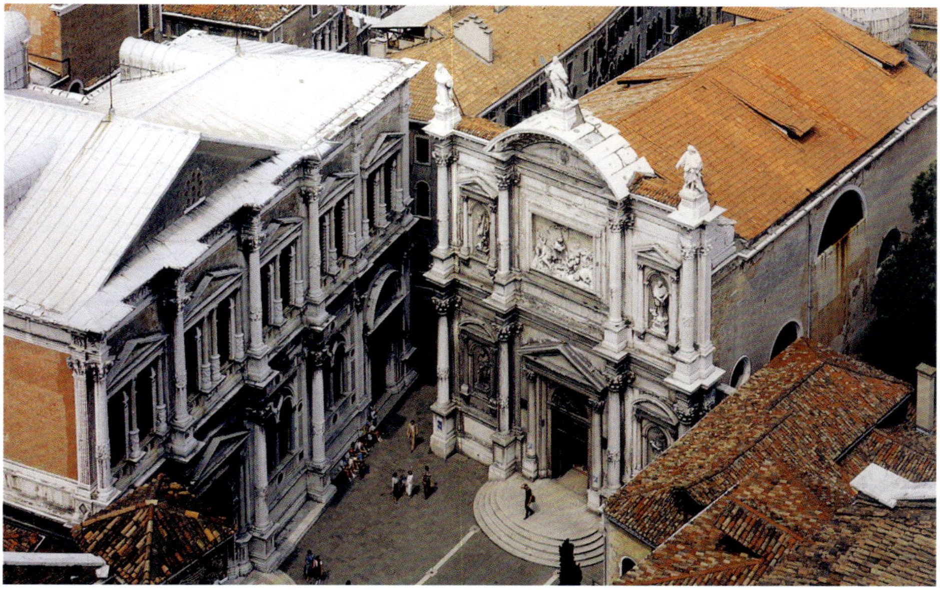

Fig. 1 - The Scuola Grande and the Church of San Rocco

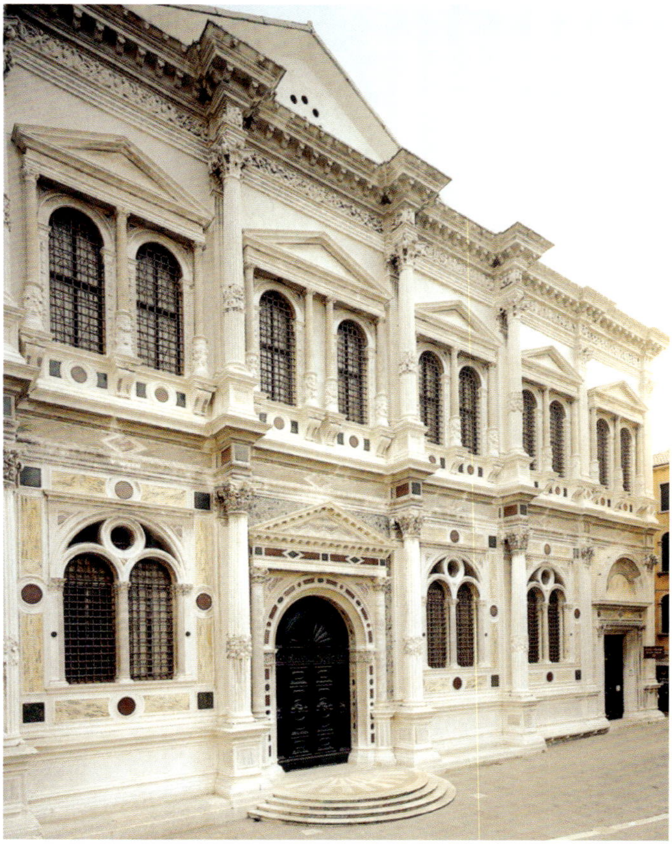

Fig. 2 - The façade of the Scuola Grande

The Sala dell'Albergo

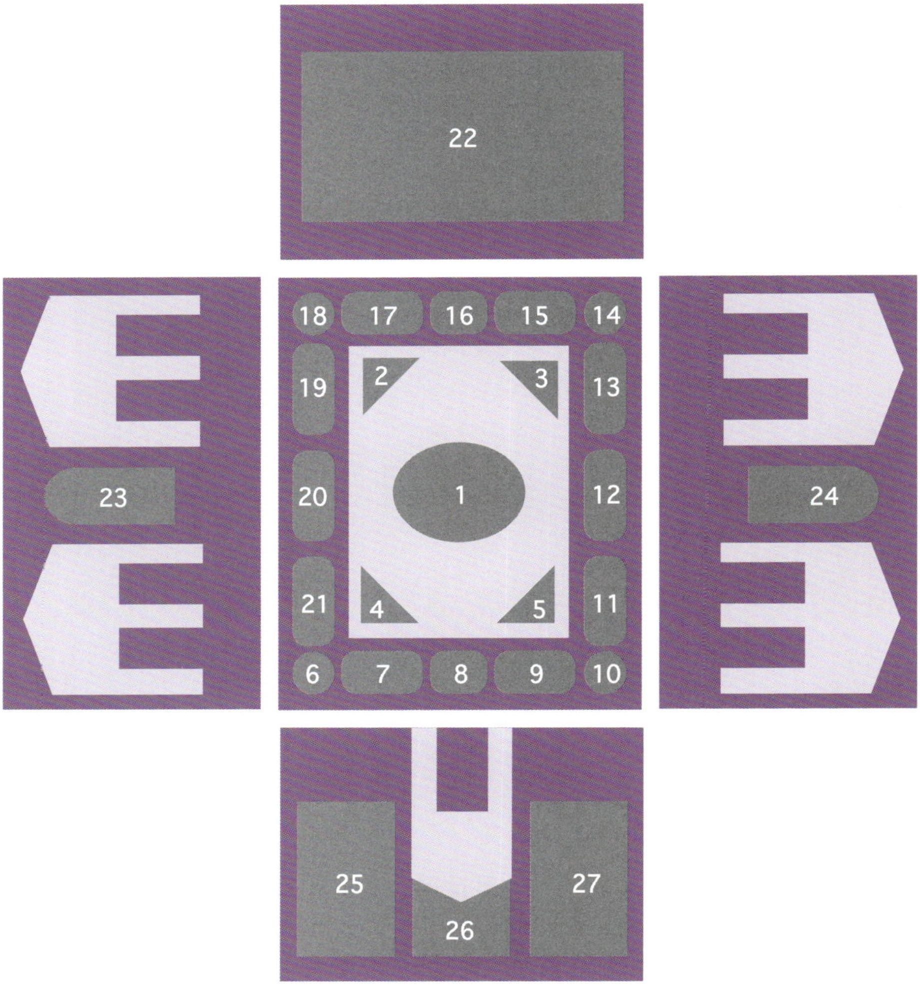

Ceiling

1. St. Roch in Glory
2-5. Putti
6. Winter
7. Female figure (Humility?)
8. Happiness
9. Female figure (Patience?)
10. Autumn
11. Goodness
12. Allegory of the Scuola di San Teodoro
13. Faith
14. Summer
15. Allegory of the Scuola di San Giovanni Evangelista
16. Allegory of the Scuola della Misericordia
17. Allegory of the Scuola di San Marco
18. Spring
19. Truth
20. Allegory of the Scuola della Carità
21. Liberality

Walls

22. Crucifixion
23. Prophet
24. Prophet
25. Christ before Pilate
26. Ecce Homo
27. Ascent to Calvary

This hall, built for the meetings of the Confraternity's governing body, was decorated by Tintoretto between 1564 and 1567. It is the artist's first commission, which begins the cycle from the ceiling's central oval – **St. Roch in Glory [1]**, ***(note 1),*** continues with the other sections, then with the giant **Crucifixion [22]** ***(note 2)*** on the wall in front of the entrance and ends with the paintings on the other walls.

Art historians have been wondering about the reason behind the theme's selection. In the other Scuole this hall was usually decorated with cycles that had as their subject matter the life of the Confraternity's patron, while this one is adorned with the depiction of the Passion of Christ. However, if we consider the fact that the Sala dell'Albergo was used for directors meeting to make decisions regarding the

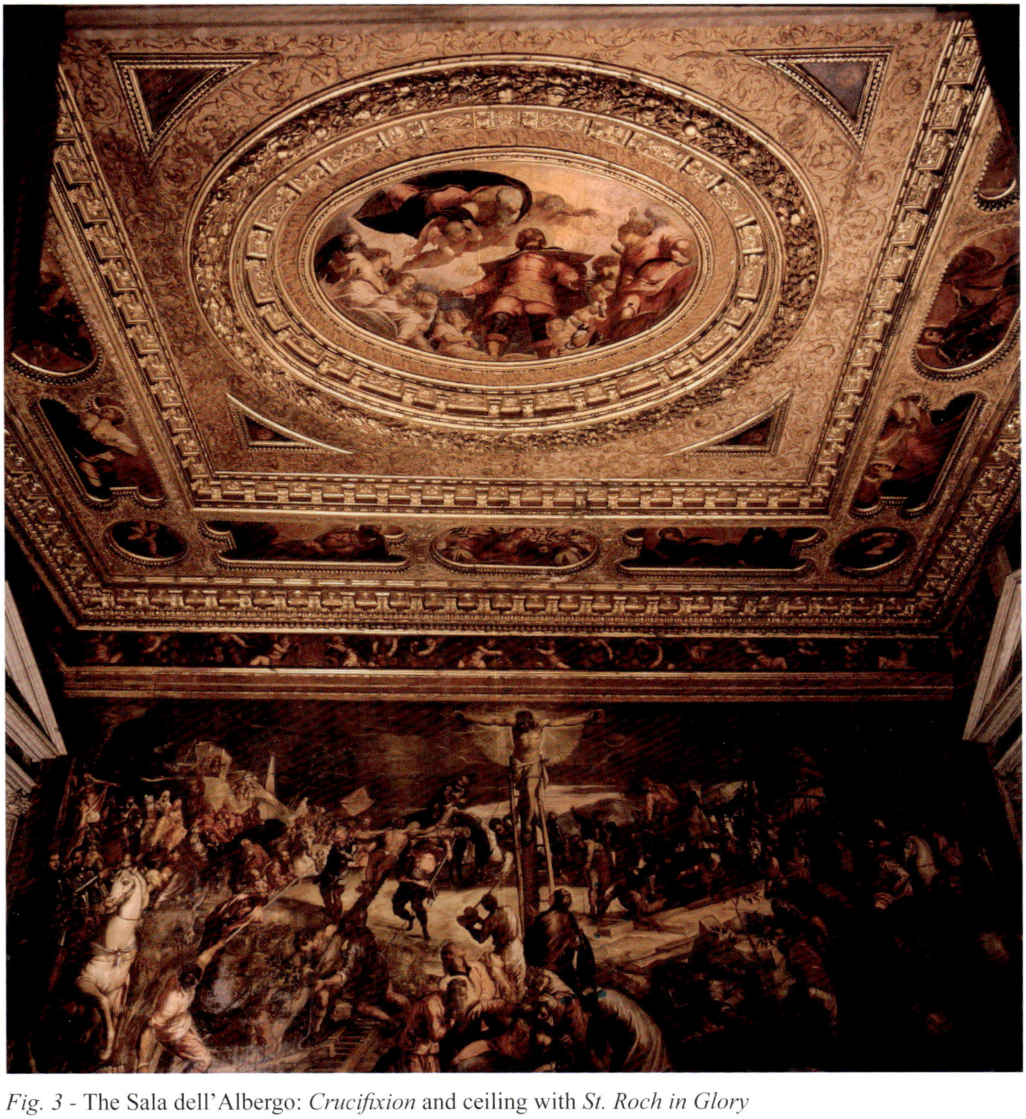

Fig. 3 - The Sala dell'Albergo: *Crucifixion* and ceiling with *St. Roch in Glory*

distribution of alms, the theme of God's love for man, manifested through the supreme sacrifice of his Son, is particularly appropriate and goes to the heart of the Christian message, being an essential foundation for any holy life. The charity that the brothers had as a model was therefore that of Christ, the same charity that inspired the patron St. Roch in his incessant assistance to the sick and needy, right up to his own self-sacrifice.

The Sala dell'Albergo was the Scuola's directive and operative center. It is here that the *Guardian grando* and his governmental colleagues gave audience. It was correctly observed that the needy, entering through the main entrance, if looked upon from the high-backed chairs on which the top Confraternity officials sat (the so-called *Banca*), presented themselves in harmony with the suffering Christ from **Ecce Homo [26]** ***(note 4)*** and immediately glanced at the heads of the Scuola, sitting directly below the **Crucifixion**. Christ therefore becomes a complete model, an object and subject of love; both the needy and the rescuers identify with him.

It should not be forgotten, as has recently been brought to light, that the Albergo, with its "Scrigni" (caskets), was also the place that conserved the Scuola's most precious relics, exhibited on occasion of St. Roch's feast day. These relics are connected to the Passion of the Lord: a thorn from the crown and a splinter from the cross. The Church of St. Roch also possessed the famous and greatly miraculous **Christ carrying the Cross** ***(fig. 4)***, along with a venerated processional wooden crucifix from the 15th century.

The cross was particularly precious, for hagiographic reasons, for the brothers of this Scuola Grande. It has already been mentioned how the cross, as a sign of health and salvation, was a determining factor in the saint's life (see p. 12).

The cross as a way to a healthy body and soul, the passion as the mystery of salvation. This is the thematic kernel that is grasped when contemplating the **Brazen Serpent** ***(note 6)*** located at the center of the Sala Superiore's ceiling in a manner as to connect the decorations of the two rooms.

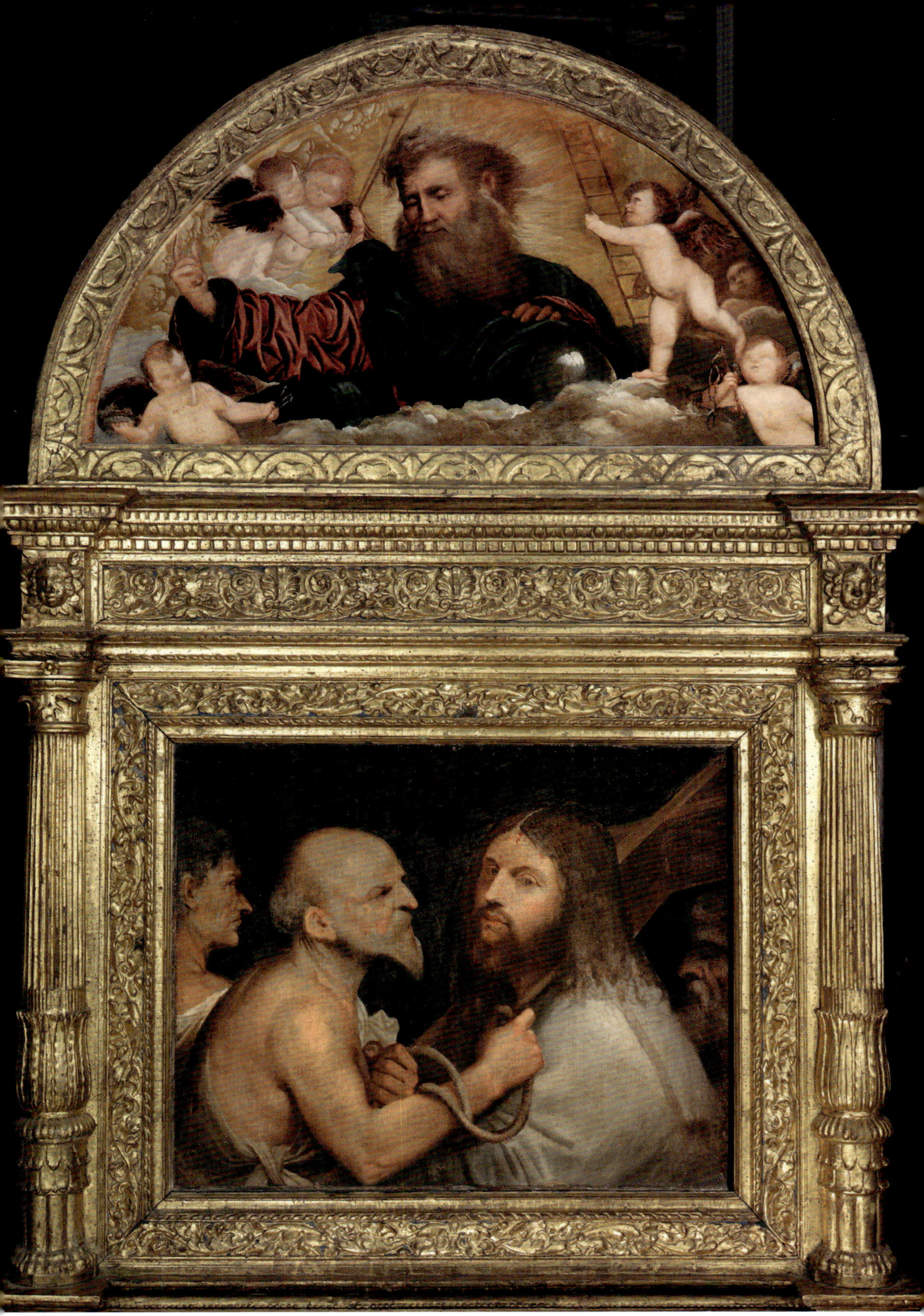

Fig. 4 - Giorgione, *Christ carrying the Cross,* 1508-1510, Sala Superiore (in the lunette: Titian, *The Eternal Father with angels*)

1. CEILING

The ceiling was the first part to be decorated by Tintoretto at the Scuola. The first painting to be created was the central oval with the scene of **St. Roch in Glory [1]** ***(fig. 5)***. Here we see the saint who, surrounded by angels from different orders, is in the heart of the beatific vision: God is in fact leaning out towards Roch, their heads are close, the contemplation is face to face. In this manner Tintoretto is expressing the complete and eternal communion with the Father that the saint experiences after death. Three putti carry God as a sign of the Trinity. It is in the wide embrace with which the Eternal Father encircles the three angelic figures, an image that calls to mind the open arms of Christ on the cross (see ***note 2***), that lies the greatest mystery of the Christian Faith: that of God who, precisely because He is love, is one and triune at the same time.

In the four circles at the top of the frame **[6, 10, 14, 18]** we find the putti that represent the four seasons ***(fig. 6),*** while in the twelve sections that run along the sides there are the symbolic representations of the Scuole Grandi of Venice (of San Marco, accompanied by a lion; of San Giovanni Evangelista, with the eagle; of Santa Maria della Carità, who holds the children in her arms; of the Madonna della Misericordia, who welcomes the brothers covering them with her mantle, in accordance with typical iconography of San Teodoro, shown as a warrior) and seven allegorical figures.

Most of these figures have been identified without difficulties, either because

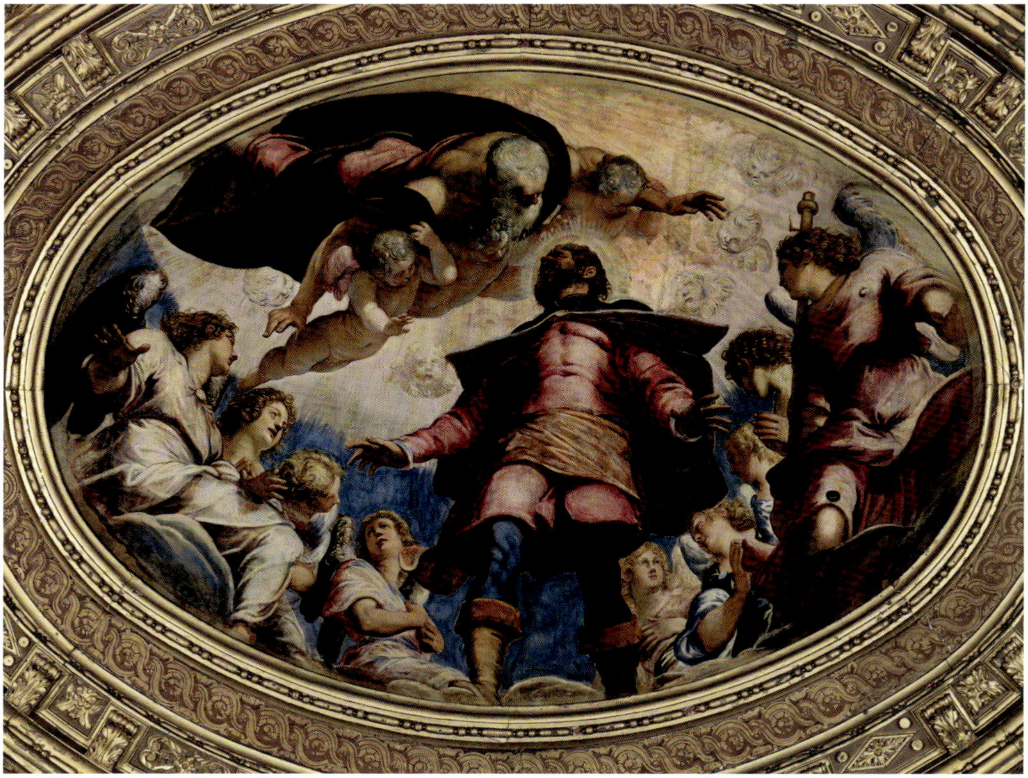

fig. 5 - St. Roch in Glory

they bear easily recognizable attributes or because the preliminary drawings on which they are based, drawings that were subtitled by Tintoretto himself, have been preserved. Recent restoration work has brought to light Tintoretto's handwriting on one of the teleri confirming the identity, previously hypothetical, of **Liberality [21]**.

A fascinating and convincing comprehensive interpretation of the ceiling helped not only to decipher all the figures, but also their relationship to one another and therefore to understand their meaning in light of a suggested theological and scriptural discourse, one whose idea they embody iconographically. According to this hypothesis, the figures would represent the main aspects of Christian love, as it is sung by St. Paul in the famous *Hymn*

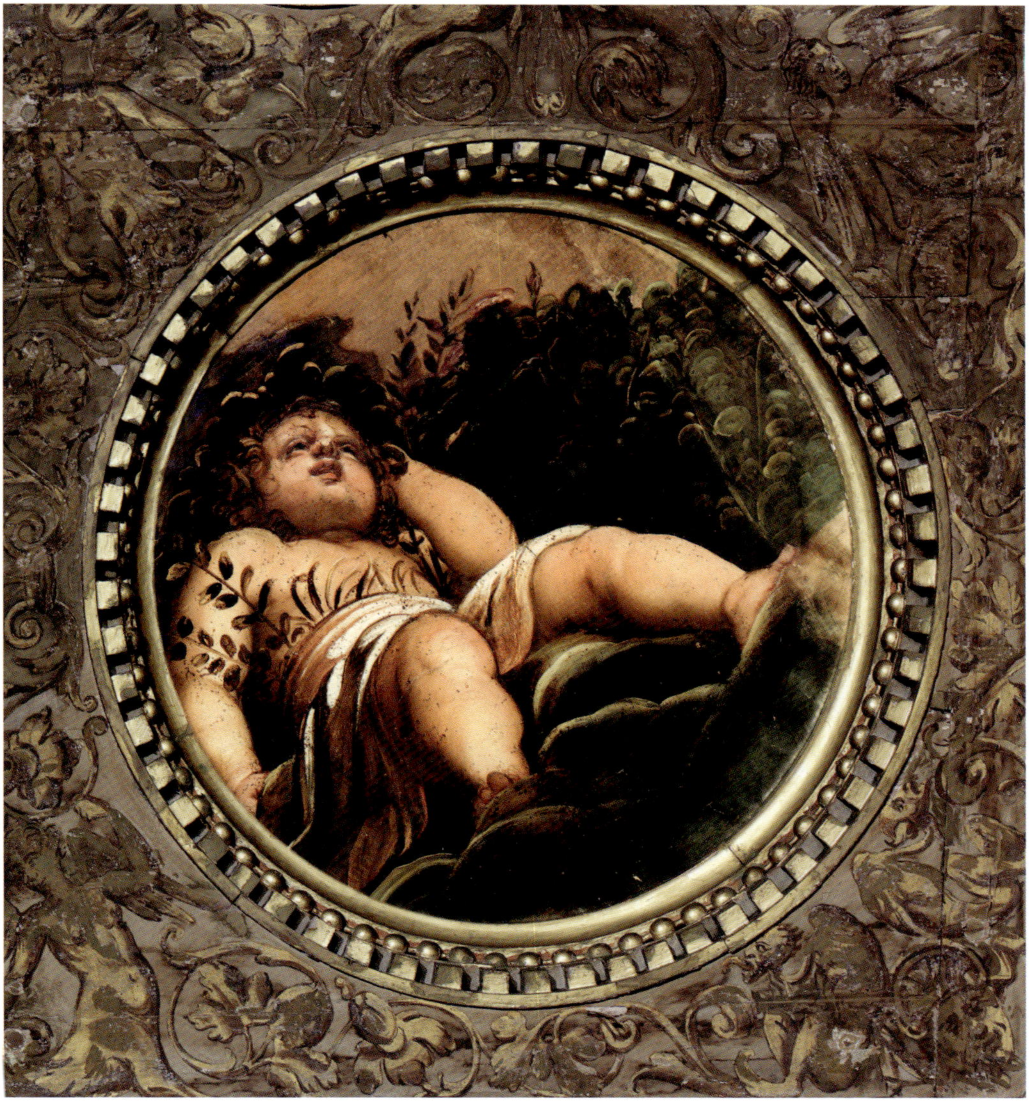

fig. 6 - Spring

to Charity in *1 Corinthians 13*: **Faith** ***(fig. 7)*** and **Truth [13, 19]**, which bares her breast as a sign of the unveiling but also as Charity in action, allude to the necessity of divine and brotherly love that must innervate them (see 1 Cor 13:2-3); the haloed figure that has her hands on her chest **[9]** ***(fig. 18)***, **Happiness [8]** ***(fig. 16)*** and the figure without a halo turned away from us **[7]** ***(fig. 14)*** represent several characteristics of Charity: patience, kindness, lack of envy, humility and respect; **Liberality [21]** is love *that does not seek its interest and does not lose its temper* (1 Cor 13:5); **Goodness [11]** ***(fig. 8)*** is love that does not hold a grudge and pursues

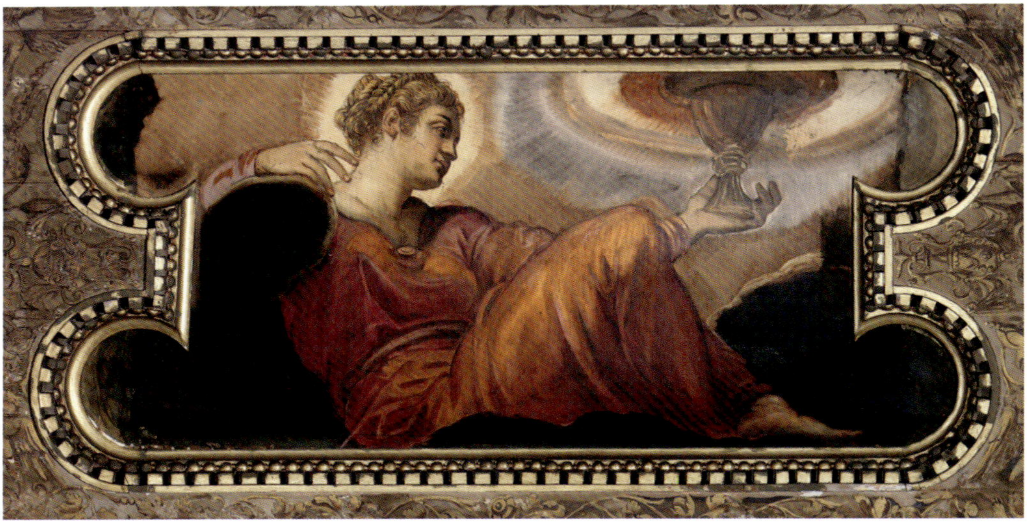

Fig. 7 - Faith. The allegorical figure is recognized thanks to the chalice, a typical attribute

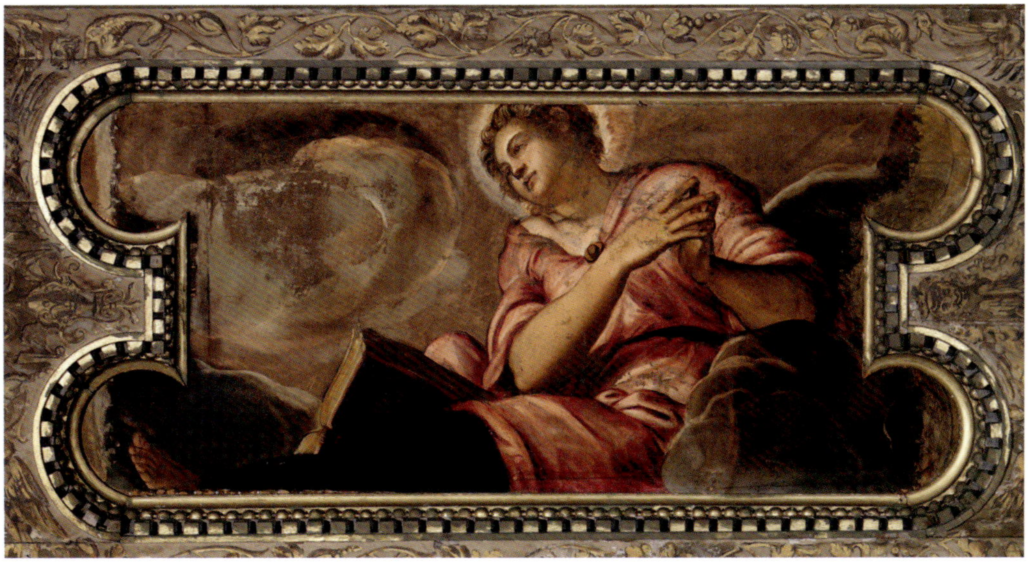

Fig. 8 - Goodness. Tintoretto depicts her with hands joined and an open book on her knees

justice (see 1 Cor 13:5-7).
The presence of the personifications of the Scuole Grandi invited all the brothers to understand and put into practice the Charity spoken of by St. Paul, working together for the common good.
In this context, while earthly time, represented by the putti as the four seasons, limits man to an indirect and partial knowledge of God (through allegory), the **St. Roch in Glory** shows the dimension that awaits every believer, that is, anyone who lives a charitable life, after death: the direct vision of Truth. In fact, in the *Hymn to Charity* it is written: *For now we see in a mirror, dimly, but then we will see face to face* (1 Cor 13:12). Therefore the two **Prophets [23, 24]** ***(fig. 9)***, located in an isolated position on the walls of the hall, are also contextualized correctly. The Passion of Christ, announced by the prophets of the Old Testament, is already a revealer of truth, transporting the believer to the field of divine reality; but it is still to be fulfilled, it is only a partial awareness that will eventually be followed by the last and perfect one: *For we know only in part, and we prophesy only in part; but when the complete comes, the partial will come to an end* (1 Cor 13:9-10).

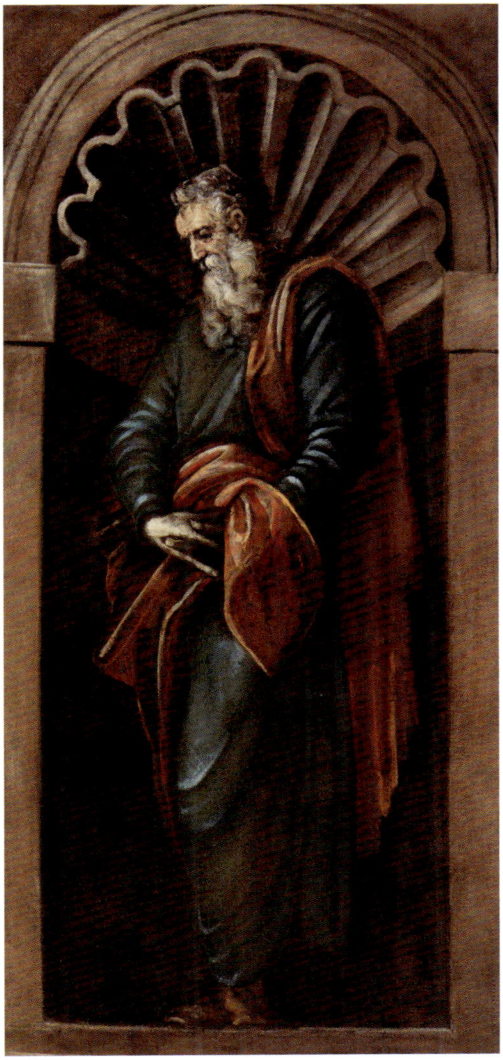

Fig. 9 - Prophet

2. CRUCIFIXION [22]

They took Jesus, therefore, and He went out, bearing His own cross, to the place called the Place of a Skull, which is called in Hebrew, Golgotha. There they crucified Him, and with Him two other men, one on either side, and Jesus in between. (...) Then the soldiers, when they had crucified Jesus, took His outer garments and made four parts, a part to every soldier and also the tunic. Now the tunic was seamless, woven in one piece. So they said to one another, "Let us not tear it, but cast lots for it, to decide whose it shall be;" This to fulfill the Scripture: "They divided my outer garments among them, and for my clothing they cast lots." Therefore the soldiers did these things. But standing by the cross of Jesus were His mother, and His mother's sister, Mary the wife of Clopas, and Mary Magdalene. When Jesus then saw His mother, and the disciple whom He loved standing nearby, He said to His mother, "Woman, behold, your son!" Then He said to the disciple, "Behold, your mother!" From that hour the disciple took her into his own household. After this, Jesus, knowing that all things had already been accomplished, to fulfill the Scripture, said, "I am thirsty." A jar full of vinegar was standing there; so they put a sponge full of the vinegar upon a branch of hyssop and brought it up to His mouth. Therefore when Jesus had received the vinegar, He said, "It is finished!" And He bowed His head and gave up His spirit. *(John 19:16-18.23-30)*

Entering the Sala dell'Albergo, the visitor's attention is immediately drawn to the figure of Christ, who, like a raised banner, is positioned at the center of the composition; the Crucifix stands out motionlessly, dominating the entire painting. All around a motley crowd has gathered, some people actively taking part, some just passively observing. While the Passion of Christ has come to an end, the other crucified men must still be raised. Tintoretto deploys in a single scene the various phases of the preparation and raising of the cross, which should be read starting from the death of Jesus, the culmination of the event on Golgotha. More generally, the entire passion cycle decorating the Sala dell'Albergo should be read starting from the crucifixion; only afterward will the visitor turn his gaze to the **Christ before Pilate,** the **Ecce Homo** and the **Ascent to Calvary [25-27]** ***(notes 3-5)***. The painter does not offer a

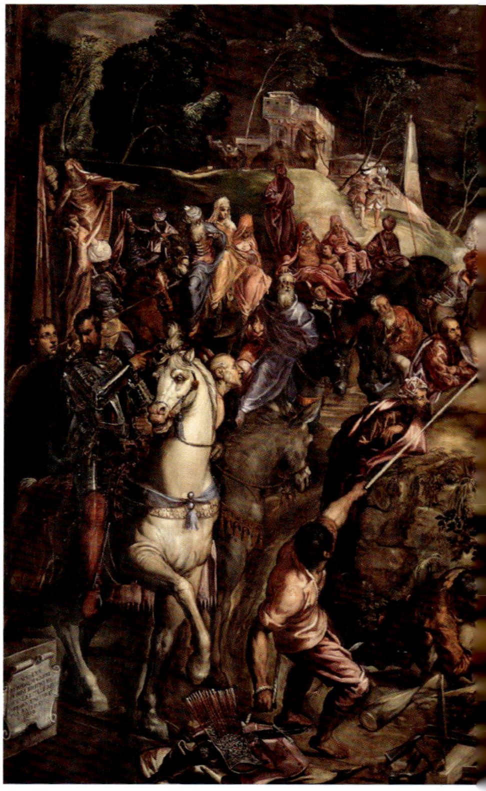

story but rather an itinerary for contemplating the passages of the Gospel, one that is projected out of the normal chronological sequence.

For Christ everything *is finished* (John 19:30): just after having said to Apostle John, who is still looking at him stupefied, "*Behold, your mother*," referring to Mary, and bowing his head, *gave up His spirit.* The Madonna, at the foot of the cross, is fainting from the pangs of a new birth ***(fig. 10)***, which, this time, contrary to the first one that occurred in joy, will occur in pain: *In the passion of the Son the soul of Mary was pierced with a sword, and that was the second birth, painful and full of every bitterness* (St. Anthony of Padua, *Sermons, First Sunday after Christmas*, § 14). This second birth, which Tintoretto depicts in the foreground, thus emphasizing its importance, certainly has an ecclesiological significance: Mary is the mother of the Church, the Christian community of which John, *the disciple who Jesus loved* (John 19:26), is the incarnation. It is in the new relationship of spiritual communion between Mary and John that Jesus sets up the original cell of the Christian people; his last breath is the gift of the Spirit that foresees the new era of the Church, given in full after his resurrection.

In the meantime Jesus is about to receive – or has already received – the sponge drenched in vinegar and down under Gol-

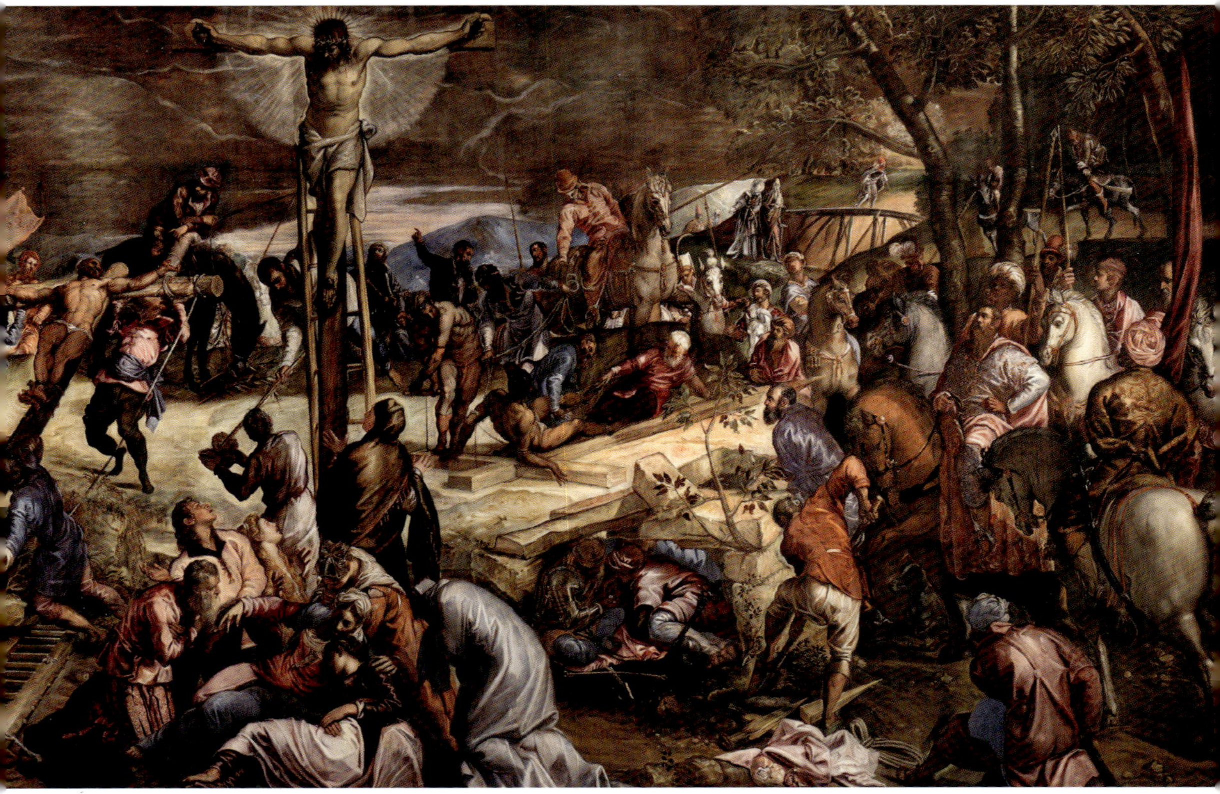

Crucifixion

gotha the soldiers are casting lots for Jesus' seamless tunic, a symbol of the unity of God's people.
The enormous halo composed of three luminous circles shining from the upper part of the Lord's body is related to the peculiar idea that John the Evangelist has of the Passion: though acting as a synthesis of the Scriptures, it is undeniable that Tintoretto's **Crucifixion** is particularly influenced by the Fourth Gospel. In fact, according to John, it is precisely the crucifixion, if perceived not as humiliation but as a majestic lifting, which is the event in which the divinity of the Son of God is demonstrated in all its glory. The halo that almost detaches him from the cross should be understood as a manifestation of divine glory, which is unleashed at the exact instant of his earthly death. The crucifixion is therefore a real *Theophany* (i.e., a Revelation of God on the perceptible plane): apart from the feet, which Christian literature has traditionally identified as the symbolic seat of his human nature, the Crucifix is placed higher than the horizon line, in a dimension that is already different from the mundane. Tintoretto, just like John, sees Christ raised on the cross like a king who towers over his people.
With the cross being the origin and culmination of the salvation story, all the events described by the prophets are collected here and the Crucified is revealed not only as a king, but also as a judge of the world: *now is the judgment of this world,* says Jesus speaking about his "lifting," or rather his death (John 12:31). Tintoretto reflects this Johannine concept of the cross by dividing the painting, as if it was almost the Final Judgment, between those who stand to the right of the Lord, that is, those who are open to the Revelation and will not be condemned, and those who, though able to see, still do not believe and therefore become enemies of the Truth. Actu-

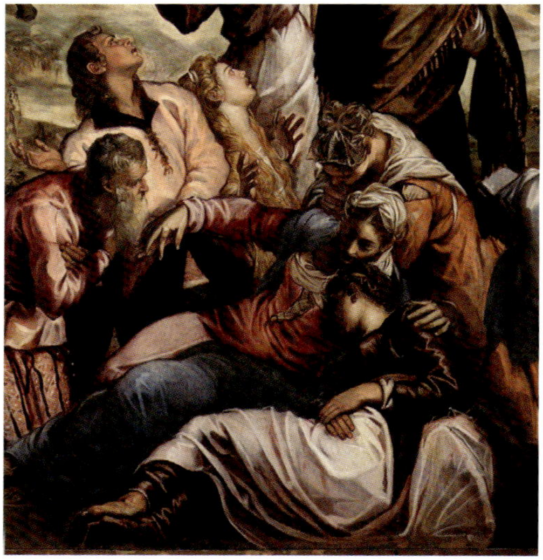

Fig. 10 - The Virgin is fainting from pains related to a new birth, which, with the gift of the Spirit through Jesus, will make her become the mother of the Church

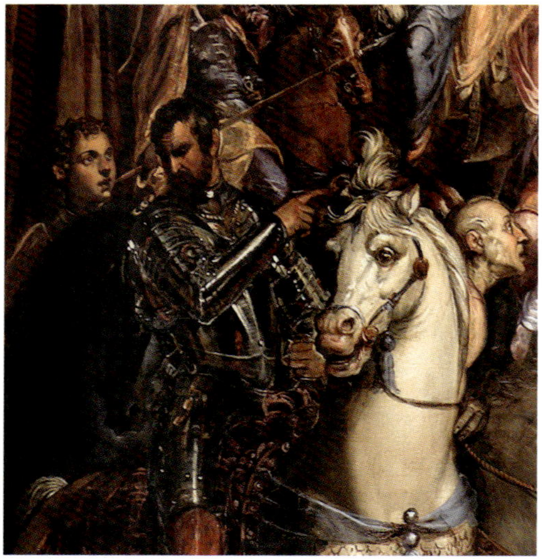

Fig. 11 - The Roman centurion's faith, here depicted, helps him see in the crucifixion not the execution of a blasphemer, but the glorification of the Son of God. His humble and respectful attitude expresses this awareness

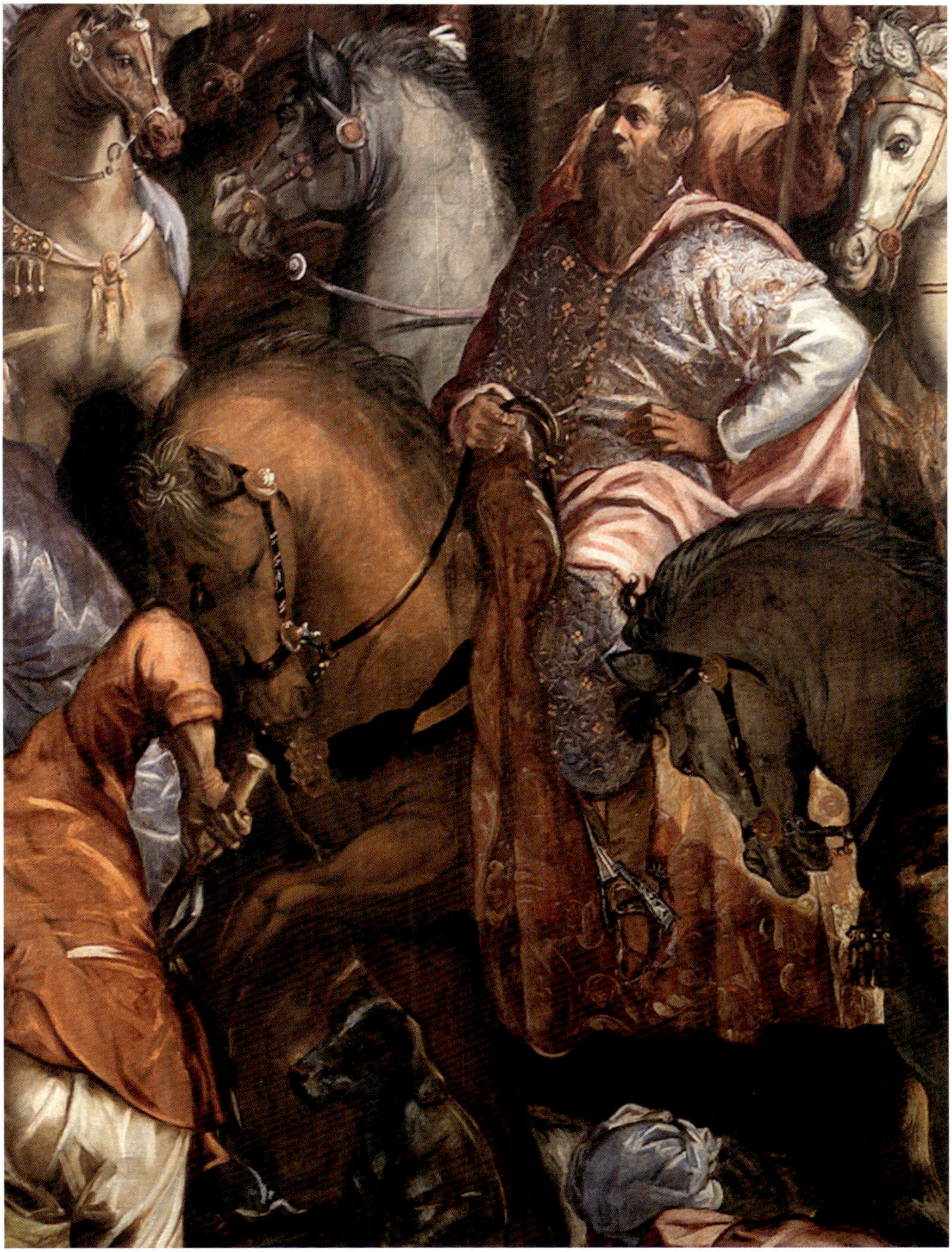

Fig. 12 - This arrogant horseman has Western features but is wearing rich Oriental clothing; he has been identified as Pilate. Under his horse a badger has a snake in his mouth, symbolizing Christ's triumph over sin

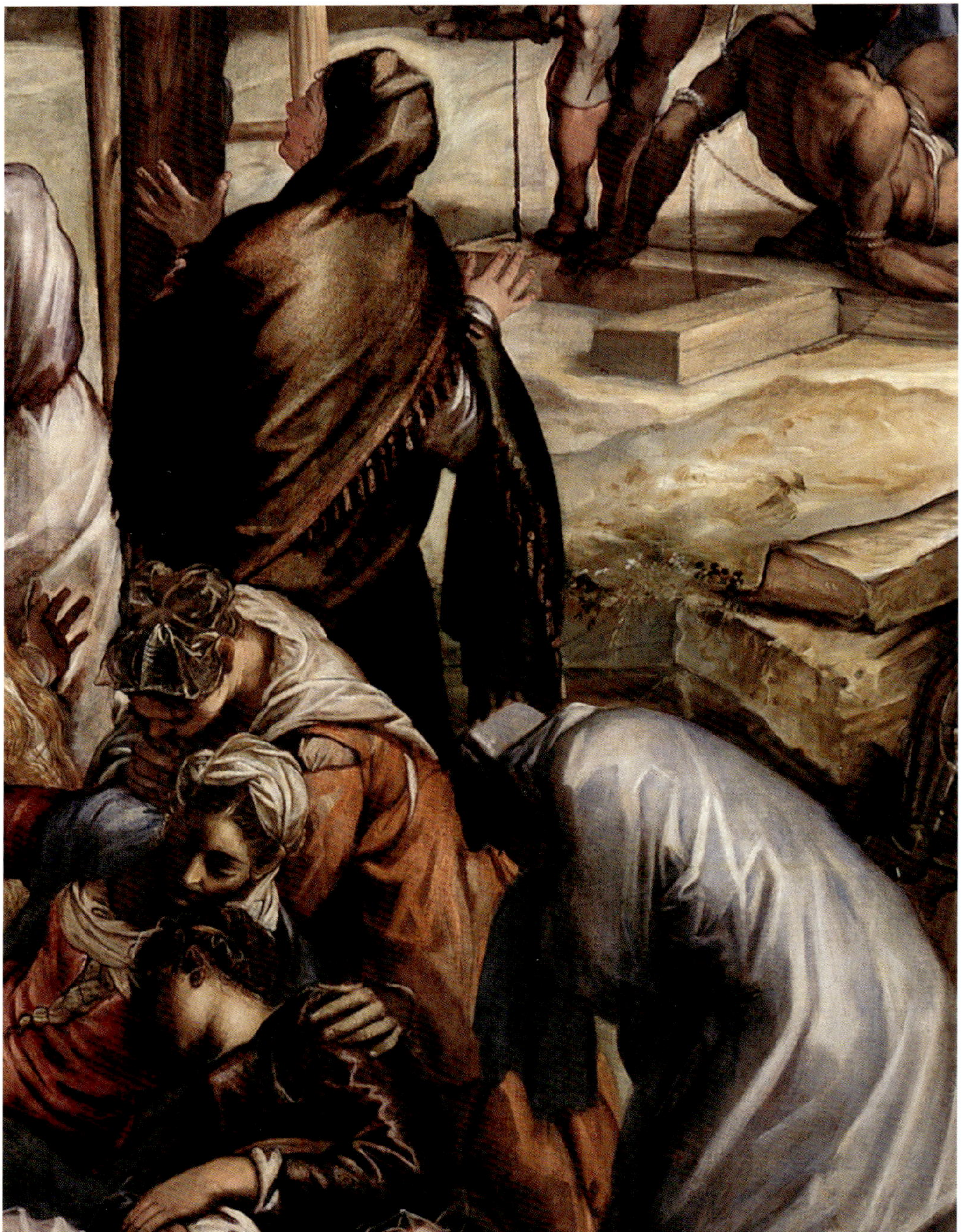

Fig. 13 - The passage from the Age of the Law to the Age of the Grace, which begins with the incarnation and culminates with the Lord's Easter, is allegorically depicted here through the personifications of Synagogue and Church: while the first is covering her face, referring to the medieval personifications that showed her blindfolded, the second, in mourning, is lamenting Christ, her Groom

ally, the distinction is not very clear (we find many positive characters on the right of the painting and vice versa), yet it is quite obvious for some key characters. To the left we see the good thief who, staring intensely at Christ, personifies the Lord's prophesy: *And I, if I am lifted up from the earth, will draw all peoples to myself* (John 12:32). On the right, instead, the bad thief turns his back to Christ and therefore remains anchored to the ground. In the foreground, on the left, the Roman centurion, with his head lowered in humility ***(fig. 11)*** and his weapons on the ground showing his good intentions, recognizes Christ as the Son of God (see Mark 15:39). Scholars have said that he, or the old penitent behind him, is the depiction of the *Guardian grando* of the era, Girolamo Rota, also remembered in the dedicatory inscription at the bottom left. On the opposite side, instead, an infidel Turk and a bearded man in Eastern clothing, probably Pilate ***(fig. 12),*** look with triumphant arrogance at the cross, personifying those who because of their pride and obtuseness fail to understand the true meaning of the event they are witnessing.

It has been hypothesized that in this *telero* Tintoretto is expressing some rather anti-Judaic sentiments, which for economic reasons had spread among the brothers of the Scuola. Here, indeed, he seems to be alluding to some issues from the polemic. From a theological point of view, it was required, for what regards Salvation, to recognize in Jesus Christ the one and only key for a correct understanding of the Old Covenant – a vision that can further be observed in the Sala Superiore, entirely built on the idea of the New Testament being the light shining on the events of the Old Testament, as well as the fulfillment of its promises (see p. 43-45). This perspective can be used, for example, to interpret the enigmatic scene that is taking place by the bridge on the right side, where a limping old aristocrat of the Temple, alluding to the patristic interpretation of Genesis 32:25-31, is pointing to the opposite direction of the Crucified, demonstrating that he is unable to recognize God's salvation. Tintoretto is also making use of the medieval tradition of depicting the Church and the Synagogue as two women at the foot of the cross: the first is wearing the black garments of mourning, lamenting Christ under the cross; the second covers her face in shame ***(fig. 13)***. The most proper Christological meaning of such allegories, which the Johannine reading of this crucifixion not only permits but also encourages, alludes to the passage – which in that precise moment is accomplished and almost anticipates the Pentecost – from the Age of the Law to the Age of the Church, coming about through the Spirit given by Christ and the birth of the new Christian community represented by Mary and John standing under the cross.

3. Christ Before Pilate [25]

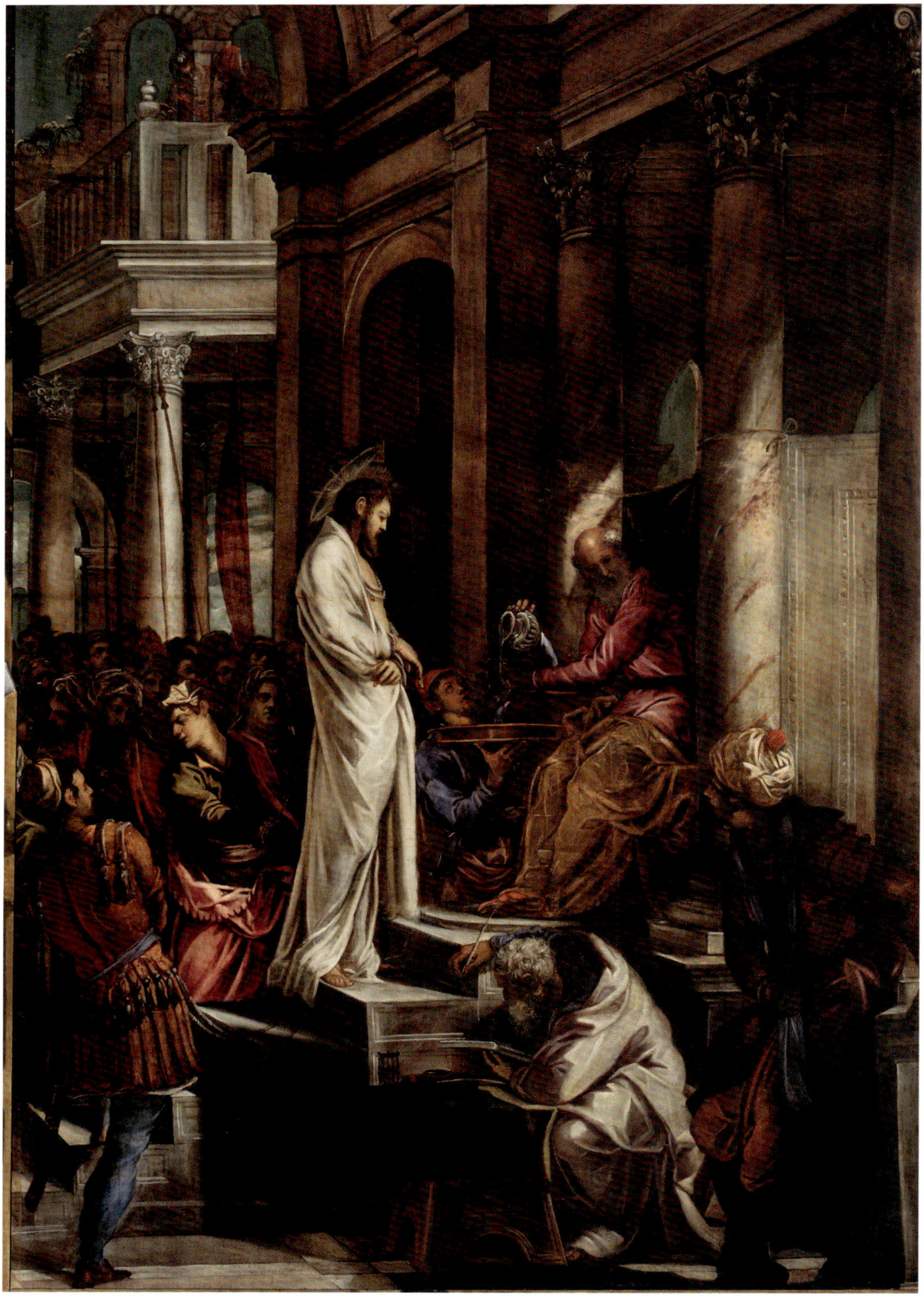

Christ before Pilate

Now Jesus stood before the governor. And the governor asked Him, saying, "Are You the King of the Jews?" Jesus said to him, "It is as you say." And while He was being accused by the chief priests and elders, He answered nothing. Then Pilate said to Him, "Do You not hear how many things they testify against You?" But He answered him not one word, so that the governor marveled greatly... When Pilate saw that he could not prevail at all, but rather that a tumult was rising, he took water and washed his hands before the multitude, saying, "I am innocent of the blood of this just Person. You see to it." And all the people answered and said, "His blood be on us and on our children." Then he released Barabbas to them; and when he had scourged Jesus, he delivered Him to be crucified.
(Mathew 27:11-14,24-26)

Tintoretto shows Christ wearing a snow-white mantle: it is this white robe that, according to Luke the Evangelist (23:11), in St. Gerome's translation, the tetrarch Herod orders him to wear after receiving him from Pilate because he was from Galilee and therefore subject to his jurisdiction. Disillusioned with Jesus for not working any miracles, Herod sends him back to Pilate after insulting him and dressing him in a white robe, which many Christian writers have referred to as the robe that at the time of Jesus was reserved for madmen.
It is precisely this paradox of Divine Wisdom judged as madness by human pride that becomes the painting's powerful thematic nucleus. Christ, brought before Pilate once more by two bullies who keep him tied at the hands and neck, embodies true knowledge, which comes from hu-

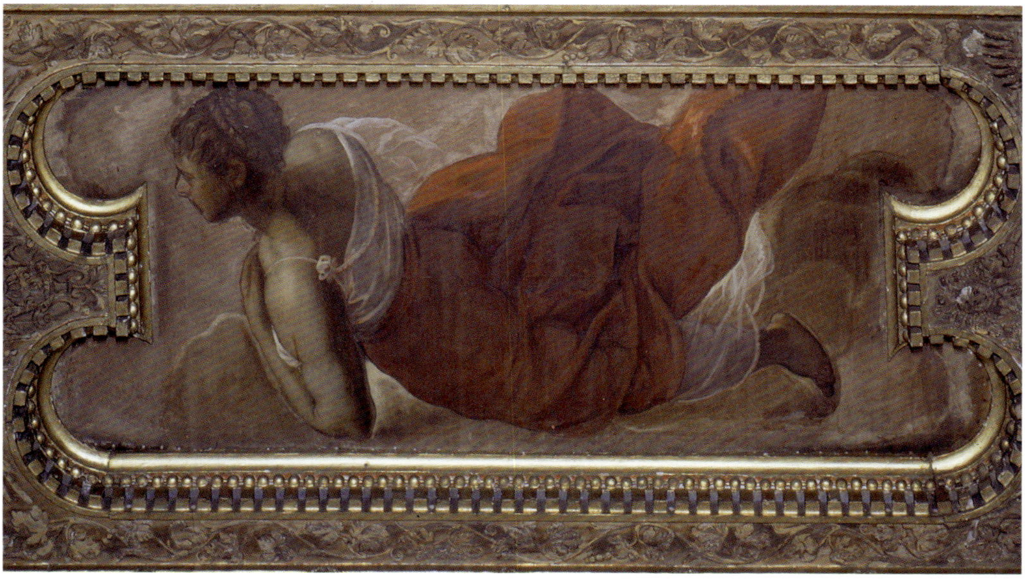

Fig. 14 - Humility (?)

mility. We hear the words of Paul, which inspire the depiction on the ceiling: *And though I have the gift of prophecy, and understand all mysteries and all knowledge, and though I have all faith, so that I could remove mountains, but have not love, I am nothing* (1 Cor 13:2). It is indeed love that nurtures **Humility**, that *does not parade itself, is not puffed up* (1 Cor 13:4), which is most probably personified by the female figure with her back turned and without a halo **[7]** ***(fig. 14)*** located imme-

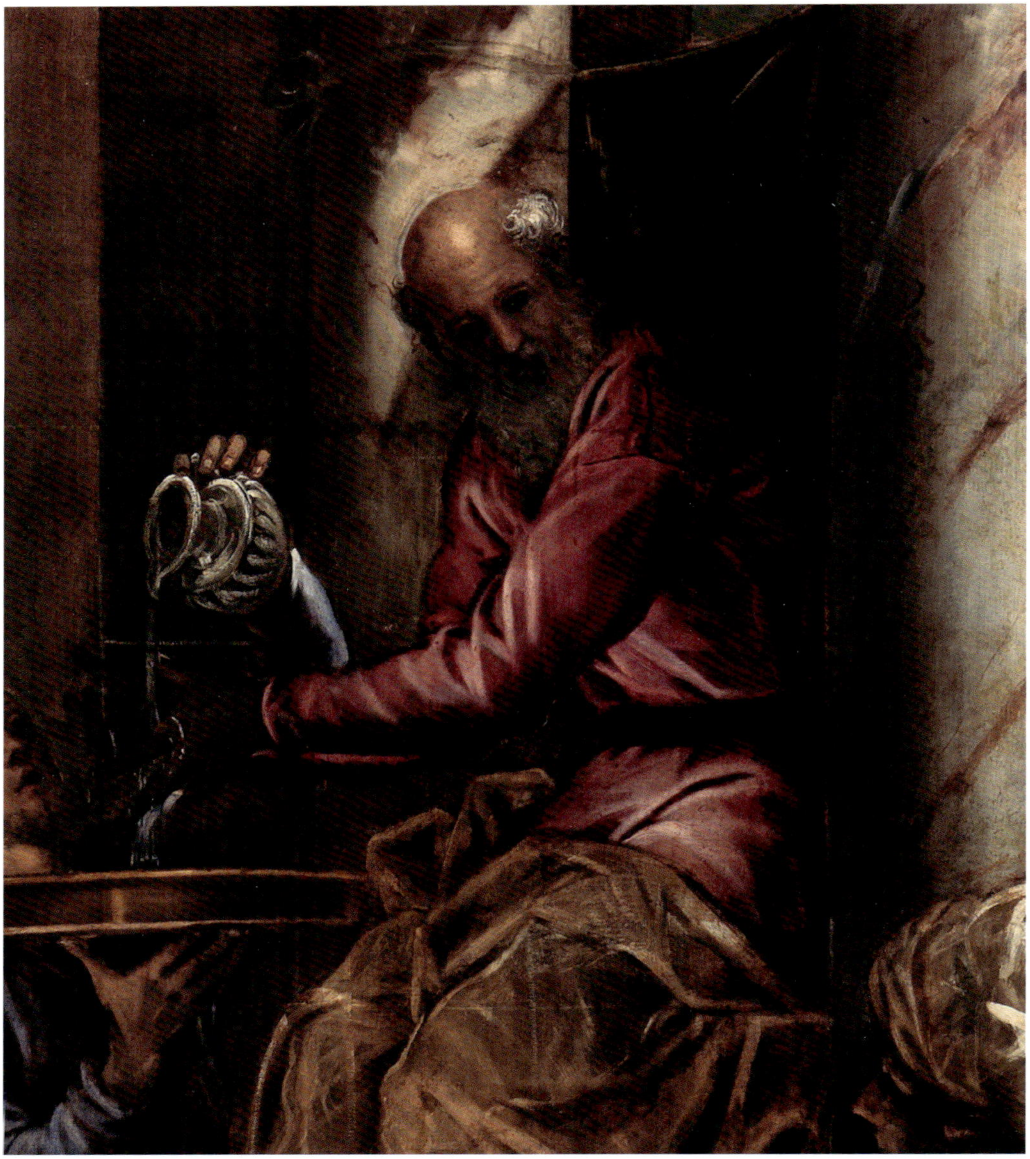

Fig. 15 - Pilate's hands remain black, even though by washing them he symbolizes the attempt to remove the guilt that is not his. But only Christ with his sacrifice can remove the sins of the world

diately above the **Christ Before Pilate.** Compared to the sacrifice of Jesus' love, those whom the world believes as learned are actually foolish, those who think they are wise are in reality mad, because God *made foolish the wisdom of this world* (1 Cor 1:20).

Pilate does not know how to recognize the radiating Truth in front of him; he looks away. Not even the old sage in the foreground, who is about to write the Roman prefect's sentence, wishes to understand and and thus prefers to stare blindly at a closed book in his left hand. With this image Tintoretto allegorically shows the presumption of scholars, which prevents them from understanding the mystery of a God appearing in the flesh and belittled for the sins of all mankind. In fact, Jesus' white robe certainly alludes to the sacrifice of the innocent for the sins of humanity: even if Pilate thinks that he will wash away with water any responsibility, his hands remain black, immersed in shadow ***(fig. 15),*** in sharp contrast with the pureness of Christ's tunic. Behind the judgment scene an ominous red drape enshrouds the bystanders who have just asked for the liberation of Barabbas. The drape symbolizes the blood of the condemned, for which the crowd assumes responsibility (see Mathew 27:25).

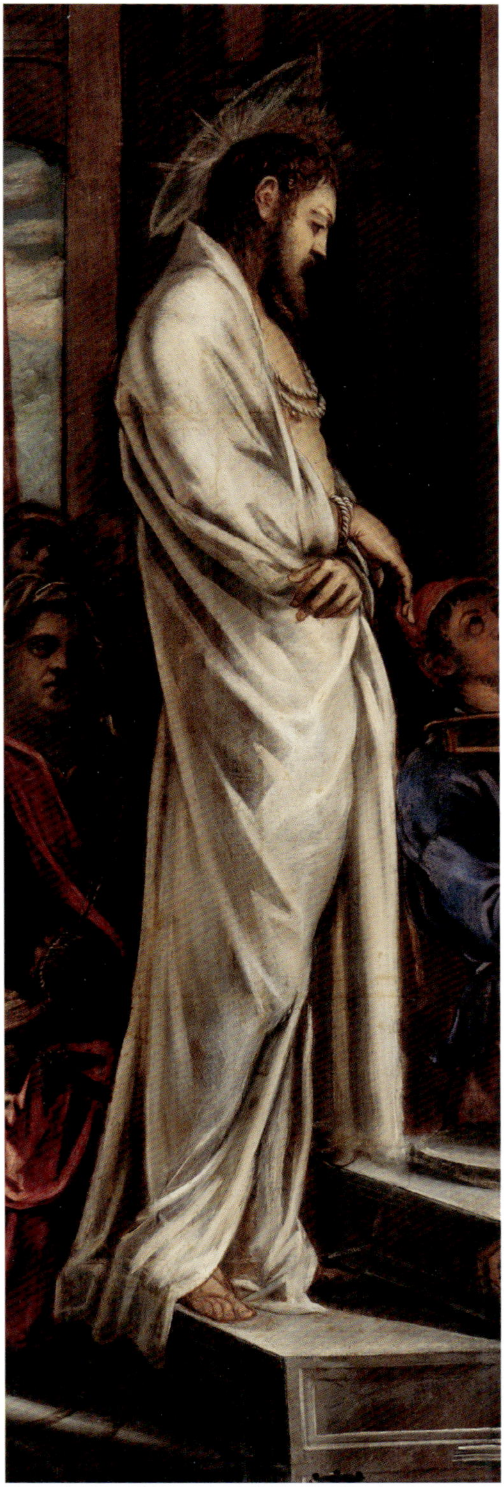

4. Ecce Homo [26]

So then Pilate took Jesus and scourged Him. And the soldiers twisted a crown of thorns and put it on His head, and they put on Him a purple robe. Then they said, "Hail, King of the Jews!" And they struck Him with their hands. Pilate then went out again, and said to them, "Behold, I am bringing Him out to you, that you may know that I find no fault in Him." Then Jesus came out, wearing the crown of thorns and the purple robe. And Pilate said to them, "Behold the Man!"
(John 19:1-5)

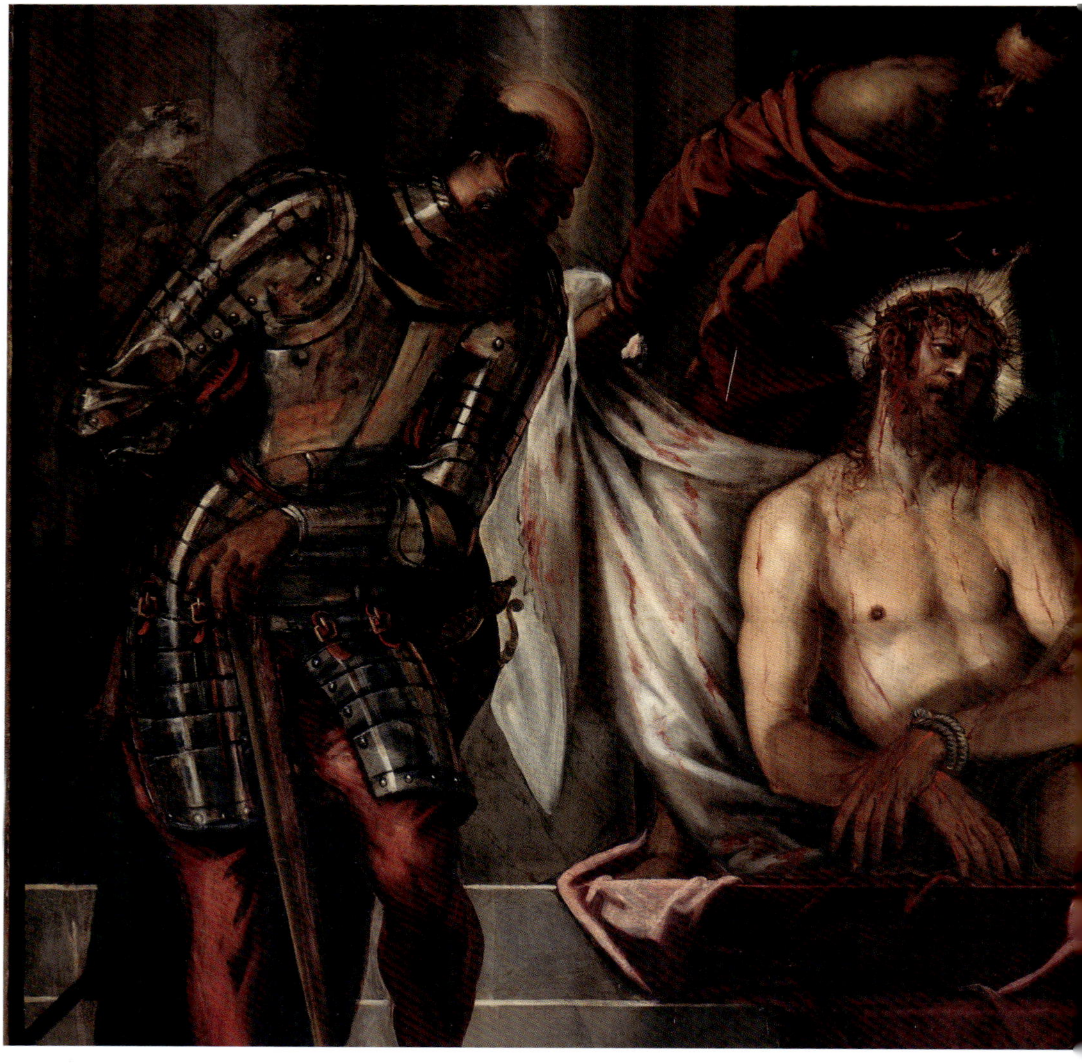

Ecce Homo

Here Tintoretto depicts one of the most dramatic but also ironically revelatory moments of Jesus' messianic regality, as related by John: Jesus, already punished by Pilate, is shown to the crowd in all his fragility as a suffering man with the crown of thorns, the purple mantle and the hyssop branch. The crowd laughs at him claiming to be the "king of the Jews". Everywhere in Chapter 19 of the Gospel According to John we find allusions to the theme of regality: while for Pilate the vision of that beaten-up man is visible proof of the absurdity of being considered king, for those who believe in Jesus, as Pilate unwittingly admits, he is *the real man («Behold the man!»)*, whose humiliation introduces a much higher regality, unshakeable by the

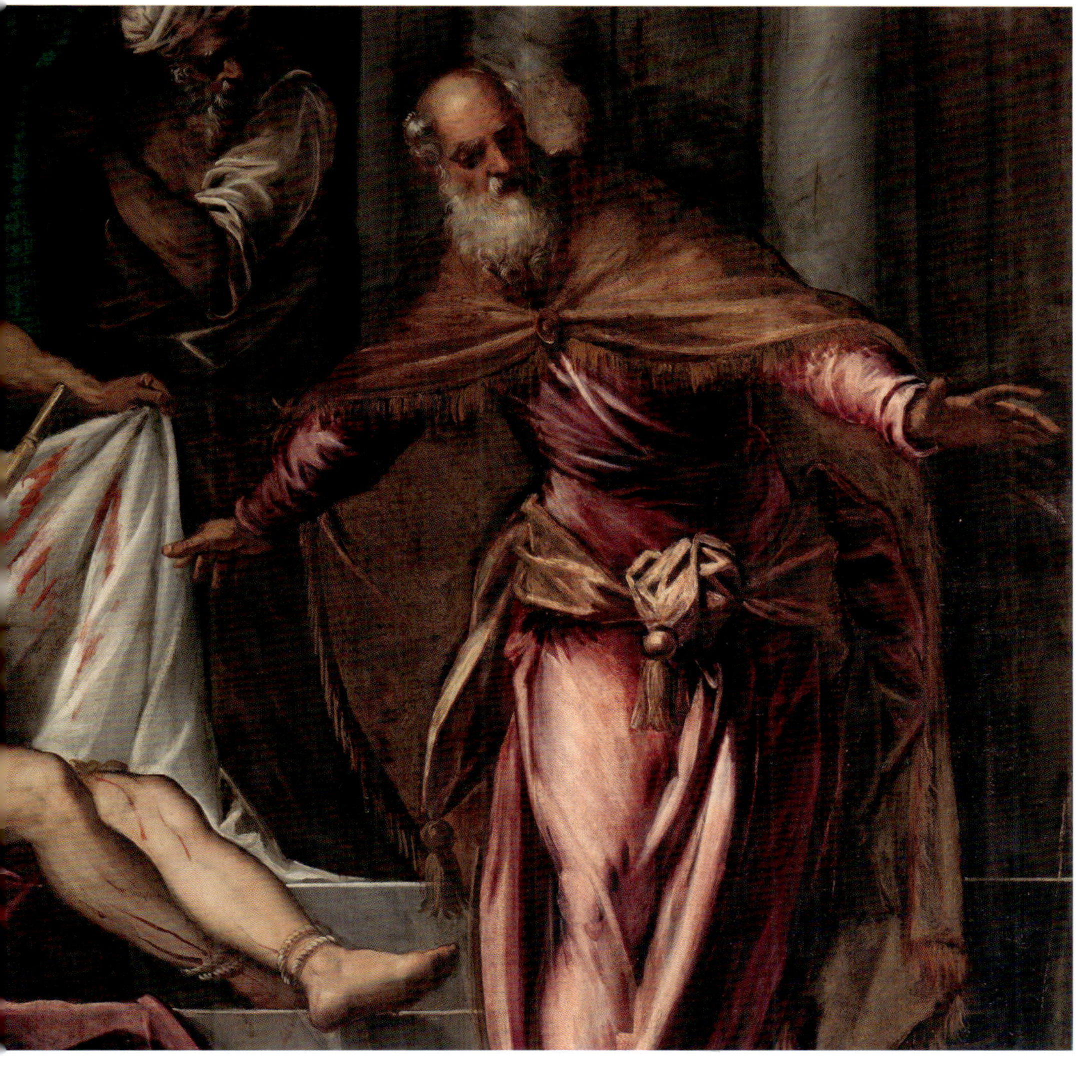

values of the world.
Therefore, it is Christ's regality that is brought to light in this painting. The axis that is created between the **Ecce Homo,** the personification of **Happiness [8]** ***(fig. 16)*** – located on the ceiling, crowned in ivy and roses and offering crowns – and **St. Roch in Glory [1]** ***(fig. 5)***, reveals the regal meaning of the crown of thorns, which in Heaven will become a crown of beatitude for those who, like the saint, have followed the teachings of Christ.
If we look at the composition of the side paintings, we will notice that the Christ of **Ecce Homo** represents their fulcrum: the powerful diagonals oriented towards the bottom of each scene indeed have this image of an ideal symmetric axis. Pilate and a jeering soldier show Christ's body – half naked, gleaming with blood, with neither

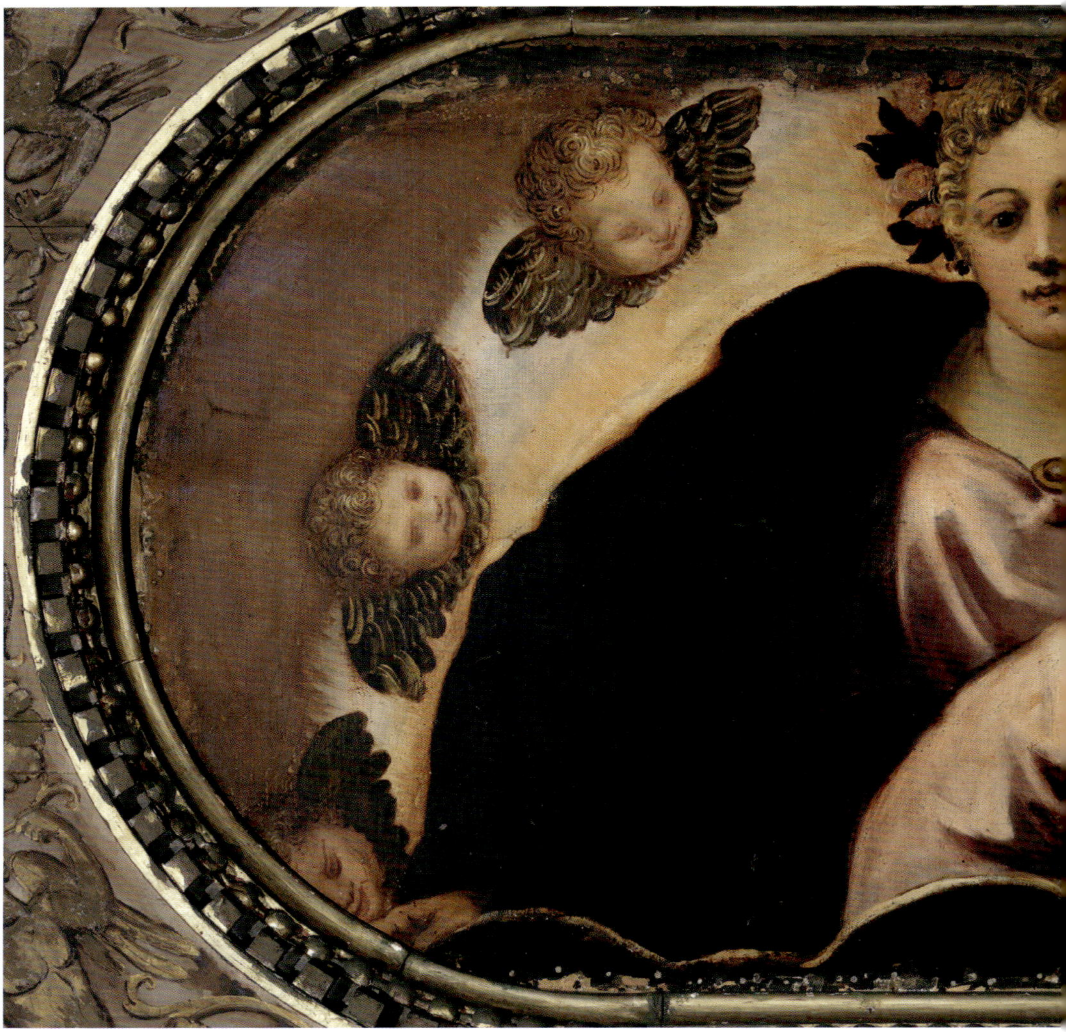

Fig. 16 - Happiness. Placing this rose-crowned allegory above Christ, the painter is expressing the regal meaning of the crown of thorns

the white robe, which an attendant unfolds like a bed sheet or a tablecloth, nor with the purple mantle, which lies on the steps – to the people (see Mathew 27:29). It was not rare in 16th century Gospel commentaries to find a relation between the presentation of Christ to the people and the celebrant's lifting of the consecrated Host. Here, perhaps, Tintoretto also wants to present the Lord's body and blood as a Eucharistic offer, placing Jesus on the Lithostrotos steps against the background of the white robe, which respectively refer to the steps and cloth of the altar.

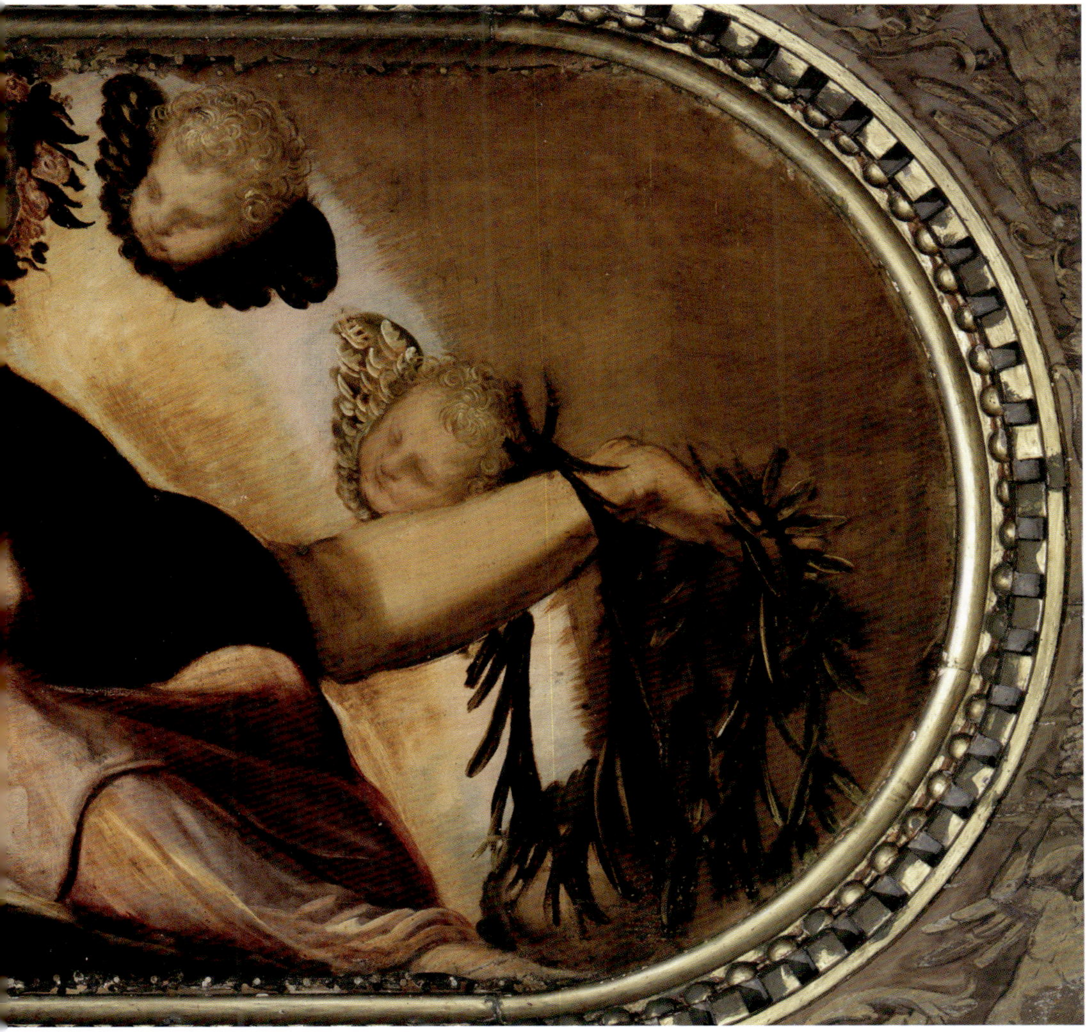

5. Ascent to Calvary [27]

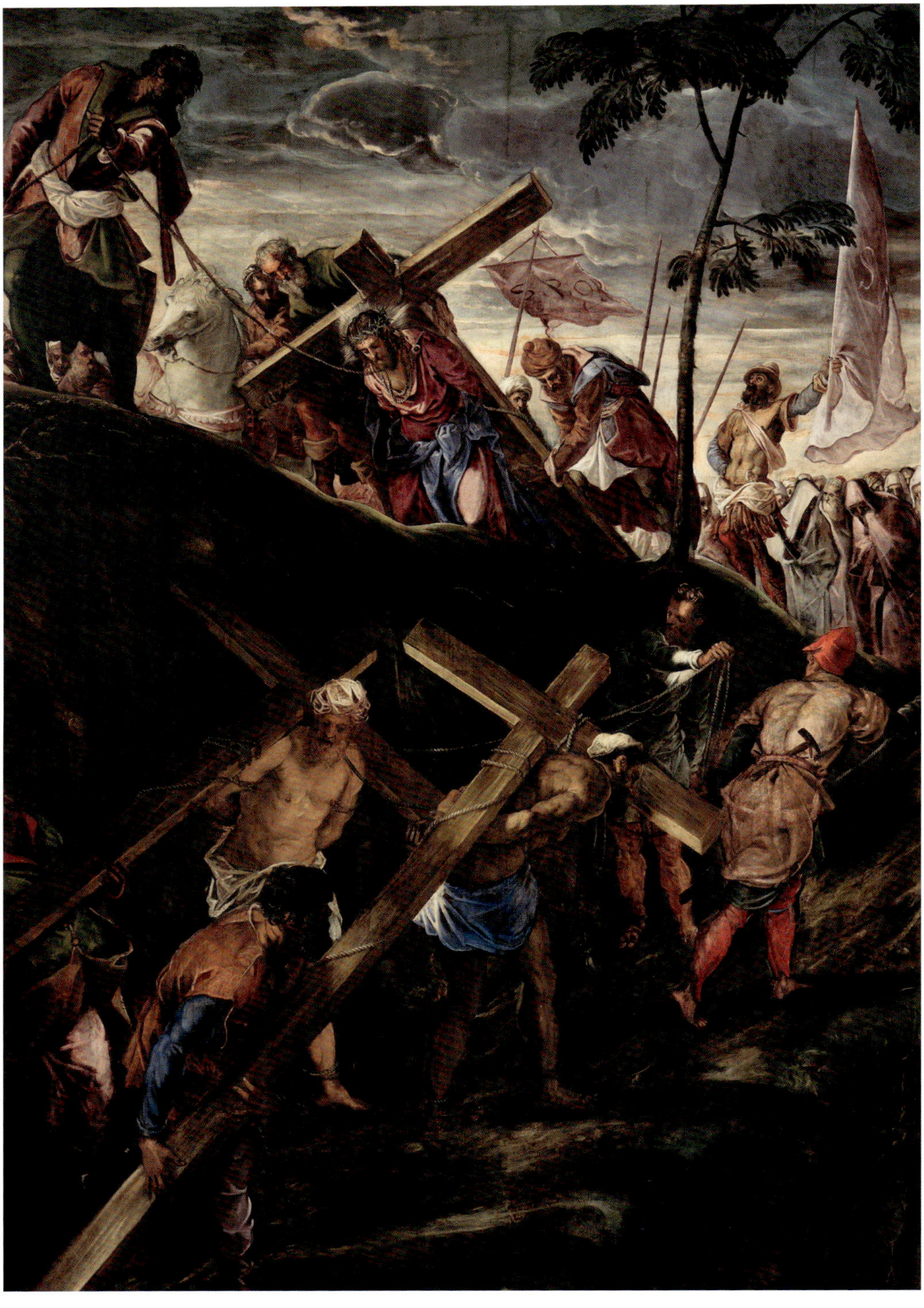

Ascent to Calvary

Now as they led Him away, they laid hold of a certain man, Simon a Cyrenian, who was coming from the country, and on him they laid the cross that he might bear it after Jesus. And a great multitude of the people followed Him, and women who also mourned and lamented Him. But Jesus, turning to them, said, "Daughters of Jerusalem, do not weep for Me, but weep for yourselves and for your children. For indeed the days are coming in which they will say, 'Blessed are the barren, wombs that never bore, and breasts which never nursed!' Then they will begin to say to the mountains, "Fall on us!" and to the hills, "Cover us!" 'For if they do these things in the green wood, what will be done in the dry?" There were also two others, criminals, led with Him to be put to death.
(Lc 23,26-32)

The Gospels only fleetingly refer to Jesus' ascent to Calvary: it is the future centuries that will devotionally spread the knowledge of this event, making it a true *Via Crucis.*
Tintoretto organizes the scene on two obliquely superimposed levels. Jesus, dragged to the place of execution by a rope around his neck, *like a lamb led to the slaughter* (Isaiah 53:7), occupies the upper part; at the bottom, from left to right, we see the two thieves. Down by the curve some women, with their faces covered and lowered in contrition, allude to the passage in the Gospel According to Luke in which Jesus, seeing them in despair, exhorts them to cry not for him but for themselves and their children, thus announcing

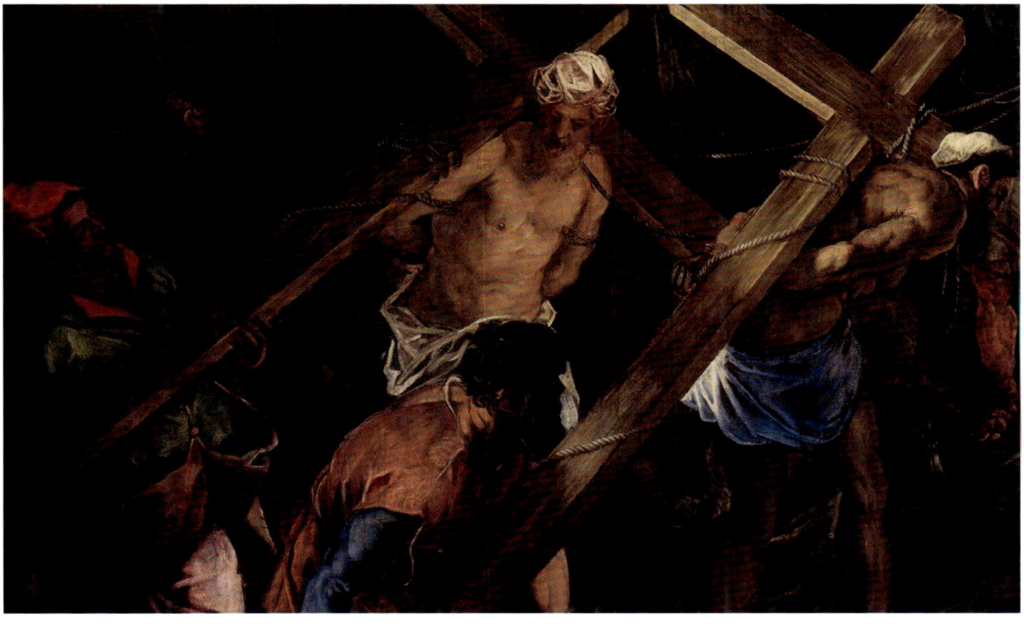

Fig. 17 - While Simon of Cyrene helps Christ carry the cross, some other characters are helping the other two condemned men: a clear encouragement for the brothers of the Scuola to perform charitable works for the needy

the imminent destruction of Jerusalem. The episode, inserted as one of the stations in the *Via Crucis,* was supposed to be interpreted not as a threat of a vengeful God but as a warning for all believers to understand the meaning of salvation in his sacrifice. Only in this way could pity become the conversion of the heart and thus salvation from eternal death. The painting's foreground seems to respond positively to this warning. The barren wombs and dry breasts, which Christ says is the most desirable condition for those who, denying him, determine their own ruin *(«Blessed are the barren, wombs that never bore, and breasts which never nursed»)*, are not but the contrary of the Charity that Tintoretto, according to tradition, almost always personifies as a fertile and nursing woman. The act of charity here is represented by the men helping the malefactors carry the crosses. It is not only Simon

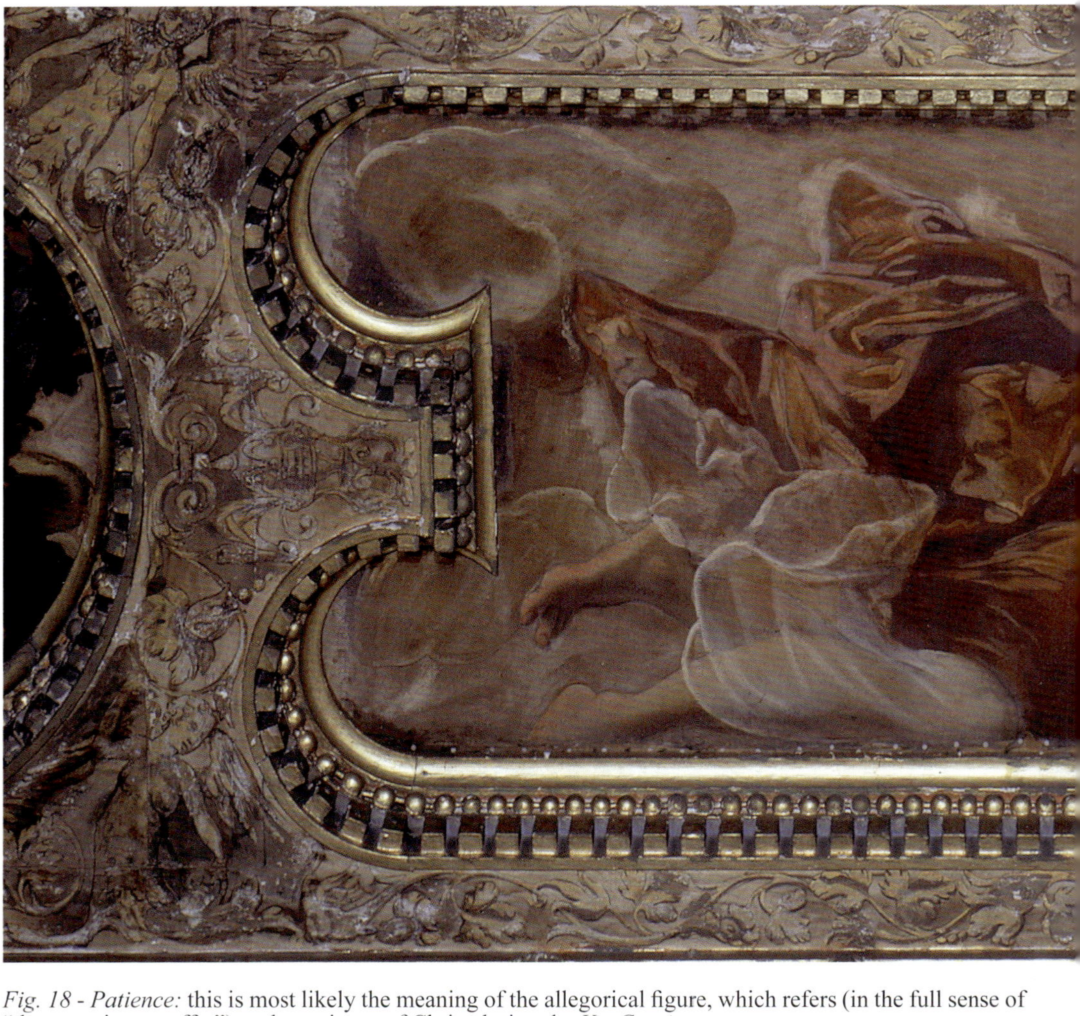

Fig. 18 - Patience: this is most likely the meaning of the allegorical figure, which refers (in the full sense of "the capacity to suffer") to the patience of Christ during the *Via Crucis*

the Cyrenian who is helping Christ carry his; others are also involved in the transportation of the crosses of the condemned ***(fig. 17).*** This is a clear message for the brothers of the Confraternity to embark upon, not only through meditation but also through daily actions and institutional tasks, the way of the Calvary, to carry with patience and goodness their own crosses and those of others (see Luke 14:27), realizing the mission of the Scuola. It is that **Patient Charity** (or rather strong, resistant and persevering in spirit), as well as good charity (kind and generous), that follows the example of the dignified, gentle patience of Christ ascending to the Calvary, the Charity that is perhaps personified by the figure who brings her hands to her chest **[9]**, located on the ceiling in alignment with this *telero* ***(fig. 18) (see note 1)***.

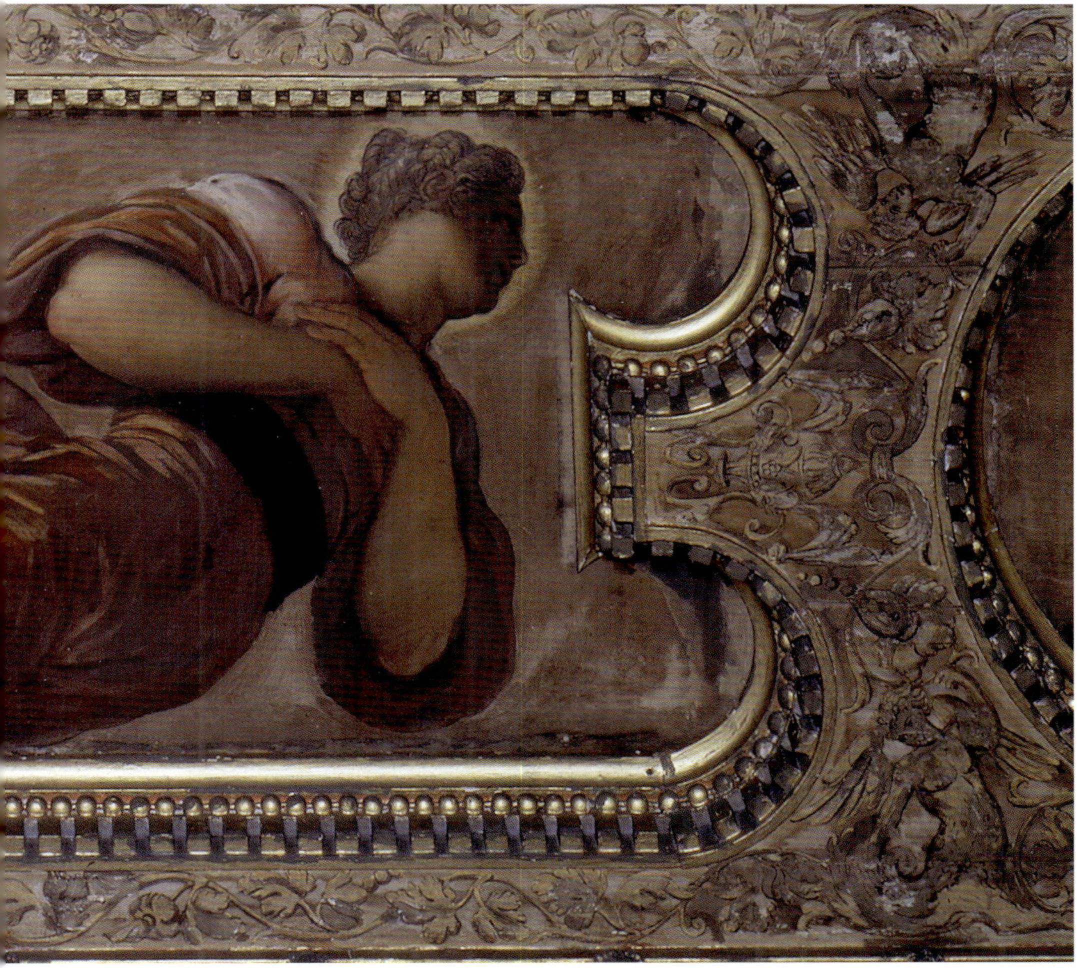

The Sala Superiore

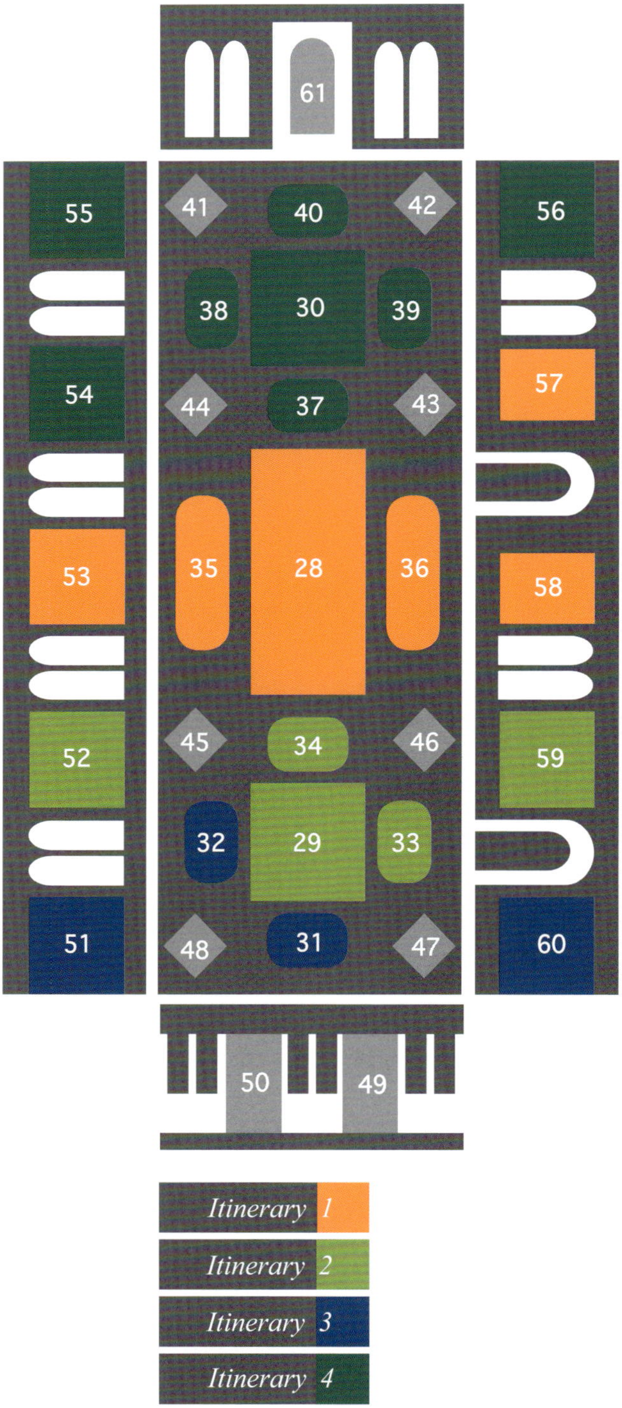

Ceiling

28. Brazen Serpent
29. Moses drawing water from the rock
30. Miracle of Manna
31. Adam and Eve
32. The Eternal Father appears to Moses
33. Pillar of Fire
34. Jonah leaves the whale's belly
35. Vision of Ezekiel
36. Jacob's Ladder
37. Sacrifice of Isaac
38. Elisha multiplies the bread
39. Elijah fed by the Angel
40. Passover
41. Abraham and Melchizedek
42. Daniel saved by the Angel
43. Elijah on the chariot of fire
44. Cain and Abel
45. Samson draws water from the donkey's jaw
46. Samuel anoints David
47. Moses saved from the waters
48. Three children in the furnace

Walls

49. St. Roch
50. St. Sebastian
51. Adoration of the Shepherds
52. Baptism of Christ
53. Resurrection
54. Agony in the Garden
55. Last Supper
56. Miracle of the Loaves and Fishes
57. Resurrection of Lazarus
58. Ascension
59. Probatic Pool
60. Temptation of Christ
61. Apparition of St. Roch

The biblical typology as a parameter for interpreting the cycle

The Sala Superiore, the main meeting room in the Confraternity, is decorated completely by Tintoretto. The artist worked here from 1576 to 1581, painting both the ceiling and the walls. The only work that was completed after is the altarpiece **Apparition of St. Roch [61]**, in 1588. It seems superfluous in relation to the original decorative cycle, yet really impressive: it is composed of 33 paintings.

If the *teleri* on the ceiling show episodes from the Old Testament, those on the walls, except for the ones dedicated to **St. Roch** ***(fig. 19)*** and St. Sebastian on the northern wall **[49, 50]**, have as their subject the life of Christ.

There is a profound relation between the ceiling and the walls, since the events of the Old Testament are understood as prefigurations of the works of Christ. This interpretation of the sacred text, which creates an interaction between the various situations and realities of the story of salvation, is called *biblical typology*: the realities of the Old Testament, called *types* (or "figures" or "models"), take life in the events and situations of the New Testament (*antitypes*). Such a reading already exists in the Gospels (for example when Jesus speaks about his Easter as a *sign of the prophet Jonah* [Matthew 12:39-40]). It was developed by the Christian tradition from its very beginning and is the foundation of some medieval variations of the illustrated Bible, such as the *Biblia pauperum*, which flanks one of the scenes from the Gospel (*antitype*), located at the center of the page, and two episodes from the Old Testament (*types*) (see box p. 44).

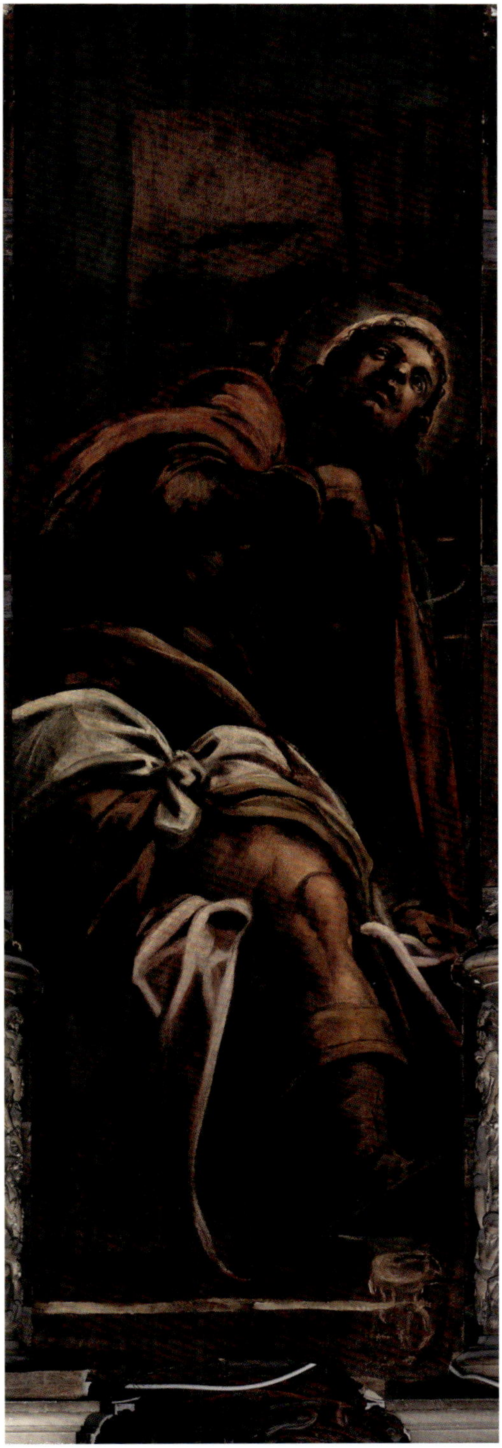

Fig. 19 - St. Roch

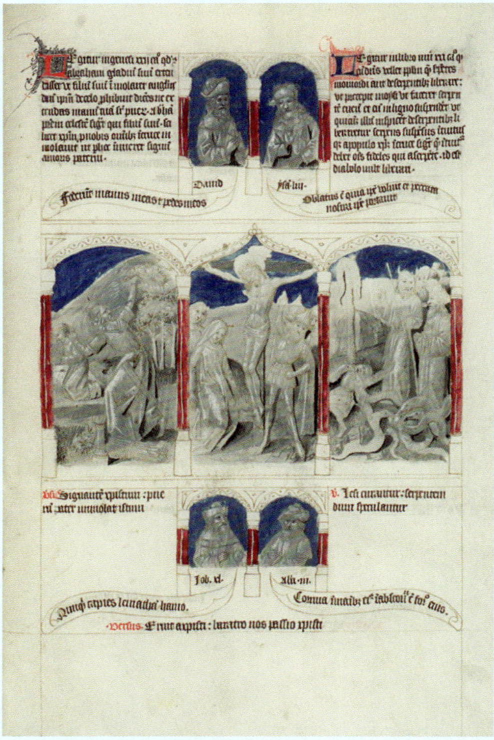

Fig. 20 - Biblia pauperum, the crucifixion page

The Biblia pauperum. Starting from the 13th century artists began depicting variations of the Bible in which the miniatures acquired their own value, separate from the text. The most famous example of this genre is the *Biblia pauperum*, in which the life of Christ is illustrated in typologies, instituting numerous connections between the Old and New Testaments. Each illustrated page from these Bibles is divided into nine sections: the central figure represents a scene from the life of Christ, in this case the *Crucifixion*. To the sides there are episodes from the Old Testament, recognized as "types," or rather prefigurations, of events from the Gospels. Here the *Sacrifice of Isaac* and the *Brazen Serpent* flank the central image as prefigurations of the death of Christ on the cross. In the upper angles there appears the paraphrase of the biblical text. Above and below the images we find citations from the Psalms and Prophets.

The Old and New Testaments are therefore considered complementary Revelations; their relationship is illuminated by the life of Christ, above all his Easter (passion, death and resurrection). The entire Old Testament in this way is one big prophecy of Christ, who is the center and culmination of history. In fact, Christ is the key that allows Christians to place all human events within God's plan of Salvation because he fulfilled the promises of the Old Testament and he is the origin of the sacramental life of the Church, giving hope of future realities that will come with the end of time.

There are three, absolutely interconnected, temporal plans:

a) The time of the Old Testament, whose realities require fulfillment and overcoming (the Hall's ceiling);

b) The time of the unique and unrepeatable life of Christ, which represents the desired fulfillment (walls);

c) The time of the Church, in which the mystery of Christ is continually expressed in the sacraments and manifests itself through an individual and communal life that follows his example and waits for his return (ceiling and walls together, interpreted in relation to the life of the Church and the ultimate reality).

It is above all the sacramental key that allows us to grasp the cycle of the Sala Su-

periore in its entirety. The scenes are not arranged according to a chronological pattern, as in the *Biblia pauperum*, but in a way as to create a discourse that, starting from biblical events – and in particular from the crucifixion as the heart of the story of salvation and origin of the sacraments – reflects upon the prominent elements of Baptism and the Eucharist. It is necessary to remember that Tintoretto decorated the Hall just after the closing of the Council of Trent (1545-1563), which was the Church's response to the Protestant Reformation. One of the most burning issues was the difference in views that Catholics and Protestants had of the sacraments, above all of the Eucharist.
The "sequela Christi", or rather the imitation of Christ, is also a theme that passes through the entire cycle; it reflects the self-awareness of the San Rocco Confraternity, which sees in charitable service the divine love received from Christ's sacrifice on the cross, always present during Mass.

The theological structure of the cycle

It is possible to identify four main thematic groups in the Hall's cycle:

I. The central painting, the biggest, constitutes the key for interpreting the entire decoration, which not accidentally begins with this depiction. The scene represented is the one of the bronze serpent being raised by Moses **[Brazen Serpent, 28]**, which saves the Israelites from venomous snakes. It is a *type* of another lifting, that of Jesus on the cross. In fact, Jesus says: *"And as Moses lifted up the serpent in the wilderness, even so must the Son of Man be lifted up, that whoever believes in Him should not perish but have eternal life"* (John 3, 14:15). By placing it at the center of the ceiling, Tintoretto places Christ's sacrifice at the center of divine initiatives for the salvation of man. To the sides of this painting we see the victory of Christ over death; the two bigger ovals, in fact, to the left show the **Vision of Ezekiel [35]** and to the right **Jacob's Ladder [36]**, respectively the prefigurations of the **Resurrection [53]** and the **Ascension [58]**, located immediately below on the walls. Thematically related to the resurrection is the **Raising of Lazarus [57]**. North and south of the **Brazen Serpent**, two "pivotal" ovals draw our attention to two thematic groups gathered around two other big paintings on the ceiling, **Moses drawing water from the rock [29]** and the **Miracle of Manna [30]**, respective prefigurations of two sacraments, the Eucharist and Baptism. **Jonah leaves the whale's belly [34]**, a type of resurrection, as well as a prefiguration of Baptism for the rebirth from water, is directly related both to the thematic central group and to the paintings of the northern group. In similar manner, the **Sacrifice of Isaac [37]** prefigures the Easter mystery and introduces the southern section as a type of Eucharistic sacrifice.

II. The theme of Baptism revolves around **Moses drawing water from the rock [29],** a prefiguration of the **Baptism of Christ [52]**, located on the eastern wall. The theme passes through the **Pillar of Fire [33]** and stops at the **Probatic Pool [59]**, symbol of the baptismal remittance of sins. **The Eternal father appears to Moses [32]** is connected to the **Baptism of Christ** with Tintoretto underlining the direct relationship between Christ and Moses through the formal reference of the hand – God's and John's – held over their heads, recalling the unction of the catechumens as in the lozenge **Samuel anoints David [46]**. The rejection of Satan, a necessary part of the baptismal rite, is recalled in the **Temptation of Christ [60]**.

III. Some of the paintings mentioned also act as a general preamble: if **Adam and Eve [31]** represents the fall of man and his necessity for redemption, the **Adoration of the Shepherds [51]** represents the birth of Christ, which is the answer to such a need. In front of this painting, on the other wall, the **Temptation of Christ** is completely different from the one of Eve on the ceiling: Christ, contrary to the progenitors, is capable of resisting Satan. **The Eternal Father appears to Moses** depicts the moment in which God orders Moses on Mount Horeb to lead the people of Israel out of Egypt towards the Promised Land: a prelude, therefore, to the years in the desert, whose important episodes occupy the ceiling's three central squares.

IV. On the other part of the ceiling the **Miracle of Manna [30]**, which depicts small pieces of bread in the form of Hosts falling on the Jews, prefigures the **Last Supper [55]**, which is

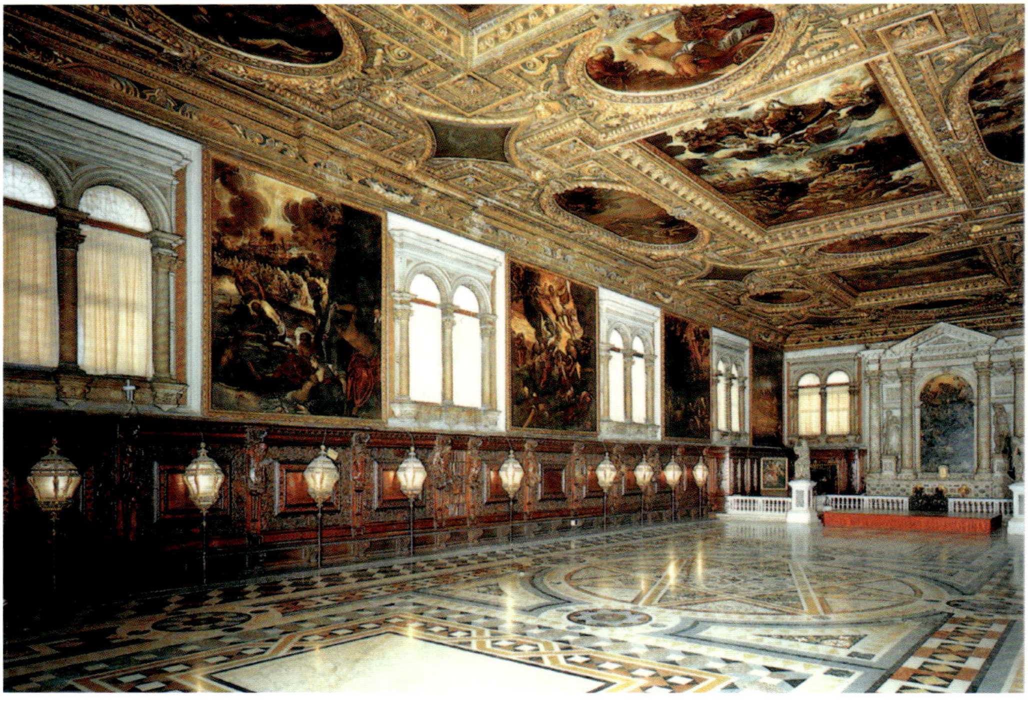

Fig. 21 - View of the Sala Superiore (ceiling and eastern wall)

the moment in which Jesus institutes the Mass. The prefiguring event of the **Miracle of the Loaves and Fishes [56]**, located at the bottom of the western wall, is when **Elisha multiplies the bread [38]**, just like the Eucharistic type and variant of the salvation bread motif descending from the sky is **Elijah fed by the angel [39]**. Completing the thematic group dedicated to the Eucharist are the **Passover [40]**, located exactly above the Hall's altar, and the **Agony in the Garden [54]**, in which an angel offers the bitter chalice to a profoundly meditative Christ, dripping on the forehead and cheeks with blood of agony, as a sign of imminent sacrifice.

The monochromatic lozenges, redone in the 18th century by Giuseppe Angeli but most probably faithful copies of Tintoretto's originals, represent variations on the main themes, enriching the entire series with fine nuances. In reality, the proposed thematic subdivision is but be a simplification. This cycle's fascination is, in fact, its elastic structure. The paintings form a fabric whose stitches are all connected: the references to form and content that the artist conveys among the various works allow us to continually discover new meanings.

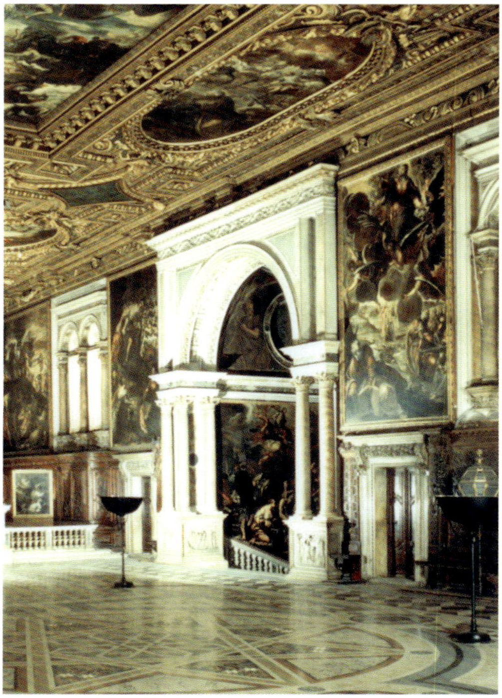

Fig. 22 - Access to the Sala Superiore and the western wall

Invention and construction of the cycle

It has still not been fully ascertained if it was Tintoretto himself who invented the iconographic scheme. The various levels of the cycle's meaning and the vastness of its conceptual architecture pose doubts that he did; it is more probable that the artist was guided, or at least supported, by one or more theologians or biblicists. The erudite brothers Alvise Cuccina and Benedetto Ferro, whom sources mention as being among those responsible for supervising the schematization of the cycle and the different stages of the Hall's preparation, definitely influenced the choice of themes. The compactness and the internal coherence of the biblical-theological discourse and the fact that the ceiling's frames had already been prepared before the start of the decoration says that the cycle systematically followed an elaborate scheme from the very beginning, contrary to the opinion, expressed by some scholars, that Tintoretto began with the idea of the central *telero* and then gradually enlarged it, "filling" the empty squares.

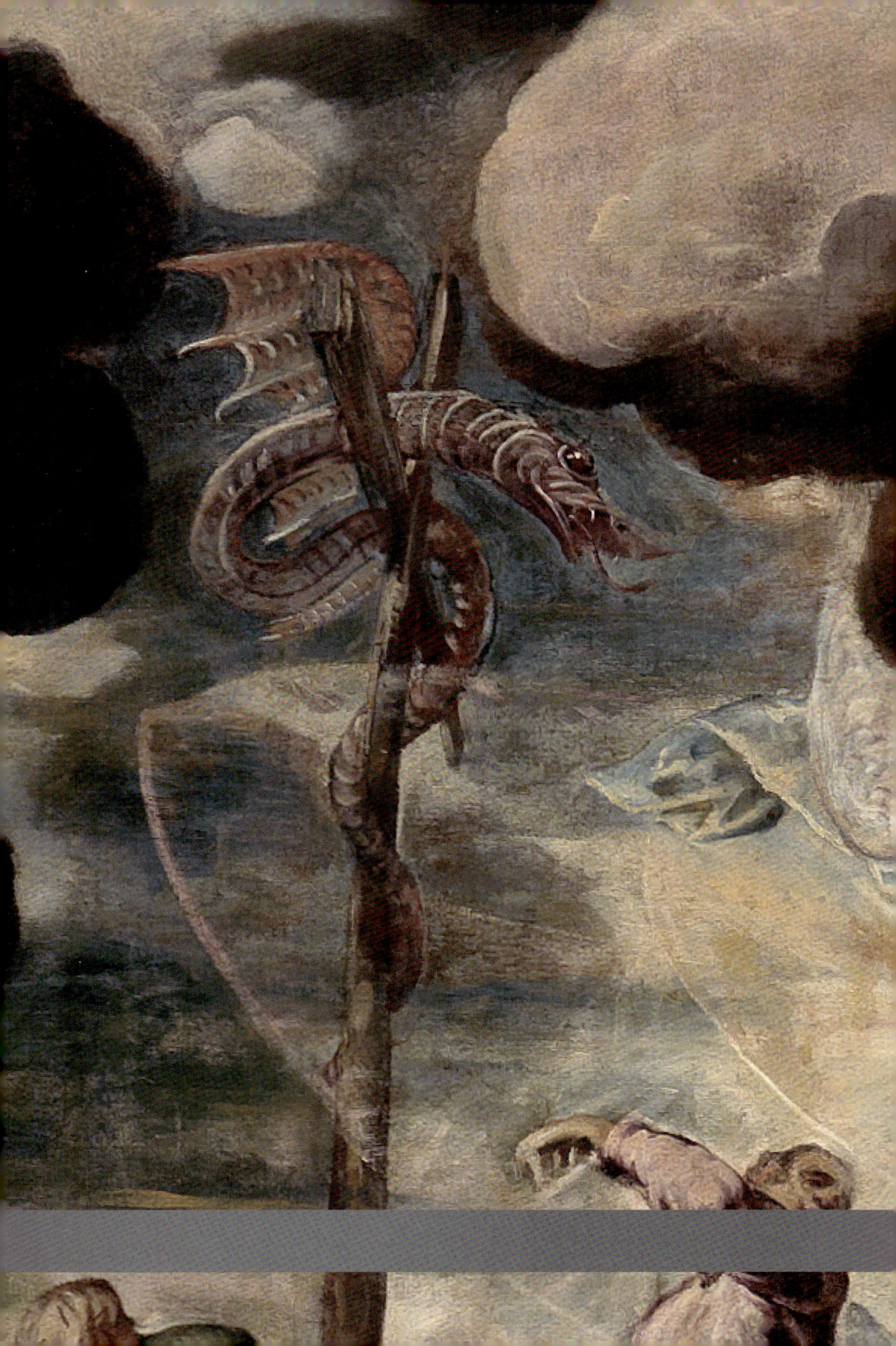

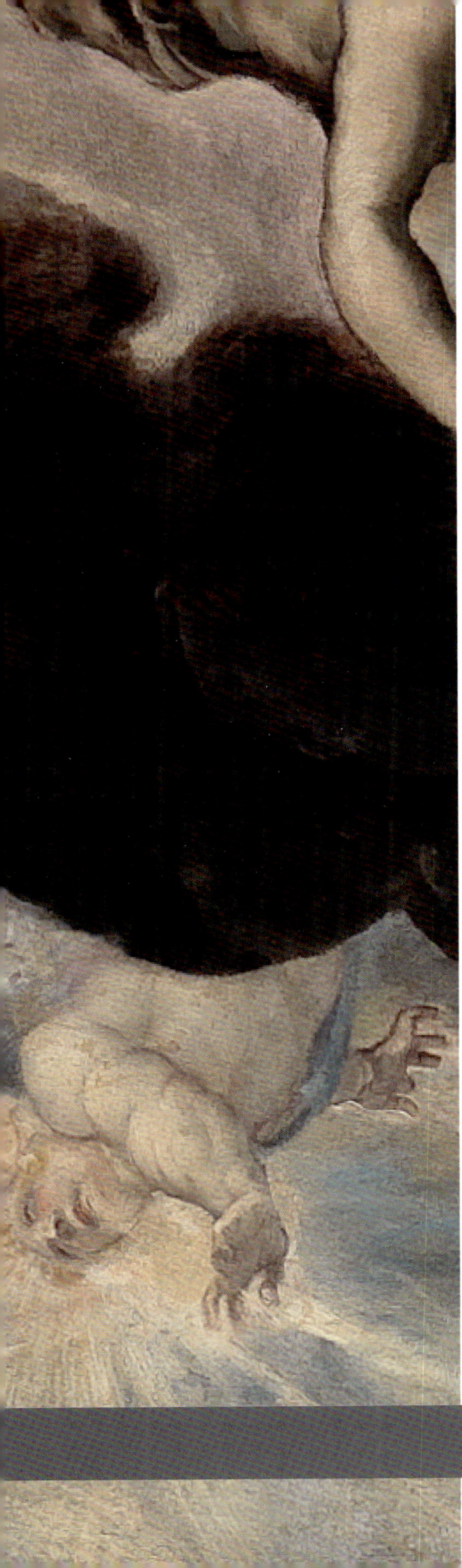

The Easter mystery as the origin of the sacraments

These *teleri* depict the Easter mystery of Christ (the passion, death and resurrection-ascension) as the origin of the sacraments, which are the protagonists of the Hall's northern and southern sections. To the sides of the **Brazen Serpent [28]**, the prefiguration of the Lord's redeeming sacrifice on the cross, we see the victory over death. The two bigger ovals to the left show the **Vision of Ezekiel [35]** and to the right **Jacob's Ladder [36]**, which are respective prefigurations of the **Resurrection [53]** and the **Ascension [58]** located immediately below on the walls.

6. Brazen Serpent [28]

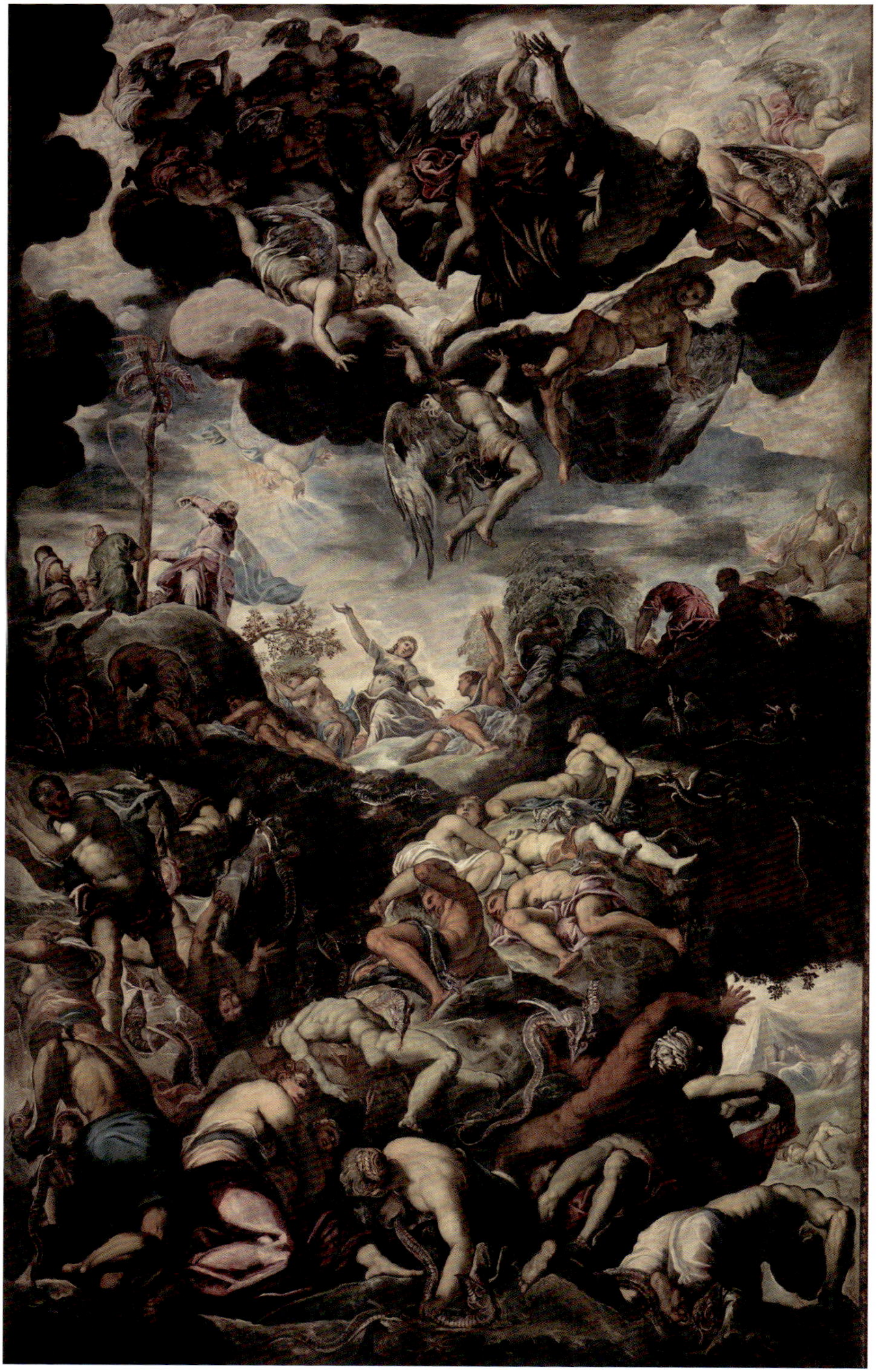

Brazen Serpent

Then the Israelites journeyed from Mount Hor by the Way of the Red Sea, to go around the land of Edom; and the soul of the people became very discouraged on the way. And the people spoke against God and against Moses: "Why have you brought us up out of Egypt to die in the wilderness? For there is no food and no water, and our soul loathes this worthless bread." So the Lord sent fiery serpents among the people, and they bit the people; and many of the people of Israel died. Therefore the people came to Moses, and said, "We have sinned, for we have spoken against the Lord and against you; pray to the Lord that He take away the serpents from us." So Moses prayed for the people. Then the Lord said to Moses, "Make a fiery serpent, and set it on a pole; and it shall be that everyone who is bitten, when he looks at it, shall live." So Moses made a bronze serpent, and put it on a pole; and so it was, if a serpent had bitten anyone, when he looked at the bronze serpent, he lived. *(Numbers 21:4-9)*

Whoever enters the Hall will linger under this painting, drawn to its centrality and dimension (840 x 520 cm); it is the key to interpreting the entire decorative scheme.
Here Tintoretto captures one of the most dramatic episodes of the Exodus: the people, forced to make a long detour, speak against God, who sends venous snakes. Having repented, the Israelites ask Moses to intercede and the Lord heals them through the lifting of the brazen serpent. In the painting an angel communicates God's message to Moses. It is by the power of an angel that, according to Hebrew tradition, and also the New Testament (see Acts 7:38; Galatians 3:19), man receives the divine will. These are the words of the Lord: whoever is bitten, looking at the copper serpent (or bronze, according to translations), shall live.
A painting that focuses on God's healing capacity is particularly suitable for the Scuola of St. Roch, who was patron of plague victims. Yet, there are many theological meanings of the scene and they cannot be simplified by merely referring to the patron saint.
Tintoretto here depicts the great biblical typology of the Lord's crucifixion, contained in the Gospel According to John where Jesus says of himself: *And as Moses lifted up the serpent in the wilderness, even so must the Son of Man be lifted up, that whoever believes in Him should not perish but have eternal life* (John 3:14-15). These words should be understood in a particular manner, in a manner that was clear to the Church Fathers and was later expressed in the illustrated sacred history texts such as the *Biblia pauperum* (see box p. 44). With the word "lifted" Jesus is not prophesizing his resurrection or ascension, but rather his crucifixion. This is part of the concept, found in the Gospel According to John, in which the cross is not a place of humiliation but rather of regal elevation and glorification. The reference to the **Crucifixion [22]** at the Sala dell'Albergo ***(note 2)***, also created according to the Johannine idea of the cross, is obvious: the main painting at the Sala dell'Albergo can be fully considered as an antitype of the one in the Sala Superiore. Christ is the new serpent that, as soon as he is exalted on the cross, will

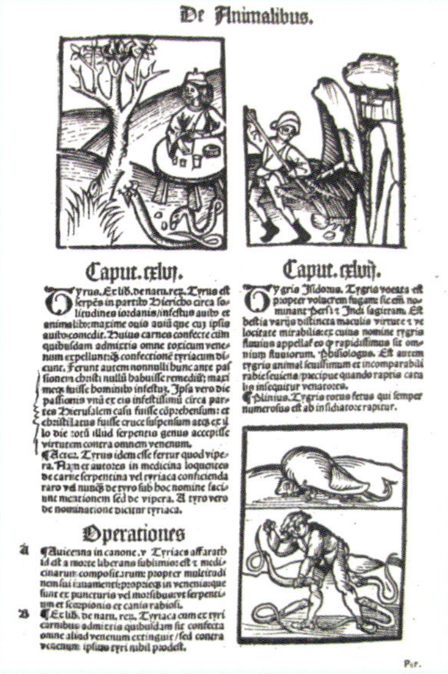

Fig. 23 - The *Hortus Sanitatis* page (1511)

The theriaca. The *theriaca (triaca)* was medicine created, according to the beliefs of the time, by Andromachus, Emperor Nero's doctor. It had the capacity to heal from any disease. The *theriaca*, initially used to contrast the effects of venomous animals, during the 16th century became a universal panacea, particularly appreciated for fighting the plague. Venetian apothecaries, who could easily use the drugs coming from the East, were known everywhere as the best experts on *theriaca*. Soon Venice acquired a monopoly on the production and exportation of the medicine, so that its preparation, in the middle of the century, became a real public spectacle. *Theriaca* worked like a homeopathic drug: to cure the venom, coming both from venomous animals and the pestilent air, the snake's meat was the essential element of the mixture.

The *Hortus Sanitatis* ***(fig. 23)***, a guide to the elementary qualities of plants, stones and animals, reprinted many times in Venice in the course of the 16th century, dedicated a large section to the origin of the name *theriaca*. Under the heading "TYRUS" it was written that the flesh of a venomous snake from the Israeli desert received the power of acting as a potent antivenin on the day of Christ's passion after one of its specimens was captured near Jerusalem and put on the cross. This would explain the origin of the term "triaca/theriaca/tyriaca," made precisely of snake meat.

defeat the serpent tempter of Eden. This contraposition can be seen at the Scuola di San Rocco: Tintoretto's salvation story begins with the serpent's temptation, which leads to death – in **Adam and Eve [31]** ***(note 15)*** – and culminates in the raising of the bronze serpent, which gives life anew. It is in this strong hope for life, founded on Christ's sacrifice and communicated through the sacraments, that we find the heart of the Tintoretto cycle, which directly associates physical healing with spiritual healing. Tintoretto painted the **Brazen Serpent** between 1575 and 1576, when Venice was in the middle of one of the most devastating plagues in its history. The intensity with which the artist painted this healing episode is explained by the social situation of the time: the plague created a desperate need to reflect upon the Easter mystery, which is the real and only origin of salvation. Therefore the salvational meaning of the bronze serpent was immediately clear for the Venetians, since it referred to the commonly used medicine in periods of infection, the so-called Theriac *(theriaca*), which functioned in a homeopathic way: in order to cure the venom,

and thus the infection, it was composed mostly of snake meat (see box p. 52). The association "Brazen serpent - Christ - *theriaca*" is documented by sources from the period: just like snake meat heals people from the snake bite, so does the sacrifice of the Christ-serpent flesh, made sin for sinners (see 2 Cor 5:21), restore them to life in the profoundest of ways: *Great mystery, to be healed by a serpent! What does it mean "to be healed by a serpent looking at a serpent"? It means to be saved from death believing in the Dead One* (Augustine, *Exposition on the Psalms*, 73:5).
According to John's Gospel, the world is judged already before the crucifixion, as a prediction of the final judgment. On the one hand, there are those who refuse to see the light, thus condemning themselves; on the other, there are those who welcome the Truth: *He who believes in Him is not condemned; but he who does not believe is condemned already* (John 3:18). Also in this case, as in the Albergo's **Crucifixion**, the episode is narrated almost as if it was the Final Judgment: many men seem to be bitten, while others on the top of the hill, turned to the bronze serpent, are healed. The serpent does not heal automatically, it is not magical; it appeals to man's freedom of choice, since it is man who must decide whether or not to receive the gift of salvation (*he who looks at it, shall live*). This is why Tintoretto places at the center of the painting (and thus at the center of the Hall) neither the cross nor the desperate crowd, but rather a female figure indicating the serpent to one of the cured ***(fig. 24)***. This is most likely the personification of *Faith's glance*; showing the cross, she seems to be alluding, for both the man in the painting and the visitors of the Halls, to the real significance of the event: the exaltation of Christ in death typologically predicted by the raising of the serpent. A similar "spiritual vision" permeates the Sala Superiore's entire decoration, based on the typological interpretation of the Scriptures: the historical situations and realities of the Old Testament find their meaning only in Christ, whom man comprehends through faith. All this is embodied by the female figure at the center of the painting; she bears the meaning of the cycle on the whole.

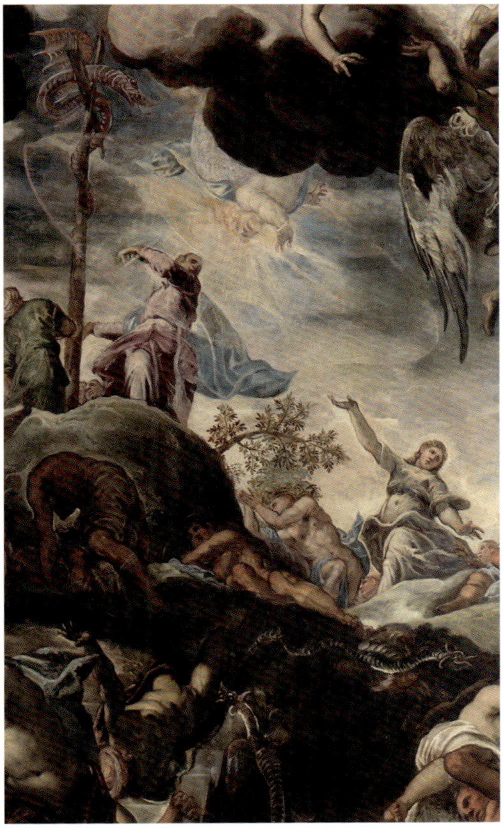

Fig. 24 - The female figure on top of the hill is wearing white and personifying Faith, showing her most traditional attribute: the cross

7. Vision of Ezekiel [35]

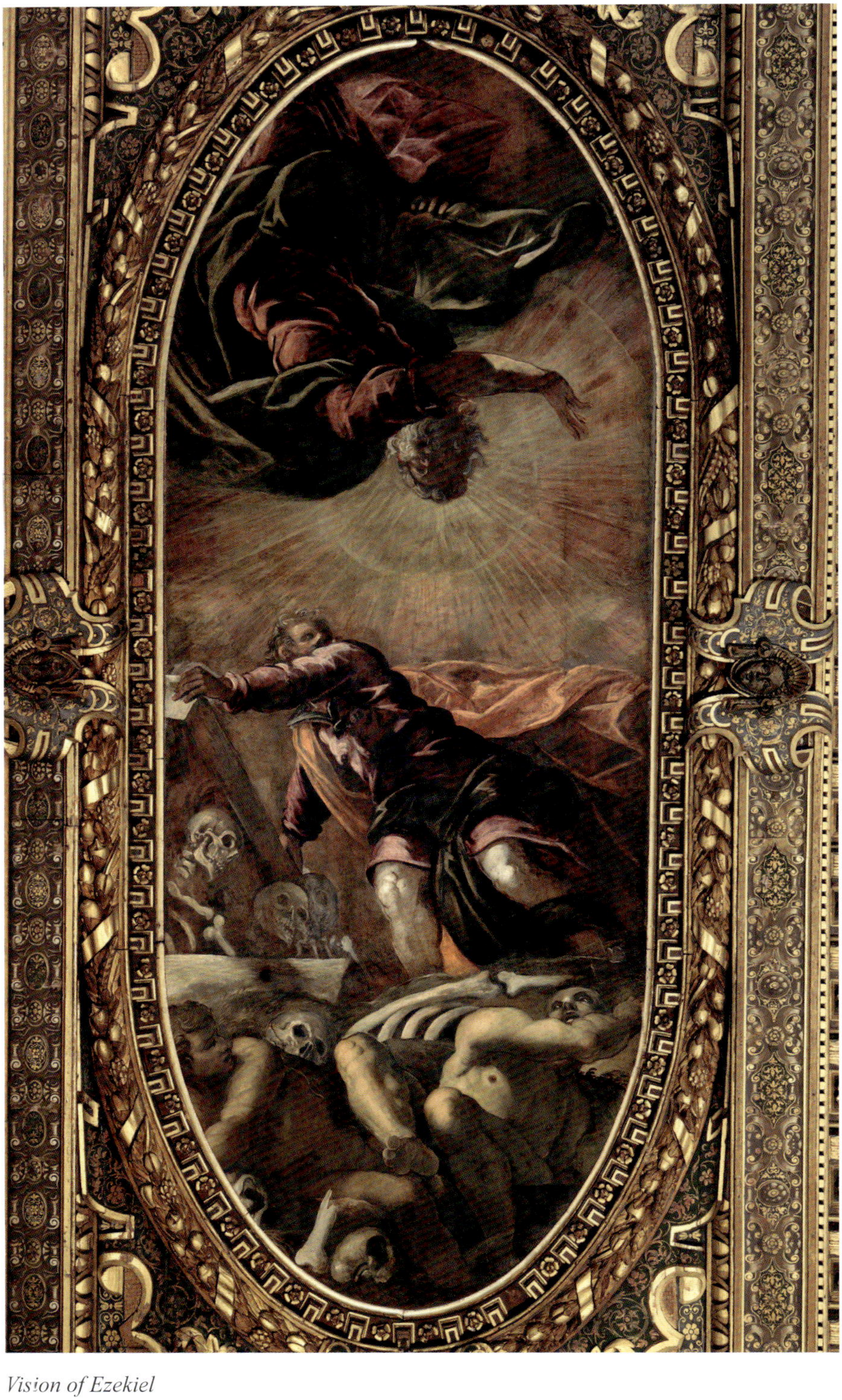

Vision of Ezekiel

The hand of the Lord came upon me and brought me out in the Spirit of the Lord, and set me down in the midst of the valley; and it was full of bones. [...] And He said to me, "Son of man, can these bones live?" So I answered, "O Lord God, You know." Again He said to me, "Prophesy to these bones, and say to them: o dry bones, hear the word of the Lord! [...] Surely I will cause breath to enter into you, and you shall live. (...)'" So I prophesied as I was commanded; and as I prophesied, there was a noise, and suddenly a rattling; and the bones came together, bone to bone. Indeed, as I looked, the sinews and the flesh came upon them, and the skin covered them over; but there was no breath in them. Also He said to me, "Prophesy to the breath, prophesy, son of man, and say to the breath, 'Thus says the Lord God: Come from the four winds, O breath, and breathe on these slain, that they may live.'" So I prophesied as He commanded me, and breath came into them, and they lived, and stood upon their feet, an exceedingly great army.
(Ezekiel 37:1-10)

Here Jesus' resurrection is typologically depicted through the vision of Prophet Ezekiel. The resurrection completes the theology of the redemption: the sacrifice on the cross does not end Jesus' story but leads to the mysteries of the resurrection and the ascension, or rather to Christ's victory over death, a theme that was already prefigured in the **Brazen Serpent** ***(note 6).***
If in the beginning Ezekiel's vision symbolically refers to the deported and imprisoned people of Israel, the Christian tradition sees in it the preannouncement of the resurrection of Christ, and therefore the resurrection of the dead. The vision is particularly dear to the Christian interpretation of the Scriptures, since it stresses that the resurrection promised by the Lord regards our person in all its constitutive elements: flesh, mind and soul. As Paulinus of Nola wrote (*Carmen XXXI*), the Ezekiel text shows that *death is of the body, life is resurrected in the body. (...) If you doubt that (...) souls can return to their vessels, then Prophet Ezekiel will be a good witness for you; the phenomenon of the Lord's resurrection was revealed to him a while back. In his vision you will understand how the imperceptible fragments of ancient men can come back to life.* Tintoretto clearly shows the correlation between this *telero* and the **Resurrection [53]** ***(note 8)*** immediately below. In fact, Ezekiel, contrary to what we read in the Bible, does not limit himself to prophesizing, but also opens a sarcophagus from which some skeletons emerge ***(fig. 25)***; the angels of the **Resurrection** below do the same by lifting the sepulcher's door.

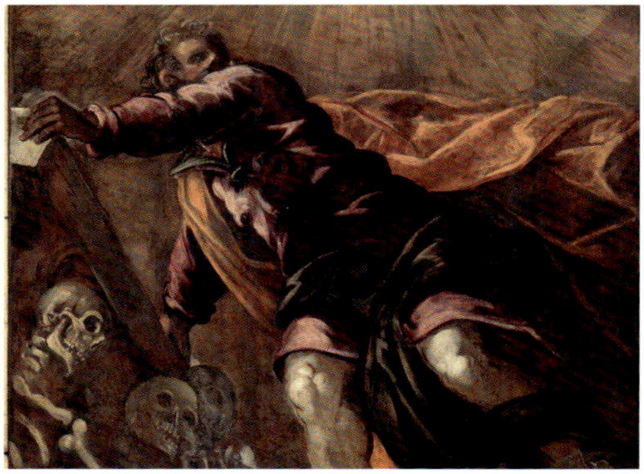

Fig. 25 - The detail of the open sarcophagus refers to the canvas of the *Resurrection*

8. RESURRECTION [53]

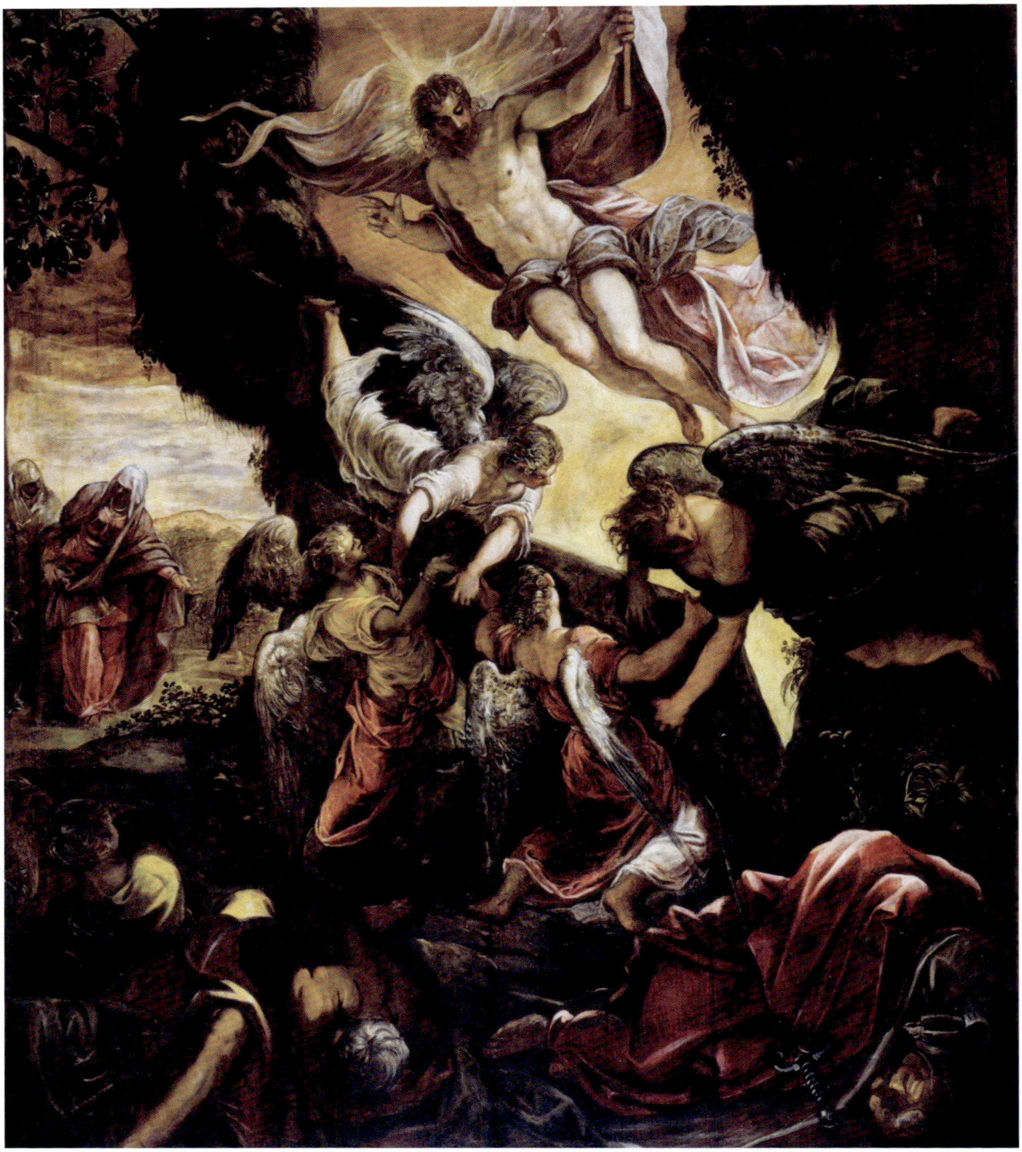

Resurrection

Now after the Sabbath, as the first day of the week began to dawn, Mary Magdalene and the other Mary came to see the tomb. And behold, there was a great earthquake; for an angel of the Lord descended from heaven, and came and rolled back the stone from the door, and sat on it. His countenance was like lightning, and his clothing as white as snow. And the guards shook for fear of him, and became like dead men. But the angel answered and said to the women, "Do not be afraid, for I know that you seek Jesus who was crucified. He is not here; for He is risen, as He said. Come, see the place where the Lord lay. And go quickly and tell His disciples that He is risen from the dead, and indeed He is going before you into Galilee; there you will see Him. Behold, I have told you." So they went out quickly from the tomb with fear and great joy, and ran to bring His disciples word. *(Matthew 28:1-8)*

In the background we see that which precedes, or rather occurs, simultaneously with the resurrection: two women heading towards the sepulcher. They are Mary Magdalene and *the other Mary, mother of James and Joseph* (Matthew 27:56), coming to visit Jesus' tomb. In the foreground the Lord rises from the sepulcher held by the angels, completely enveloped in light. Jesus has thus accomplished the reconstruction of the temple as he had prophesied: "*Destroy this temple, and in three days I will raise it up." (...) But He was speaking of the temple of His body* (John 2:19.21). As already noted, a reference to this event can be found in the **Resurrection of Lazarus [57]** – a miracle that symbolizes the resurrection of the body of every man in Christ (see John 11:26) and therefore directly related to the **Resurrection** – through the use of an edificatory metaphor of the rocks: both Lazarus and Jesus sit upon one rock, the latter indicating a third rock with his right hand ***(fig. 26).***

Tintoretto depicts the resurrection of Christ with great vigor. It is a real explosion of light, frightening the soldiers to death, the same soldiers who had been placed to guard the sepulcher to make sure the disciples would not steal the Master's body after three days and then say that, as he had predicted, he rose from the dead (see Matthew 27:62-66).

The guards are depicted by the lower edge of the painting: in the left corner a guard covers his face with an arm; another, with his back bent and face lowered to the ground, protects himself from the light; the last one, to the right, covers himself completely with his mantle. The guards are important eyewitnesses of the historical reality of the resurrection (thus they are all the more reliable since they were sent by enemies of Christ). They are eyewitnesses of the extraordinary event in the moment of its occurrence. This is emphasized in writings such as the apocryphal Gospels (see box p. 123), for example the Gospel of Nicodemus. We can see in one soldier's effort to keep his face turned to the Lord – even though his arm is blocking his eyes – his desire to admit the truth, which will be rejected by his superiors, that is, by those who, even with the proof in front of them, *do not want* to see: *You*

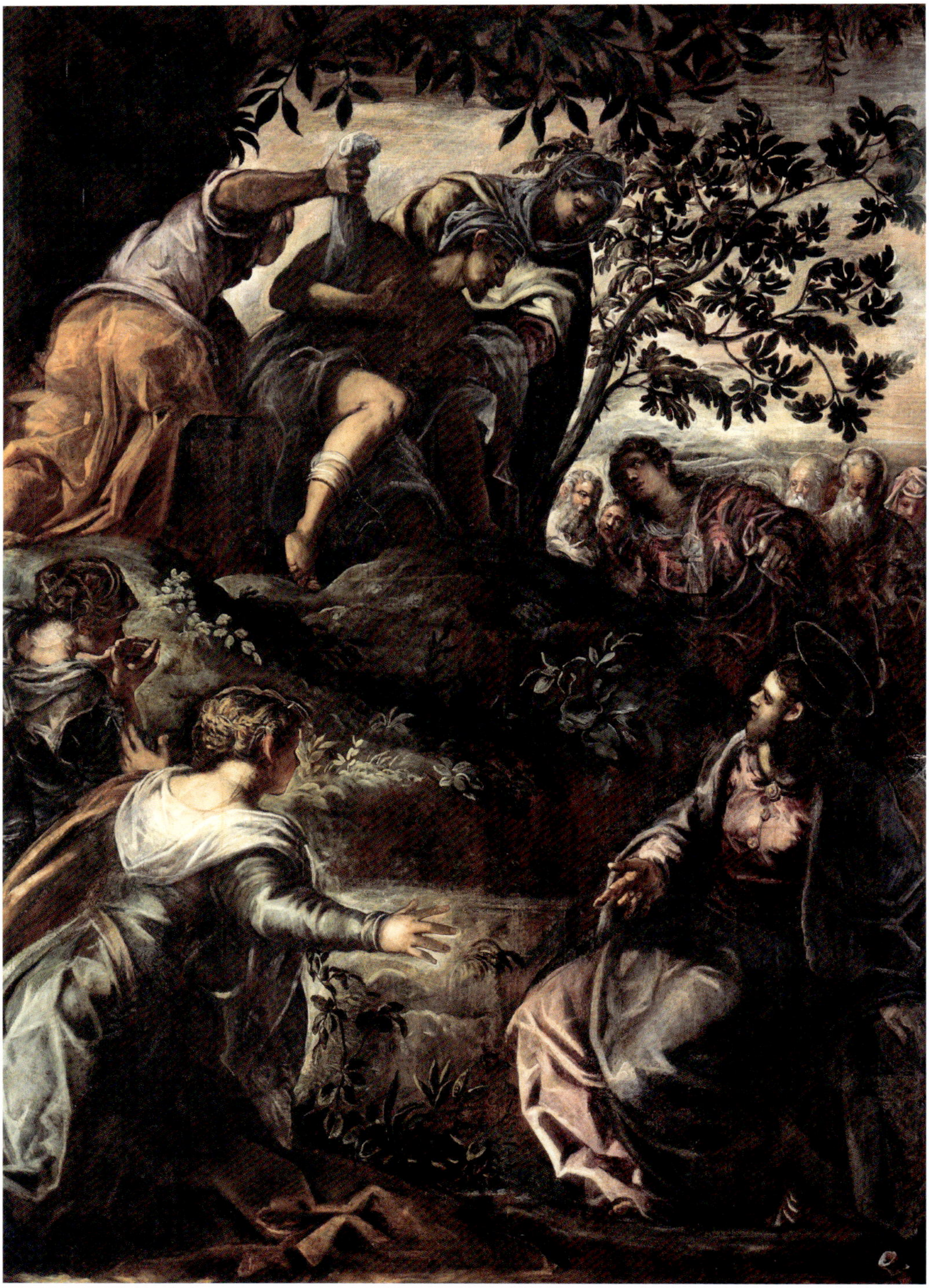

Fig. 26 - Resurrection of Lazarus. When resurrecting Lazarus Jesus points to a stone, alluding perhaps to his own resurrection as the reconstruction of the Temple

have seen so many signs in that man and still you do not believe; how can you then believe in us? (*Gospel According to Nicodemus,* 13).
Popular tradition identifies one of the guards by the sepulcher as Longinus, the centurion who under the cross, even though almost blind, had seen (that is, recognized) Jesus as the Son of God, and who later, after having from pity pierced Christ's side with a lance, had his eyes healed with the blood from the wound. Longinus is the saint of the *fides ex visu*, the faith based on sight. Seeing spiritually, with faith, meaning knowing how to interpret an event according to its real meaning, even if it is apparently paradoxical: only he who sees spiritually like the centurion recognizes in the evil of the crucifixion a glorification. Tintoretto depicts this concept perfectly in the Albergo's **Crucifixion [22]** ***(note 2)***. It also means, as seen in the **Brazen Serpent [28]** ***(note 6)***, being capable of reading the story as a sequence of divine works, whose center and interpretative key is the Easter of Christ. Seeing spiritually ultimately means to recognize the complete similarity between the current rite and the historical-salvational event: resurrected, Christ's body and blood become bread and wine in reality. The faithful recognize the substance of Christ's body and blood in the Eucharist, even though the material characteristics of the bread and wine are not changed.

All this seems to be implied by the triangulation that gives structure to the entire painting, which is fundamental for its theological interpretation. If in fact the guard has his face turned to the Lord, the latter's glance, like the one of the angel positioned at the extreme right of the group, is directed at a precise point in the painting where we see a pitcher and bread ***(fig. 27),*** symbols of the Eucharist. From this moment on it seems that Jesus is saying, "My body for you is consecrated bread," substantially they are one and the same.

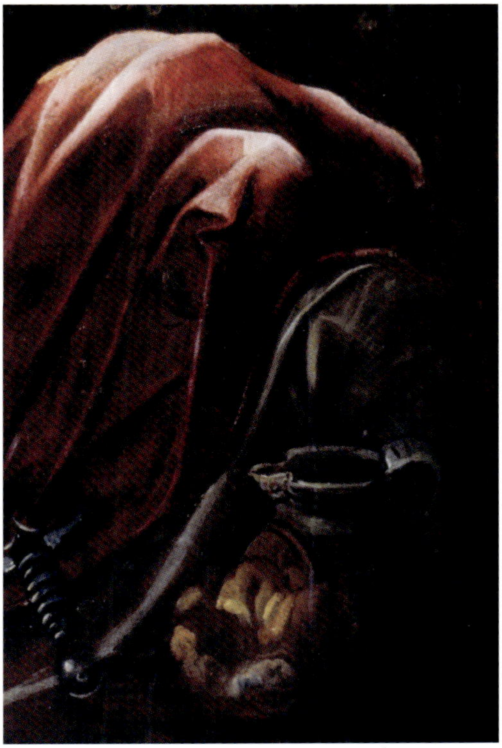

Fig. 27 - The pitcher and the bread in the foreground on the right of the painting are symbols of the Eucharist

9. Jacob's Ladder [36]

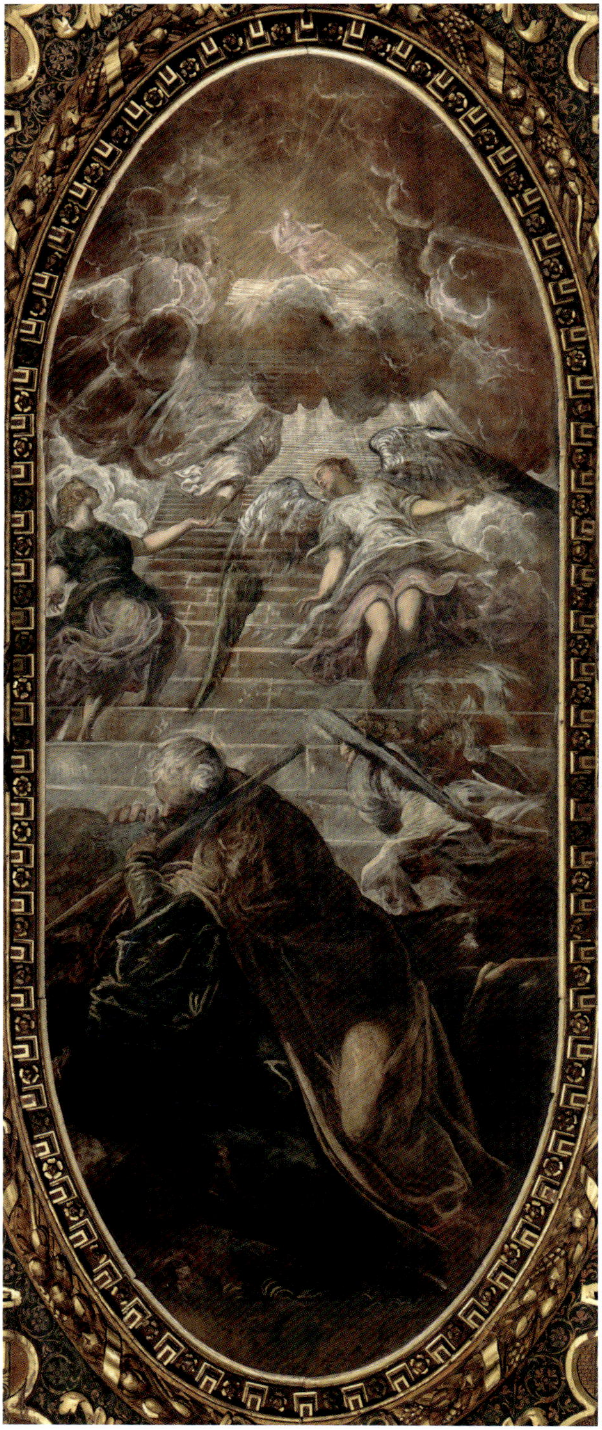

Now Jacob went out from Beersheba and went toward Haran. So he came to a certain place and stayed there all night, because the sun had set. And he took one of the stones of that place and put it at his head, and he lay down in that place to sleep. Then he dreamed, and behold, a ladder was set up on the earth, and its top reached to heaven; and there the angels of God were ascending and descending on it. And behold, the Lord stood above it and said: "I am the Lord God of Abraham your father and the God of Isaac; the land on which you lie I will give to you and your descendants. Also your descendants shall be as the dust of the earth; you shall spread abroad to the west and the east, to the north and the south; and in you and in your seed all the families of the earth shall be blessed. Behold, I am with you and will keep you wherever you go, and will bring you back to this land; for I will not leave you until I have done what I have spoken to you."
(Genesis 28:10-15)

Jacob's Ladder

Jacob's dream represents an intense encounter between man and God, in which the latter repeats the promises already made to Abraham and Isaac (see Genesis 15;22;26). The ladder symbolizes the connection between the human and the divine spheres, and yet respects the transcendence of God. Such is Tintoretto's *telero*, in which the sky and the earth are linked on the one hand by the ladder and on the other, separated by a mantle of clouds.
The episode is clearly meant to be a prefiguration of the **Ascension [58]** ***(note 10)***, according to an established typological reading. Here the artist prefers to depict the prefiguration of Jacob's ladder rather than the one, which was more common to the times, of **Elijah on the chariot of fire** (which the creator of the iconographic scheme includes **[43]**, but leaves for one of the adjacent monochromes). The reason is that this episode is symbolically related to the crucifixion, and therefore to the **Brazen Serpent [28]** ***(note 6)***. In fact, Christian interpretation of Jacob's dream has always insisted on the ladder being a symbol of the cross. Cromatius of Aquileia writes: *the ladder that rose from the earth to the sky is Christ's cross through which we reach the sky (Sermons,* 1:6). Other Church Fathers see Christ on top of the ladder, since it was the cross that was raised like a ladder of access to Heaven. The figure of God that Tintoretto positions on the last step, who resembles the Son rather than the Father and who has his arms extended as those of the Crucified ***(fig. 28)***, seems to be alluding to this interpretation.
Jacob's dream also has, as already noted by scholars, interesting Eucharistic implications, which Tintoretto wittingly demonstrates. Here Jacob is strangely depicted as an old man, even though the Bible says that he is a young man looking for a wife (he is in fact on his way to uncle Laban's to marry one of his daughters). It is possible that the painter intended to unite the episode of the dream with that of the return to Bethel, something that Jacob does later in the story. On that occasion, after another appearance of God, Jacob erects a stela on which he performs libation (see Genesis 35:1-15); this sacrifice to God was interpreted by many texts that were well-known in the 16th century, such as the *Moralized Bible* (a sort of comment on the Scriptures which gives explanations of paraphrased stories, accompanied by miniatures), as being a figure of the Last Supper, and thus the Eucharist.

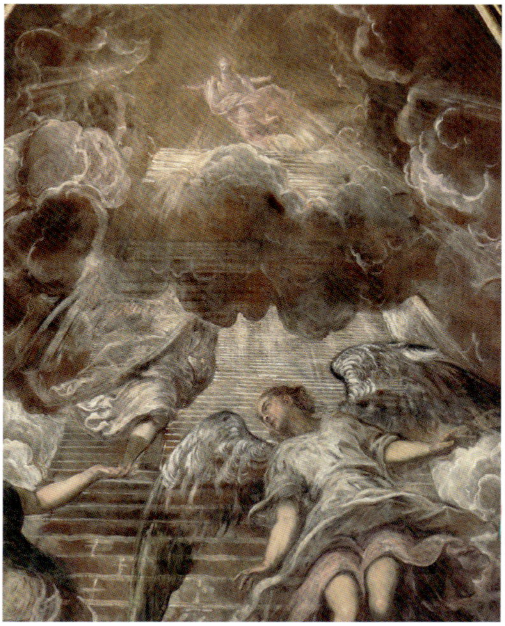

Fig. 28 - God's position at the top of the ladder is a reference to the Crucifixion; Christian tradition has often associated Jacob's vision with the cross

10. Ascension [58]

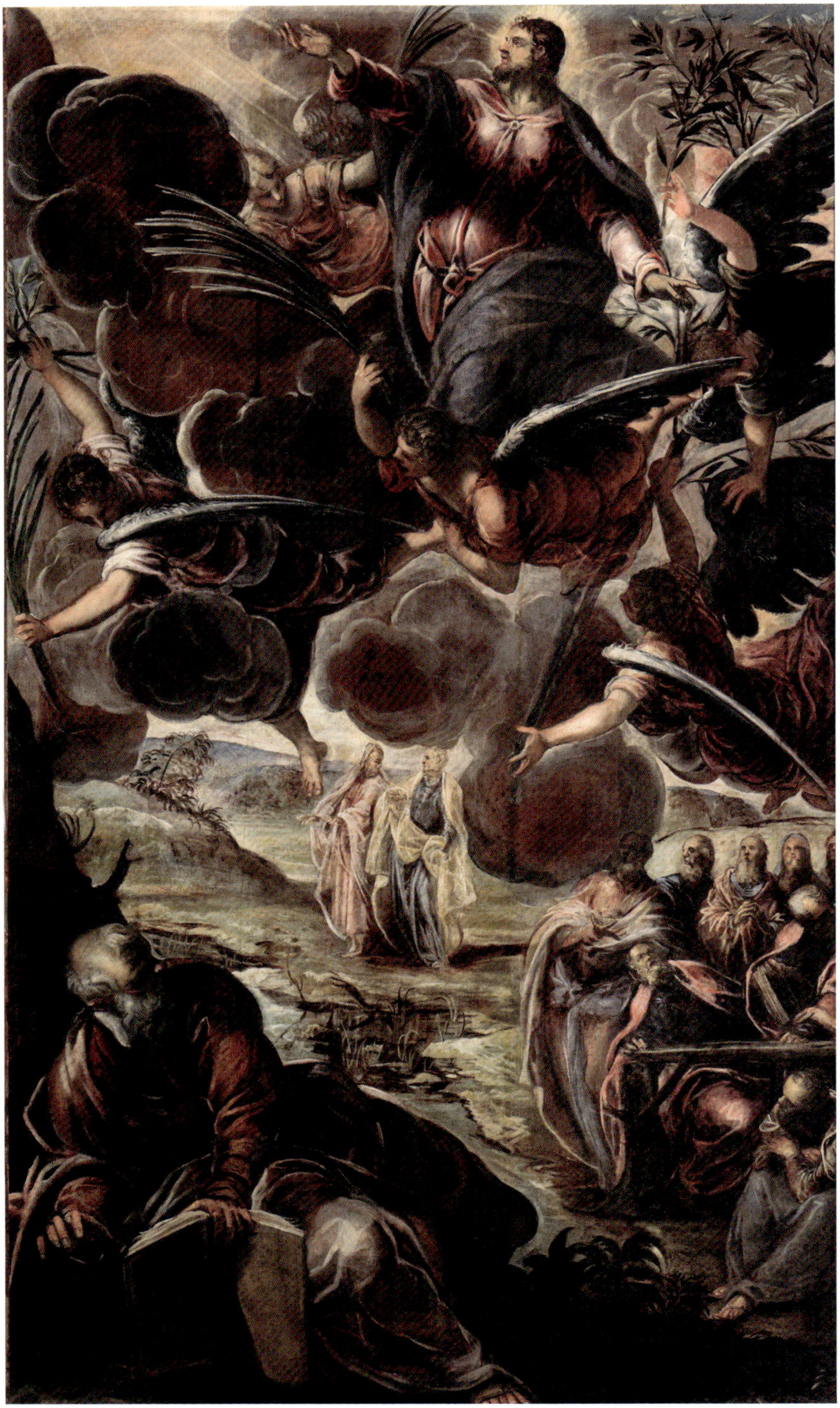

Ascension

The former account I made, O Theophilus, of all that Jesus began both to do and teach, until the day in which He was taken up, after He through the Holy Spirit had given commandments to the apostles whom He had chosen, to whom He also presented Himself alive after His suffering [...]. And being assembled together with them, He commanded them not to depart from Jerusalem, but to wait for the Promise of the Father, "which," He said, "you have heard from Me; for John truly baptized with water, but you shall be baptized with the Holy Spirit not many days from now. (...)". Now when He had spoken these things, while they watched, He was taken up, and a cloud received Him out of their sight. *(Acts 1:1-5.9)*

Luke tells us about the ascension both in his Gospel (see Luke 24:36-53) and in the Acts. The comparison and integration of the two texts is essential for correctly interpreting this painting. In both texts the apostles are sitting at a table: Tintoretto depicts them in this position on the right part of the painting. While, taken from the Acts, there is the detail of the cloud that distances Christ from the apostles during the ascension ***(fig. 29)***, from the Gospel there is the detail of a book that one apostle is holding, alluding to the *intelligence of the Scriptures* acquired by the Eleven thanks to what Christ tells them before ascending: *All things must be fulfilled which were written in the Law of Moses and the Prophets and the Psalms. (...) Thus it is written, and thus it was necessary for the Christ to suffer and to rise from the dead the third day, and that repentance and remission of sins should be preached in His name to all nations* (Luke 24:44-47).

In the foreground we see the Evangelist, or rather the narrating voice that introduces the event: in the prologue of the Acts Luke turns directly to his friend Theophilus, explaining that the ascension is the end of a long journey, begun with the works and teachings of Jesus and concluded with his death and resurrection (see Acts 1:1-2).

But who are the two characters speaking so emotionally in the background? To find the answer let's return to the texts. Jesus appears before the apostles to ask them for something precise: to be witnesses of his resurrection *to the end of the earth* (Acts 1:8; Luke 24:46-48). The Acts interprets the ascension as the end of the Easter apparitions: it is the resurrection that is the heart of the Christian message, propagated by the apostles during their missions. The two men in the background are therefore the protagonists of the first apparition of the resurrected Christ: the disciples who are returning from Emmaus to Jerusalem to tell the Eleven *about the things that had happened on the road, and how He [the Lord] was known to them in the breaking of bread* (Luke 24:35).

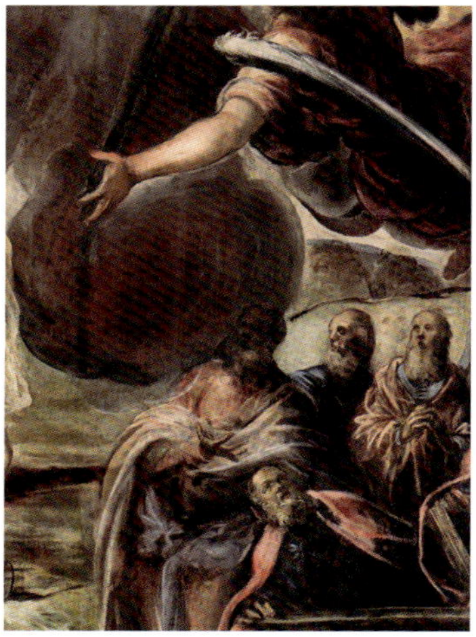

Fig. 29 - As in the story from the *Acts of the Apostles*, a cloud covers the faces of the apostles when Christ ascends

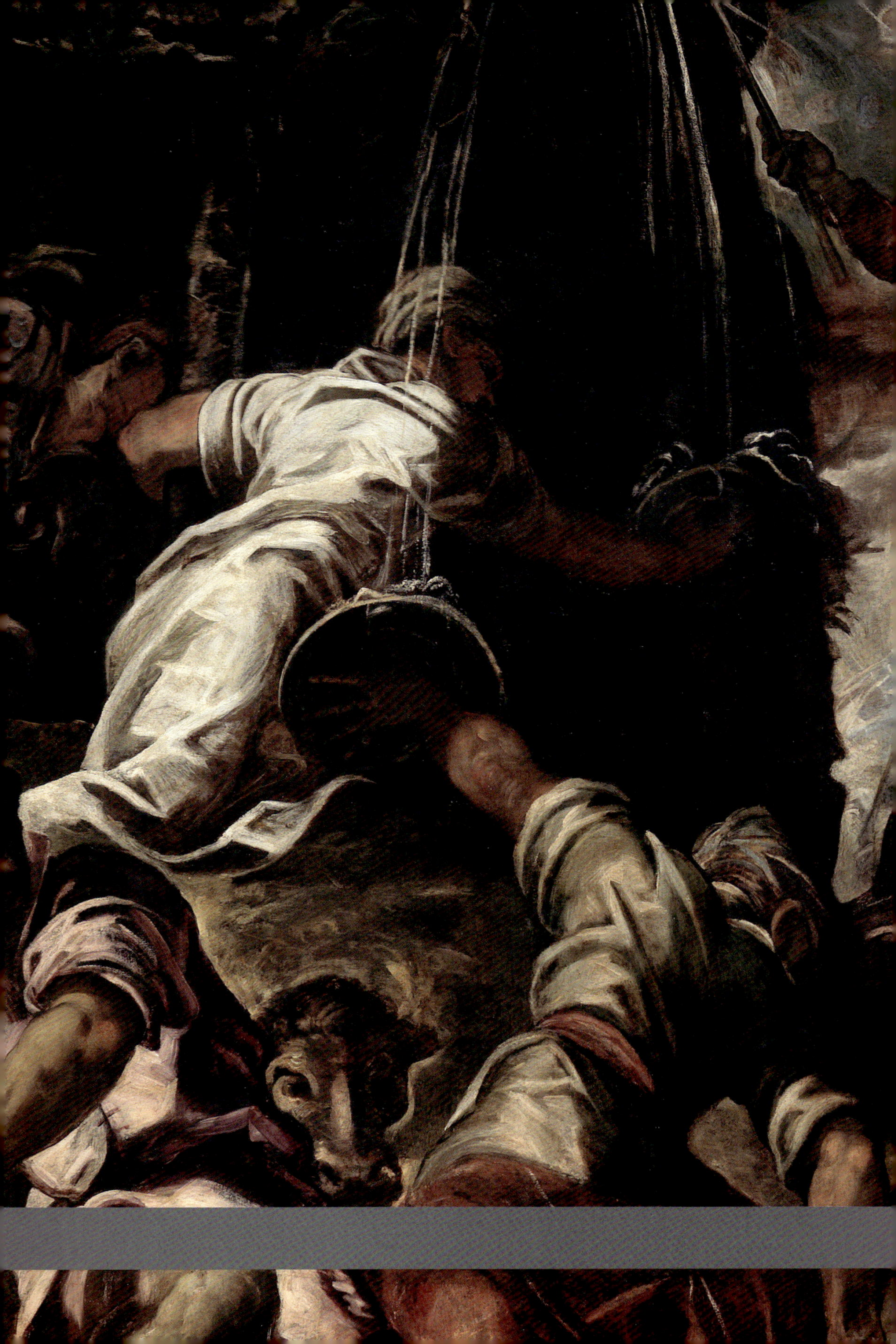

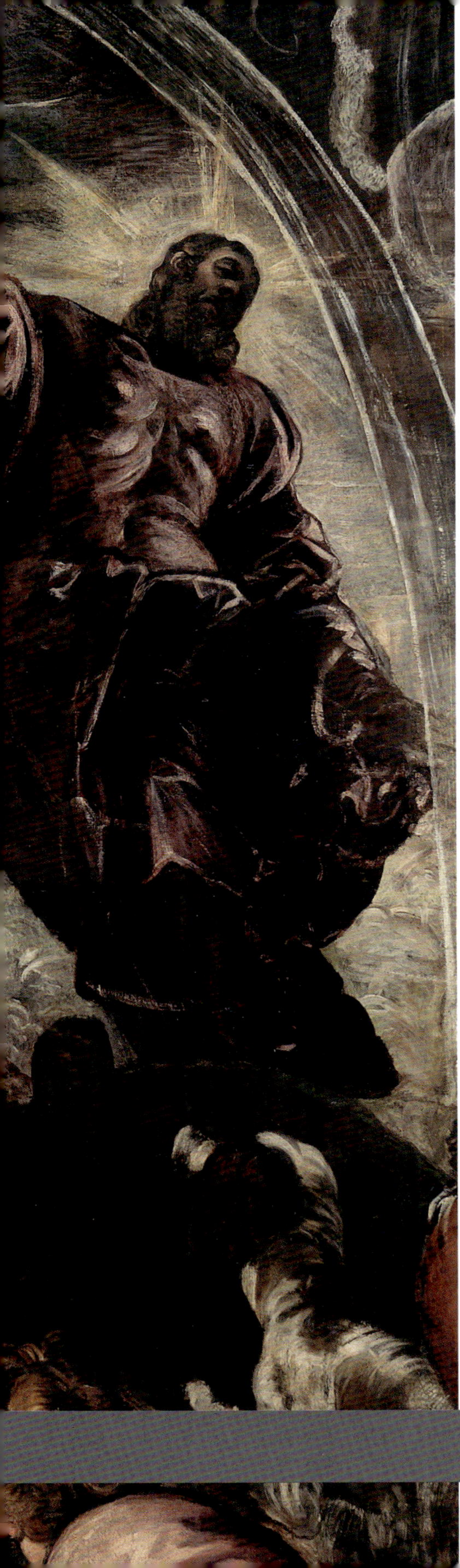

The Baptism

Moses drawing water from the rock [29], the main *telero* in the northern section, is the prefiguration of the Baptism, through which man is given the salvation of the cross of Christ, who is the protagonist of the middle section. Introduced by the episode with **Jonah [34]**, which is the prefiguration of Baptism with the rebirth from water, the baptismal theme is reflected in the **Baptism of Christ [52],** then in the **Pillar of Fire [33]** and finally in the **Probatic Pool [59]**, which is the symbol of the baptismal remission of sins.

11. Jonah leaves the whale's belly [34]

Now the word of the Lord came to Jonah, "Arise, go to Nineveh, that great city, and cry out against it; for their wickedness has come up before Me." But Jonah arose to flee to Tarshish from the presence of the Lord. He went down to Joppa, and found a ship going to Tarshish; so he paid the fare, and went down into it (...) But the Lord sent out a great wind on the sea, and there was a mighty tempest on the sea, so that the ship was about to be broken up. Then the mariners were afraid, (...) and they said to one another, "Come, let us cast lots, that we may know for whose cause this trouble has come upon us." So they cast lots, and the lot fell on Jonah. (...) And he said to them, "Pick me up and throw me into the sea; then the sea will become calm for you. For I know that this great tempest is because of me." (...) So they picked up Jonah and threw him into the sea, and the sea ceased from its raging. (...) Now the Lord had prepared a great fish to swallow Jonah. And Jonah was in the belly of the fish three days and three nights. (...) So the Lord spoke to the fish, and it vomited Jonah onto dry land. Now the word of the Lord came to Jonah the second time, saying, "Arise, go to Nineveh, that great city, and preach to it the message that I tell you." So Jonah arose and went to Nineveh, according to the word of the Lord. *(Jonah 1:1-5.7.12.15.17; 2:10; 3:1-3)*

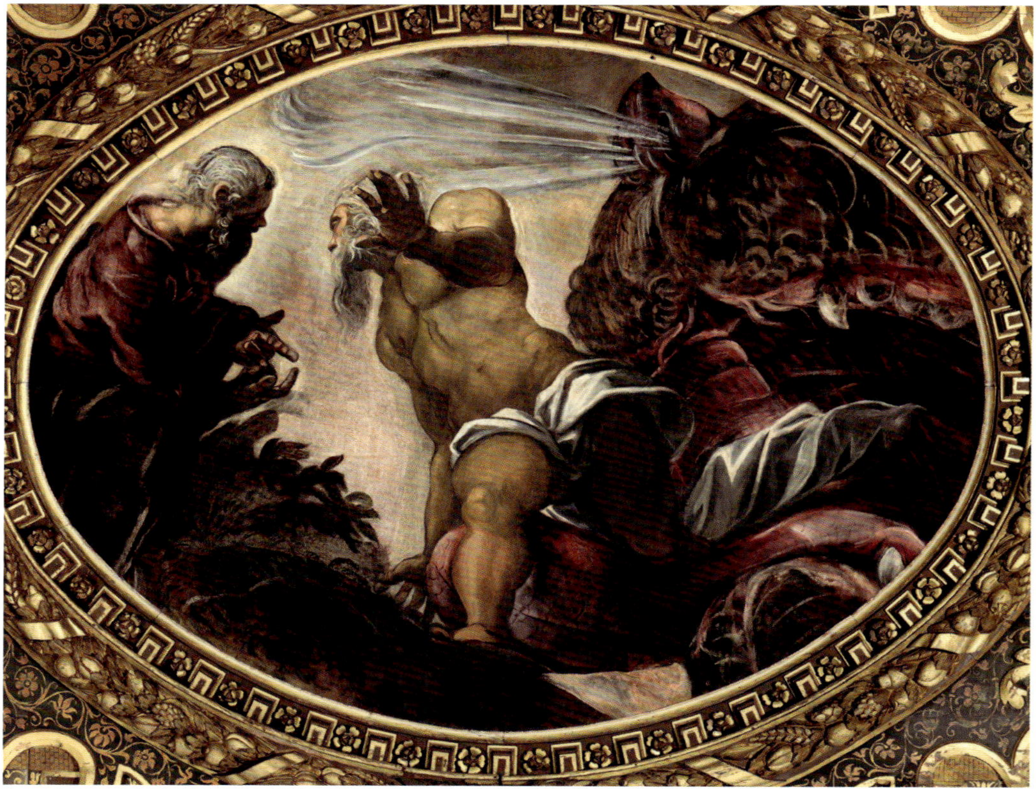

Jonah leaves the whale's belly

The *telero* with Jonah is a pivotal painting. Jonah remains in the sea monster's belly for three days, only then to be vomited up onto the shore. The whale swallows him but it does not devour him; it saves him, according to Divine Will. As predicted by Christ, who ciphers his passion in the *sign of prophet Jonah* (Matthew 12:39), the Fathers of the Church interpret Jonah's adventure in an allegoric manner: like Jonah, who fell from the ship into the belly of the cetacean, so did Christ descend from the cross into the sepulcher and into death; like Jonah, who sacrificed himself for his shipmates, so did Christ die for the salvation of mankind; like Jonah's preaching, which reached the citizens of Nineveh only after he had been spit up by the fish, so did the prophetic message of the Lord reach the pagans only after his resurrection (see Augustine*, Letters*, 102:34).

Therefore Jonah is an Old Testament model of the resurrection, linking himself to the central thematic group of the paintings. But he also clearly represents the spiritual rebirth from water that every Christian experiences during Baptism, connecting himself thus to the paintings in the northern group: it is not by chance that a strong spray of water coming from the whale's nostrils hits the prophet's head as he leaves from the fish's jaws. The interaction between God and Jonah is intense. The prophet does not directly look at God: even though the Lord is depicted on his level, Jonah's eyes are directed elsewhere. This alludes to what the Lord told Moses: *You cannot see my face, for no man shall see me and live* (Exodus 33:20). In fact, it is like this in many paintings on the ceiling where God is covered by a cloud of glory, which simultaneously veils and unveils him. Jonah does not see God directly, but lends him his ear so that he can speak to him, as specified in the Bible, *a second time* (Jonah 3:1). The command is still the one of getting up and going to Nineveh to preach conversion. The painting does not alter the irony of the biblical story, in which Jonah, after many vicissitudes, returns to where he started: God is reminding him wisely, with the typical gesture of rotating the index finger and the thumb, which still today means the inconsistency of a real alternative.

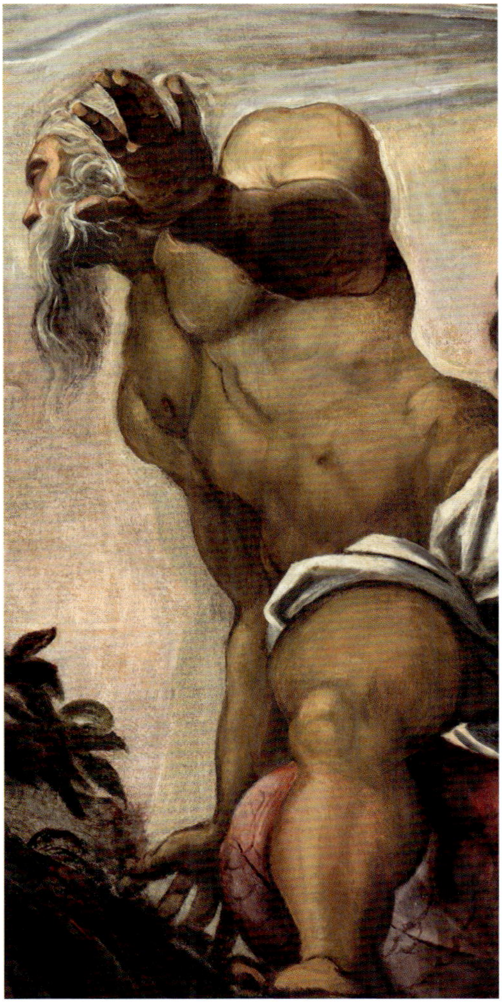

12. MOSES DRAWING WATER FROM THE ROCK [29]

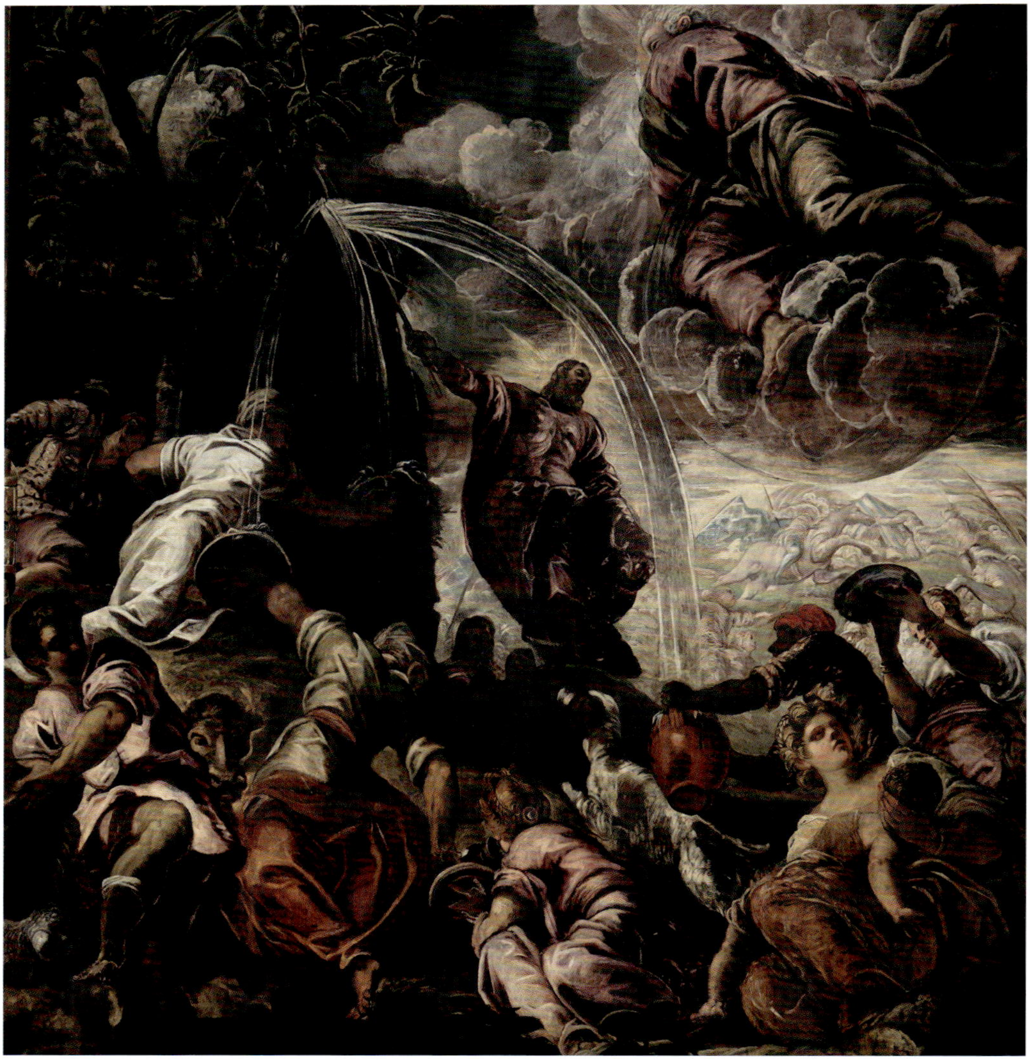

Moses drawing water from the rock

Then all the congregation of the children of Israel set out on their journey from the Wilderness of Sin, according to the commandment of the Lord, and camped in Rephidim; (...) And the people thirsted there for water, and the people complained against Moses, and said, "Why is it you have brought us up out of Egypt, to kill us and our children and our livestock with thirst?" So Moses cried out to the Lord, saying, "What shall I do with this people? They are almost ready to stone me!" And the Lord said to Moses, "Go on before the people, and take with you some of the elders of Israel. Also take in your hand your rod with which you struck the river, and go. Behold, I will stand before you there on the rock in Horeb; and you shall strike the rock, and water will come out of it, that the people may drink." And Moses did so in the sight of the elders of Israel. So he called the name of the place Massah and Meribah, because of the contention of the children of Israel, and because they tempted the Lord, saying, "Is the Lord among us or not?" *(Exodus 17:1-7)*

During their walk through the desert the exhausted Israelites ask Moses to procure them some water. God commands Moses to take a rod – the same rod with which Moses would *do the signs* (see Exodus 4:17) – and strike the rock, from which springs forth the water to quench the people's thirst. It is precisely this moment that Tintoretto depicts: the Israelites are leaping to collect the water that is pouring out in potent streams from the rock's crack.
The scene is constructed in a way as to imply a prefiguration of a moment in the story of Christ, without however having the connection be explicit. In fact, Tintoretto, substituting the fountain that normally represented the miracle with the spurting water, is referring to a precise scene, that of the angels collecting the gushing blood and water from Christ's side during the crucifixion ***(fig. 30)***. The rock struck by Moses is therefore, according to an old typological interpretation, the prefiguration of Christ's body pierced by the Roman soldier's lance (see John 19:34). In this manner Moses' miracle clearly refers to Christ's sacrifice and to the sacraments that in it have their roots. Jesus himself had compared his passion to a *baptism* (see Mark 10:38; Luke 12:50), and the Church interpreted the blood and the water pouring from the Lord's rib as signs of Baptism and the Eucharist, sacraments of the new life in Christ: it is from his pierced side that gushes the living water of baptismal grace. Tintoretto alludes to this by "conforming" Moses' rod to the cross: taking a closer look, we see, in fact, that the rod is in reality a cross that is outlined against the dark background of the rock ***(fig. 31)***. The rebirth from water in the painting is symbolized by the fig plant, whose lush foliage we see above on the left: in a land that the Bible describes as a completely arid desert, Tintoretto inserts a plant that symbolizes the Promised Land par excellence, thus alluding to what the people will obtain only at the end of the long journey through the desert.
A passage from St. Paul will better illustrate the reason for which the painter decided to depict the continuation of the biblical story behind this miracle. In fact, in the background we find the battle be-

tween the Israelites and the Amalekites taking place in Rephidim. Amalek is the archenemy, precisely because he is inconvertible (see Exodus 17:16). Moses came to mediate in the victory for Israel, holding up the *rod of God* (Exodus 17:9) during the clash. The Bible relates that when Moses lifted his arms, Israel was winning, but when he lowered them, the enemy had the upper hand. Then Moses stood up on a rock while Aaron and Hur held up his arms; this allowed the Israelites to defeat Amalek. The rock, which in this episode returns to support Moses, for St. Paul represents Christ, the spiritual rock that accompanies the Hebrews in the desert (see 1 Cor 10:1-4): according to Jewish tradition, in fact, the rock from which the water was drawn had miraculously followed the Israelites in their migration. Just like the

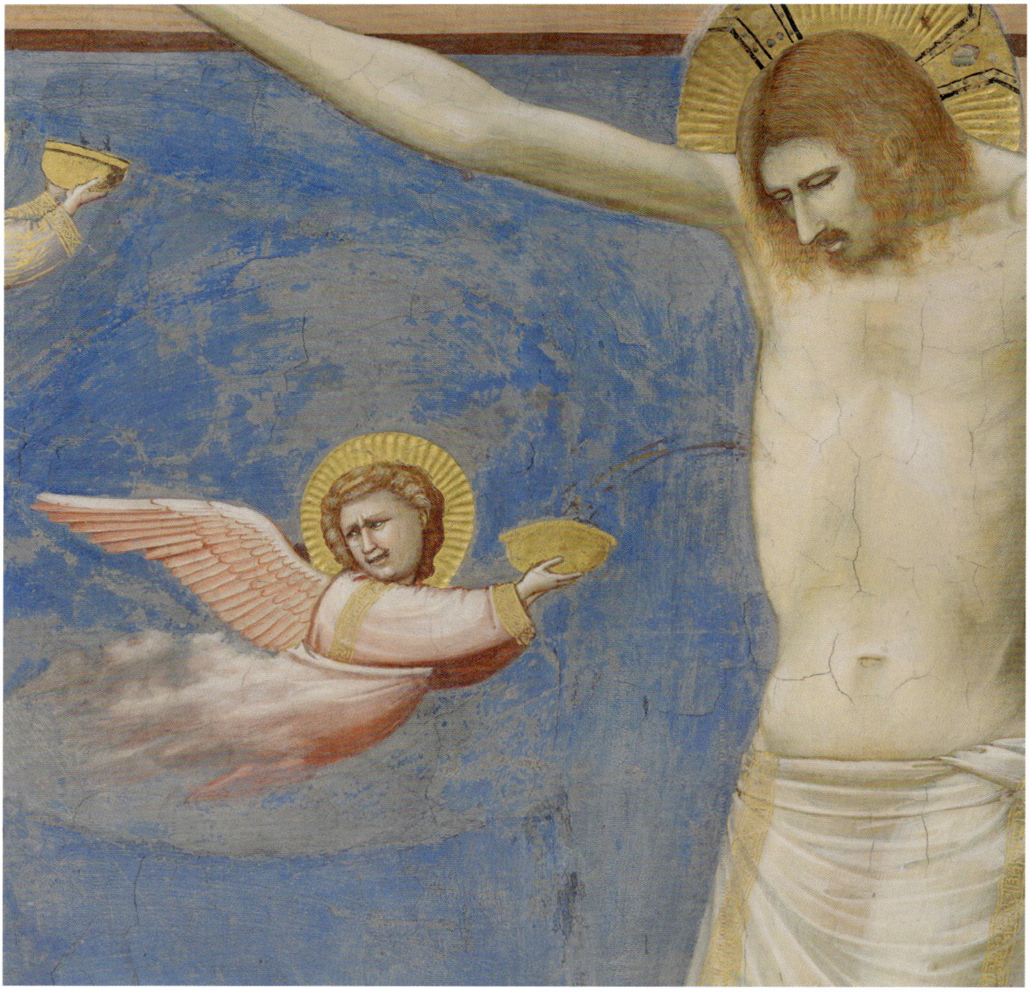

Fig. 30 - Giotto, *Crucifixion* (1303-1305), Padua, Cappella degli Scrovegni, detail. Painting the water gushing out, which the Israelites are collecting in containers, Tintoretto is consciously referring to a particular figurative tradition that shows angels collecting the blood and water spurting out of Christ's side

rod, the rock is therefore a sign of salvation that depends on the will of God and prefigures his embodiment in Christ, the fountain of the Spirit that quenches the baptized: *everyone drank the same spiritual drink: they drank from the spiritual rock that accompanied them, and that rock was Christ* (1 Cor 10:4).

Just as for the **Brazen Serpent [28]** ***(note 6),*** the historical dimension should not be forgotten when interpreting this painting. Similar to the serpent-*theriaca*, the water also has significant medicinal value. There were many legends that evolved around the so-called "healthy waters," which were considered miraculous when fighting the plague and which, precisely in the years of the Sala Superiore's decoration, due to the spread of the contagion, were very sought after. We can easily understand how the visitors identified with the characters in the painting who were saved by the miraculous streams of water just when they thought they were going to die of thirst. Certainly the visitors imagined, based on their own or others' experience, the pilgrimages to the salutary wells (as the one in Santa Croce on the island of Giudecca) with the aim of drawing water to protect themselves from the deadly epidemic.

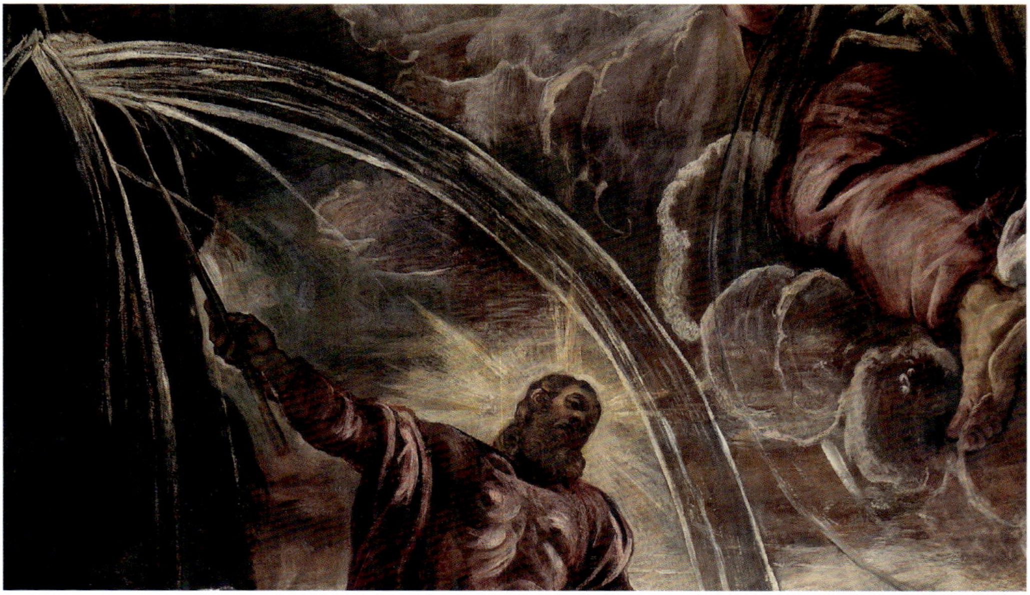

Fig. 31 - Moses' stick takes the form of a cross that stands out against the dark rock

13. Baptism of Christ [52]

It came to pass in those days that Jesus came from Nazareth of Galilee, and was baptized by John in the Jordan. And immediately, coming up from the water, He saw the heavens parting and the Spirit descending upon Him like a dove. Then a voice came from heaven, "You are My beloved Son, in whom I am well pleased." *(Mark 1:9-11)*

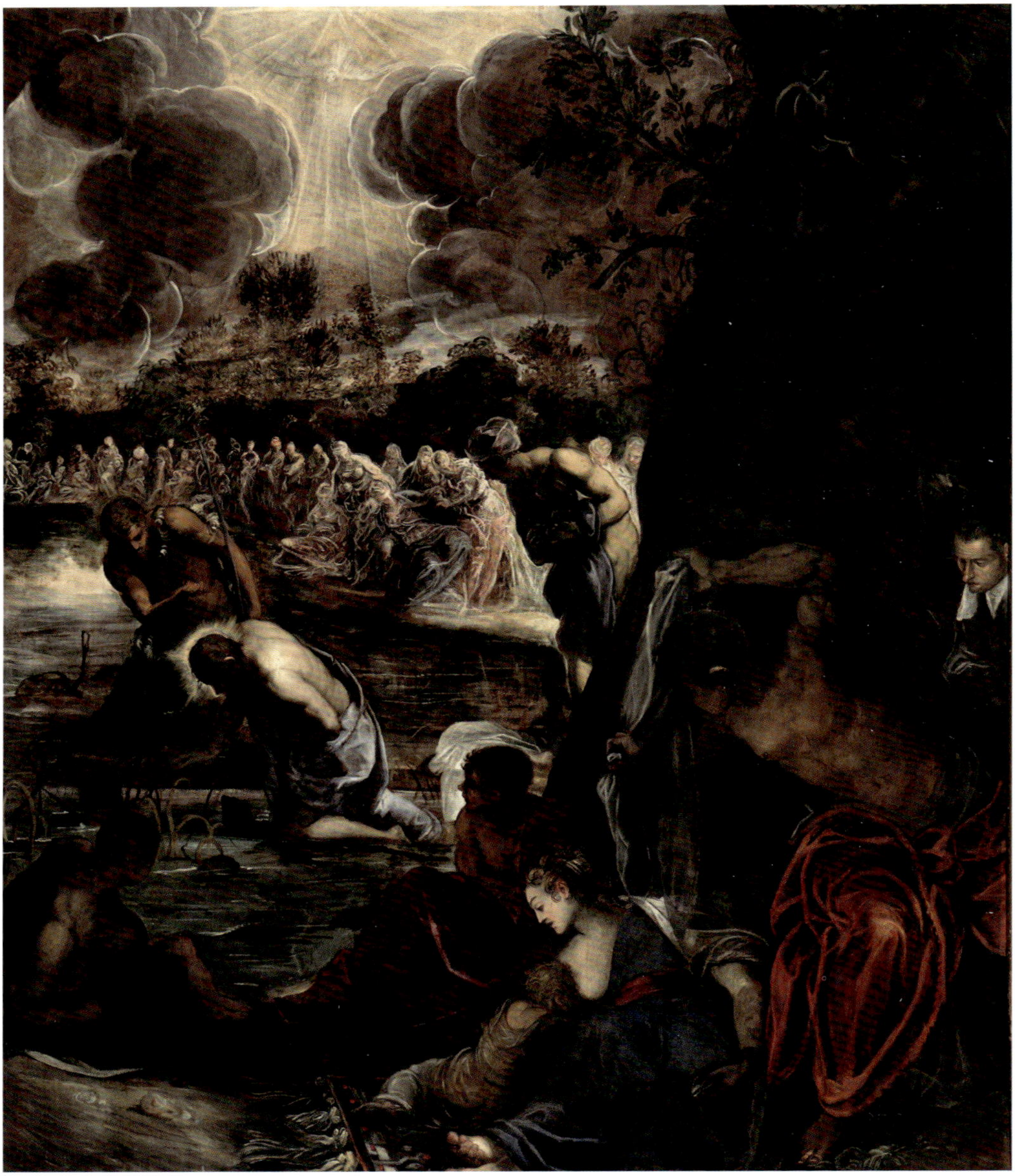

Baptism of Christ

For every Christian Baptism is the death of sin by means of a life in Jesus Christ (see Romans 6:11): *Therefore we were buried with Him through baptism into death, that just as Christ was raised from the dead by the glory of the Father, even so we also should walk in newness of life* (Romans 6:4). To receive Baptism means in fact to be buried in the water of Jordan, to die together with Christ, and thus shed the old human in us. This is what the figure who is approaching the Baptist behind Christ is doing: leaving his clothes, or rather his old sinful birthday suit, he is shedding the slave in himself. The sacrament remits the sins in a drastic way. Contrary to what Luther thought, original sin, as the Council of Trent specified, is washed away and man can call himself innocent before the Lord. There is a powerful link between the mystery of the cross and the sacrament of Baptism, since it is only with the sacrifice of God that water becomes redemptory. St. Augustine writes: *Baptism (...) would not be water of salvation if it was not consecrated by Christ, who shed his blood for us, that is, if water was not the sign of the cross (Sermons,* 352:1,3). Tintoretto places great emphasis on this aspect: behind Christ, as if seeing her son crucified, Mary already seems to be swooning ***(fig. 32)***.

Baptism gives man the three theological virtues: Faith, Hope and Charity. Perhaps it is them that Tintoretto wanted to depict on the *telero*, placing them in the foreground, outside the event, in a dimension that is not part of the story but rather of the sacrament. Hope, the figure with the nude torso in the near foreground, knows that which it still cannot see. Faith, instead, by the grace of God sees the deepest mysteries in the present, namely, that God, in Christ, is present in all reality and history: it is the figure dressed in red on the shores of the Jordan, looking through the darkness; the veil covering Hope's eyes is drawn away from her face. Faith and Hope are depicted here as complements, since Faith *is the substance of things hoped for* (Hebrews 11:1). Charity is depicted in the usual nursing pose between the other two virtues, as their most precious fruit.

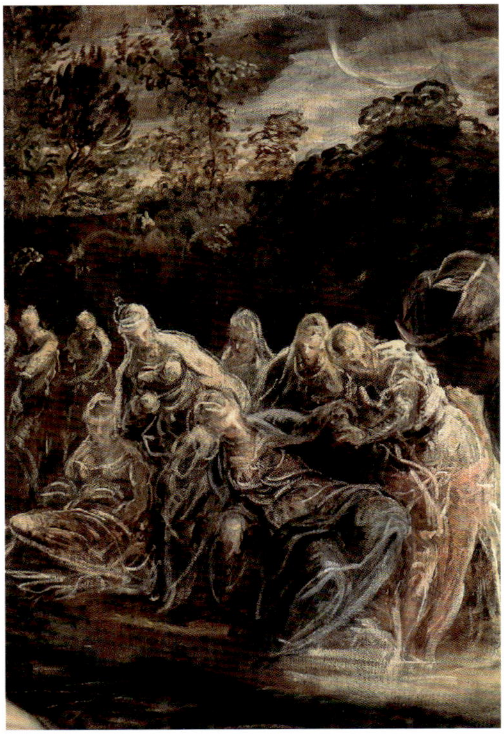

Fig. 32 - The Virgin is present during her son's baptism, swooning as if already under the cross (see *Crucifixion*, ***fig. 10***). This shows the strong connection between this moment and the passion

14. Probatic Pool [59]

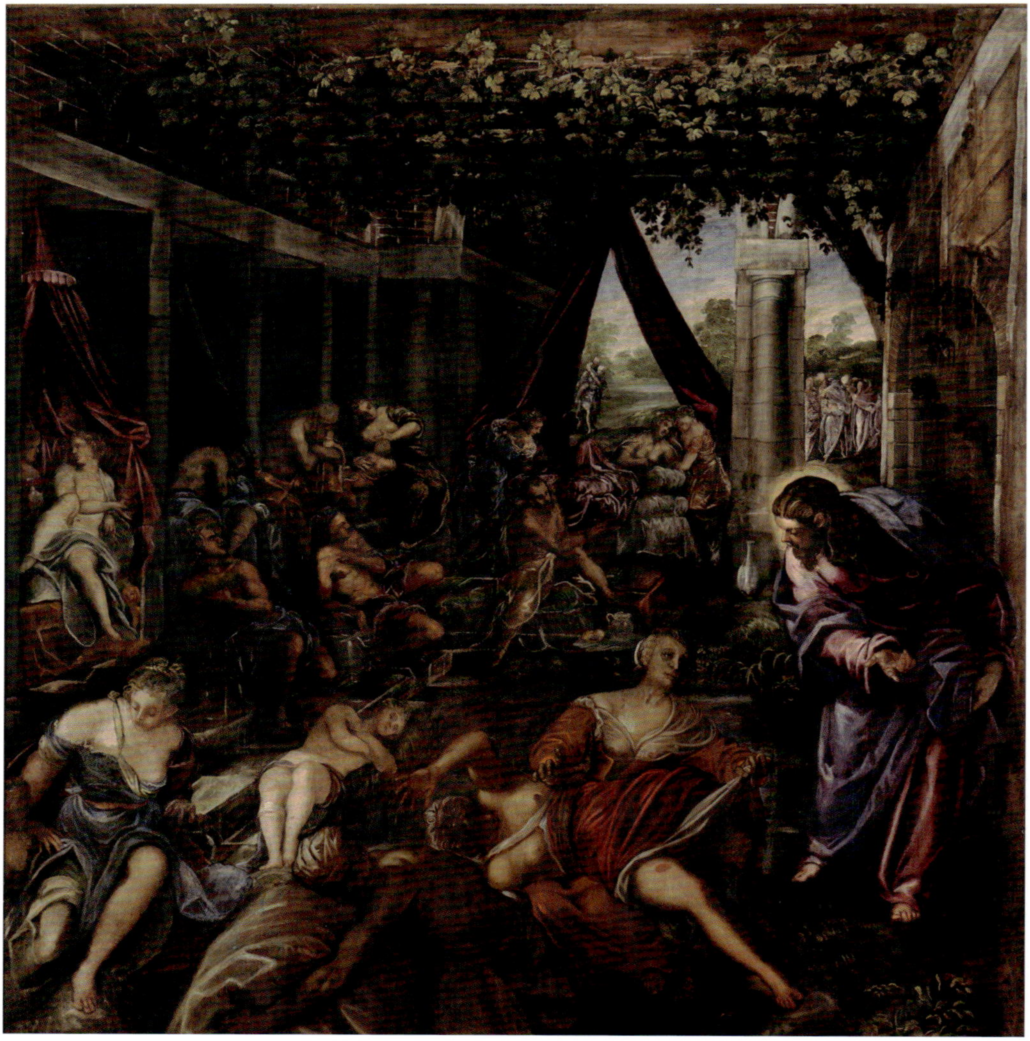

Probatic Pool

After this there was a feast of the Jews, and Jesus went up to Jerusalem. Now there is in Jerusalem by the Sheep Gate a pool, which is called in Hebrew, Bethesda, having five porches. In these lay a great multitude of sick people, blind, lame, paralyzed, waiting for the moving of the water. For an angel went down at a certain time into the pool and stirred up the water; then whoever stepped in first, after the stirring of the water, was made well of whatever disease he had. Now a certain man was there who had an infirmity thirty-eight years. When Jesus saw him lying there, and knew that he already had been in that condition a long time, He said to him, "Do you want to be made well?" The sick man answered Him, "Sir, I have no man to put me into the pool when the water is stirred up; but while I am coming, another steps down before me." Jesus said to him, "Rise, take up your bed and walk." And immediately the man was made well, took up his bed, and walked. *(John 5:1-9)*

If in **Moses drawing water from the rock [29]** ***(note 2)*** the miraculous spring is the prefiguration of the salvational water used for Baptism, whose establishment is shown in the **Baptism of Christ [52]** ***(note 13)***, the **Probatic Pool** is the episode of Jesus' life in which the passage from man's old to new condition, represented by Bap-

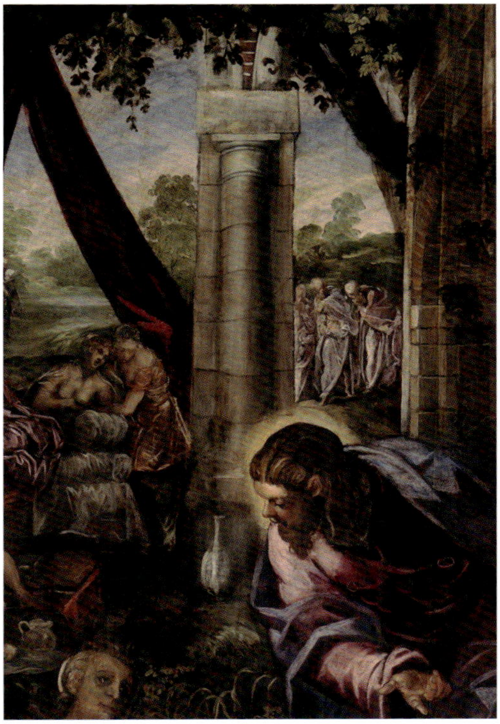

Fig. 33 a - Probatic Pool, detail

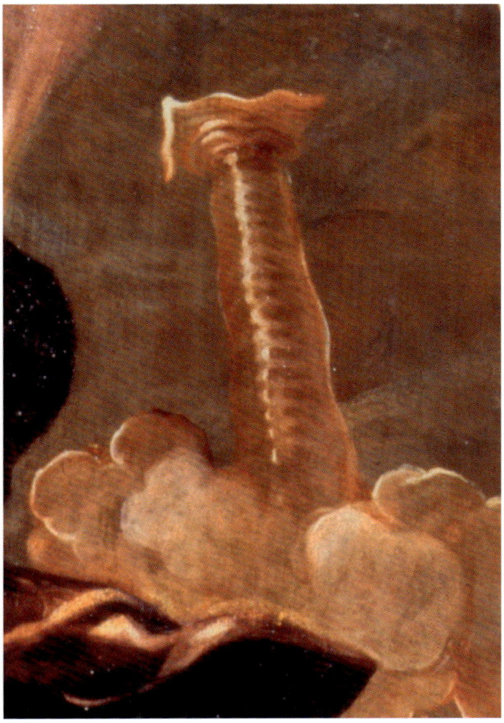

Fig. 33 b - Pillar of Fire, detail

According to the Bible, a pillar of water and of fire accompanied the Israelites as they left Egypt. Now it is Christ who is the new pillar in which every Christian is baptized in water and Spirit

tism, is emphasized the most. Christians have always interpreted the water of the pool, which cures corporal maladies, as a figure of Baptism, which heals the maladies of the soul: the healing from paralysis alludes to the liberation from sin, which, while disfiguring man, has made him spiritually blind, sick, lame and paralytic.

Jesus' healing is greater and much more important than the one offered by the probatic pool, which is only physical and temporary. Christ is the new pillar of clouds and fire in whose name everyone can be baptized in water and Spirit (see John 1:32-34): it is not by chance that Tintoretto paints a pillar behind Jesus' head, referring directly to the oval located immediately above on the ceiling with the **Pillar of Fire [33]**, also highly symbolic of baptism ***(fig. 33)***.

Christ therefore represents the news; his love is *the fulfillment of the Law* (Romans 13:10). In order to realize this love, Tintoretto "invents" a scene that does not di-

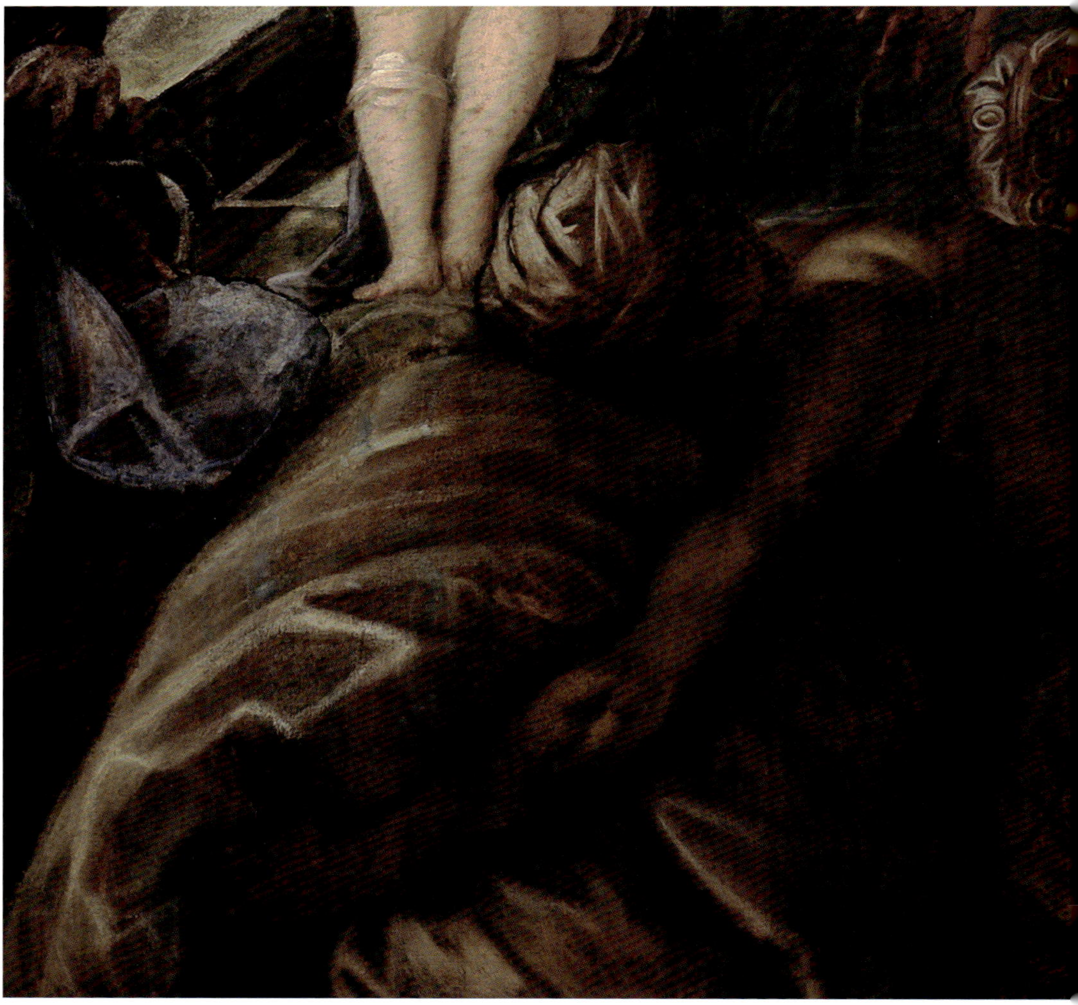

rectly belong to the Gospel. We see in fact that the protagonist is no longer the paralytic, who has already been healed: he occupies the lower area of the painting and is taking the bed away as Jesus commanded (*fig. 34)*. Another person is now drawing the Master's attention: it is an old woman showing him the sores of the plague's initial stage on the thighs of the young girl she is holding. St. Augustine talks about the probatic pool as a place in which suffering, like sin, passes from the condition of the individual to that of the community. In this sense Christ's healing becomes a perfect example of the social, charitable mission of the Scuola Grande di San Rocco. Tintoretto also wishes to express that good works have their raison d'être in faith and the sacraments. That is why the Lord, with his right hand, is indicating a point outside the painting, as if alluding to the brothers united in the Hall, whose healing the sick woman ideally seeks, but also to a painting located right in front (the **Baptism of Christ**), to emphasize the sacramental nutriment of love for one's neighbor.

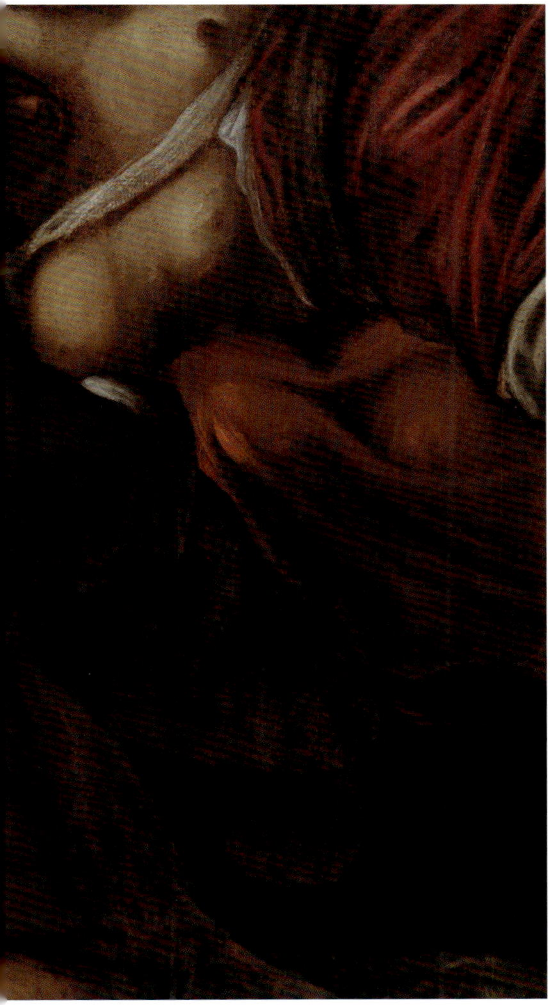

Fig. 34 - While the miracle's paralytic occupies the lowest part of the painting, the protagonist is a young woman afflicted with the plague. We are in the Scuola di San Rocco, the saint of the plague: the episode is narrated in a way as to remind the brothers of their charitable duties

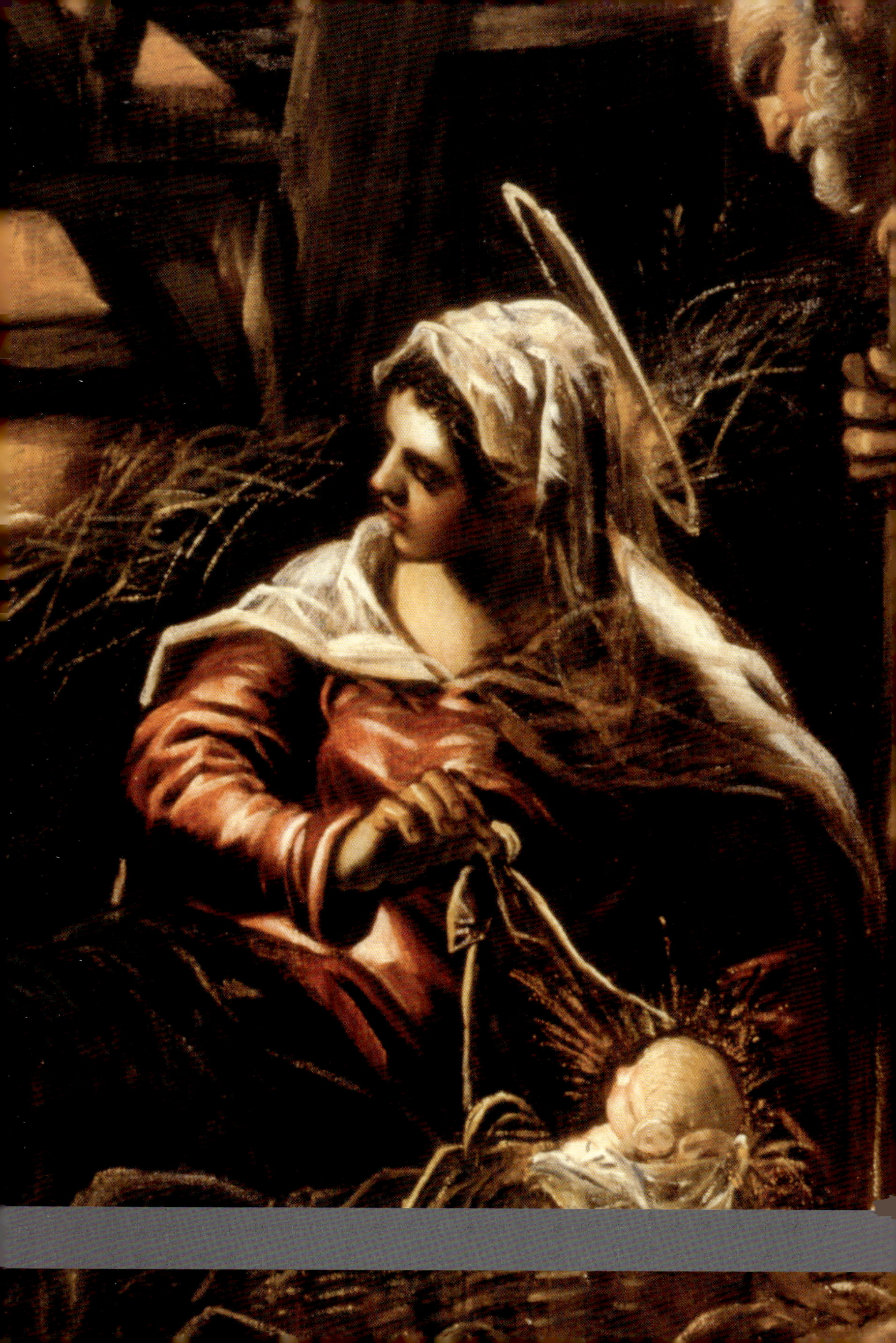

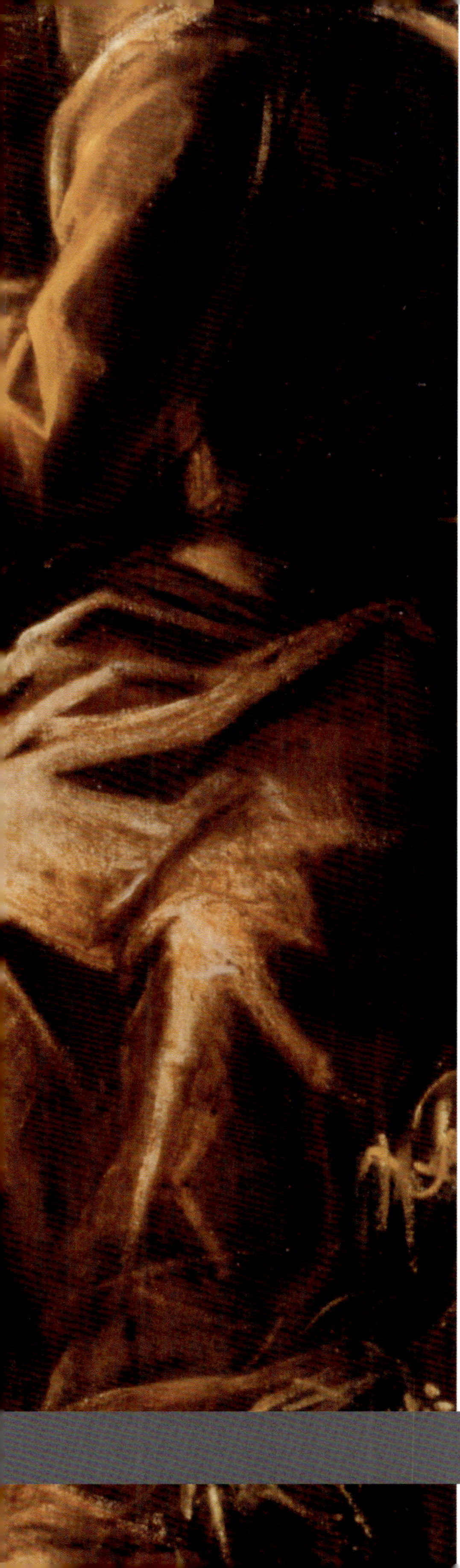

Preamble

The cycle of the Sala Superiore opens with some paintings that act as a preamble: if **Adam and Eve [31]** marks the beginning of man's history in the *world* (John 7,7) and his need for redemption, the **Adoration of the Shepherds [51]** responds to this need, since the incarnation of the Son of God is the primary condition of salvation. **The Eternal Father appears to Moses [32]** depicts the moment in which God commands Moses on Mount Horeb to lead the people of Israel out of Egypt and into the Promised Land. It is thus a prelude to the years in the desert, whose prominent episodes are described on the ceiling's three central squares.

Itinerary 3

15. ADAM AND EVE [31]

Now the serpent was more cunning than any beast of the field which the Lord God had made. And he said to the woman, "Has God indeed said, 'You shall not eat of every tree of the garden'?" And the woman said to the serpent, "We may eat the fruit of the trees of the garden; but of the fruit of the tree which is in the midst of the garden, God has said, 'You shall not eat it, nor shall you touch it, lest you die.'" Then the serpent said to the woman, "You will not surely die. For God knows that in the day you eat of it your eyes will be opened, and you will be like God, knowing good and evil." So when the woman saw that the tree was good for food, that it was pleasant to the eyes, and a tree desirable to make one wise, she took of its fruit and ate. She also gave to her husband with her, and he ate. Then the eyes of both of them were opened, and they knew that they were naked; and they sewed fig leaves together and made themselves coverings. *(Genesis 3:1-7)*

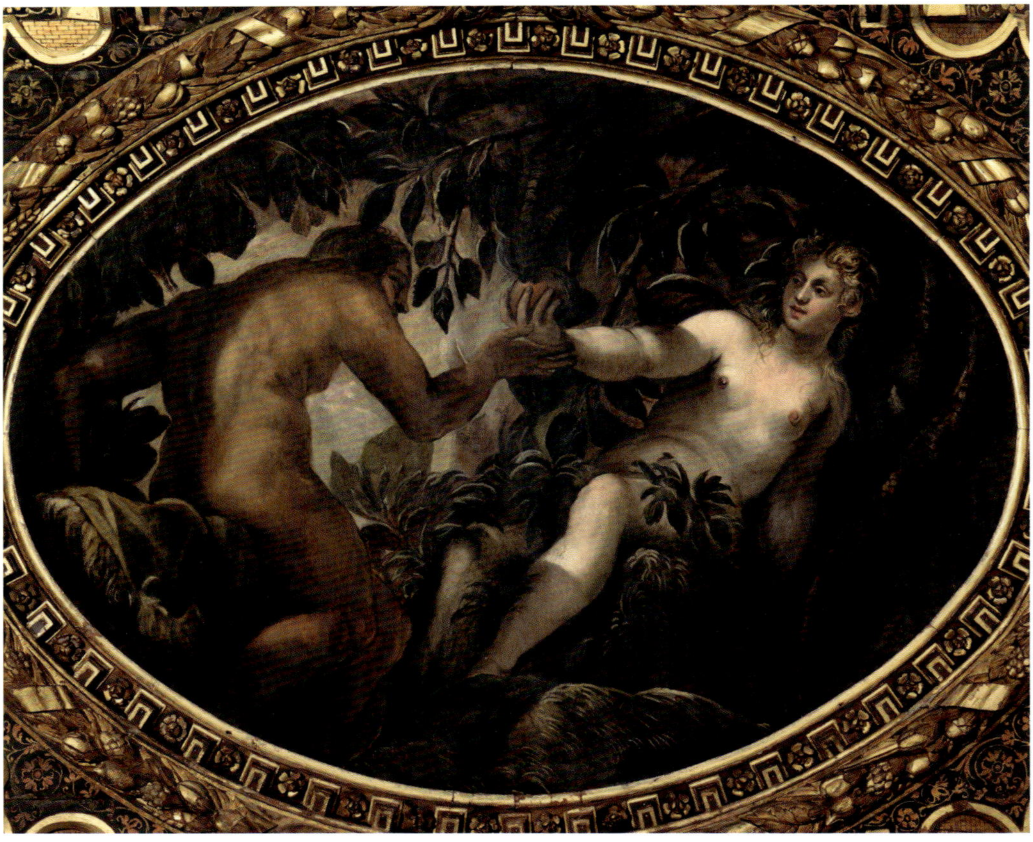

Adam and Eve

Let's inquire into the meaning of the painting starting from the most obvious fact: that, in respect to the others, it is turned upside down. Adam and Eve's sin is the starting point of man's history outside of Eden. Though challenging the Protestants over the importance given to sin, 16th century Catholic theology continued recognizing the significance of the story of Christ starting with the fall of man: the sacred story begins with the sin of the progenitors, is fulfilled in the incarnation and culminates in Christ's reparative sacrifice; he makes the removal (that is, the elimination) of original guilt possible with Baptism.
This theological context would explain the painting's different orientation in respect to the rest of the decoration. Adam and Eve are depicted as a real antecedent and one that is simultaneously overcome: it marks the fallen condition of every man, which Baptism remedies completely. It is not by chance that the visitor looks first in one direction to understand the painting, but then, in order to proceed, must look in the opposite direction. Baptism is, in fact, *resurrectio*, the lifting of the first, mortal fall that allows man to be grafted from Adam to Christ. This is why our glance, after having literally turned away from sin, is drawn along the verticality of the ceiling's decoration towards **Moses drawing water from the rock [29]** ***(note 12)***, a figure of the healing Baptism, and then towards the **Brazen Serpent [28]** ***(note 6)***, the figure that brings about the healing (the crucifixion).
The scene that Tintoretto depicts is the one from Genesis 3:6: Eve has taken and tasted the forbidden fruit and is offering it to Adam. The progenitors are sitting on animal hide ***(fig. 35)***, a symbol that foresees, just like the fig leaves into which Adam has placed his hand, their new existential condition, marked by evil and death (see Genesis 3:21). Adam's brownish complexion alludes to his origin – that is, the earth from which he was shaped and from which he received his name – and reveals his destiny: *the Lord sent him out of the garden of Eden to till the ground from which he was taken* (Genesis 3:23).
With the exile begins man the sinner's journey back to the Father. This journey is fulfilled in the redemption through the incarnated Son: Tintoretto summarizes this by contrasting Adam in the shade with shining Child Jesus in the **Adoration of the Shepherds [51]** ***(note 16)***, located immediately below on the east wall.
On the other wall, instead, Tintoretto shows the evangelical antitype of the progenitors' sin, that is, the **Temptation of Christ [60]** ***(fig. 36)***. Both the Gospel According to Matthew and the Gospel According to Luke speak about this episode: *Now when the tempter came to Him, he said, "If You are the Son of God, command that these stones become bread." But He answered and said, "It is written, 'Man shall not live by bread alone, but by every word that proceeds from the mouth of God.'"*
The association between **Adam and Eve** and the **Temptation of Christ** is evident thanks to the devil's aspect, which, as already noticed by many scholars, greatly resembles that of Eve: she and Lucifer have the same charm. The two temptations are aligned so as to draw attention to the element that distinguishes them: Jesus, contrary to Adam, does not yield but points to the wood – a subtle allusion to the tree

of the cross on which he will be crucified ***(fig. 37).*** The passage from Adam to Christ is in fact marked by the Eucharistic experience of the cross. In his words to Satan Jesus quotes a line from Deuteronomy. In this line God remembers having given his people efficacious signs, such as the manna, demonstrating his fulfillment of the old promise. The manna is therefore not some simple nourishment, but rather the consequence of the word of God, that is, the *word that proceeds from the mouth of the Lord* (Deuteronomy 8:3). The citation is important in order to understand the painting according to the theological context surrounding it. Jesus does not refuse the old manna, but goes beyond: if the manna was already miraculous food, but limited to nourishing material life, the real bread coming from the sky is Jesus in person, the new word from God and, in a Eucharistic sense, his blood and body offered on the cross to become the essential nourishment for eternal life.

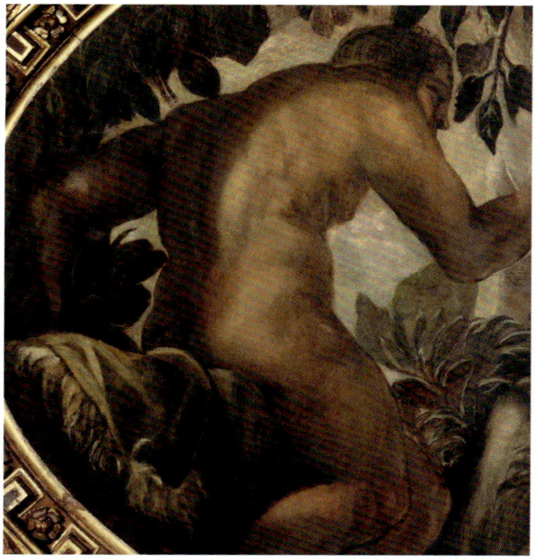

Fig. 35 a - Adam and Eve, detail

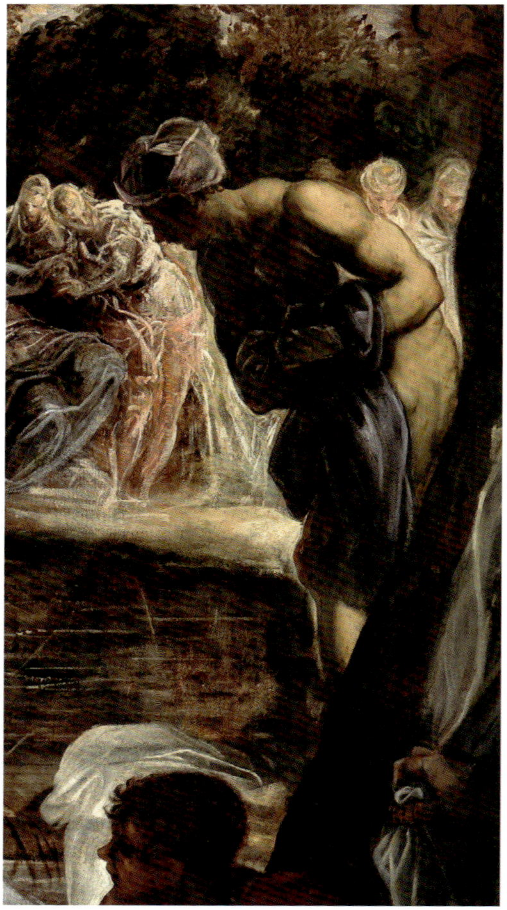

Fig. 35 b - Baptism of Christ, detail

Animal skin, which Adam will soon wear, is in the foreground symbolizing man's new mortal condition. Whereas in the *Baptism of Christ* the neophyte who is about to be baptized is shedding the clothes of sin: as St. Paul wrote, the baptized sheds the clothes of the old man to dress himself in Christ

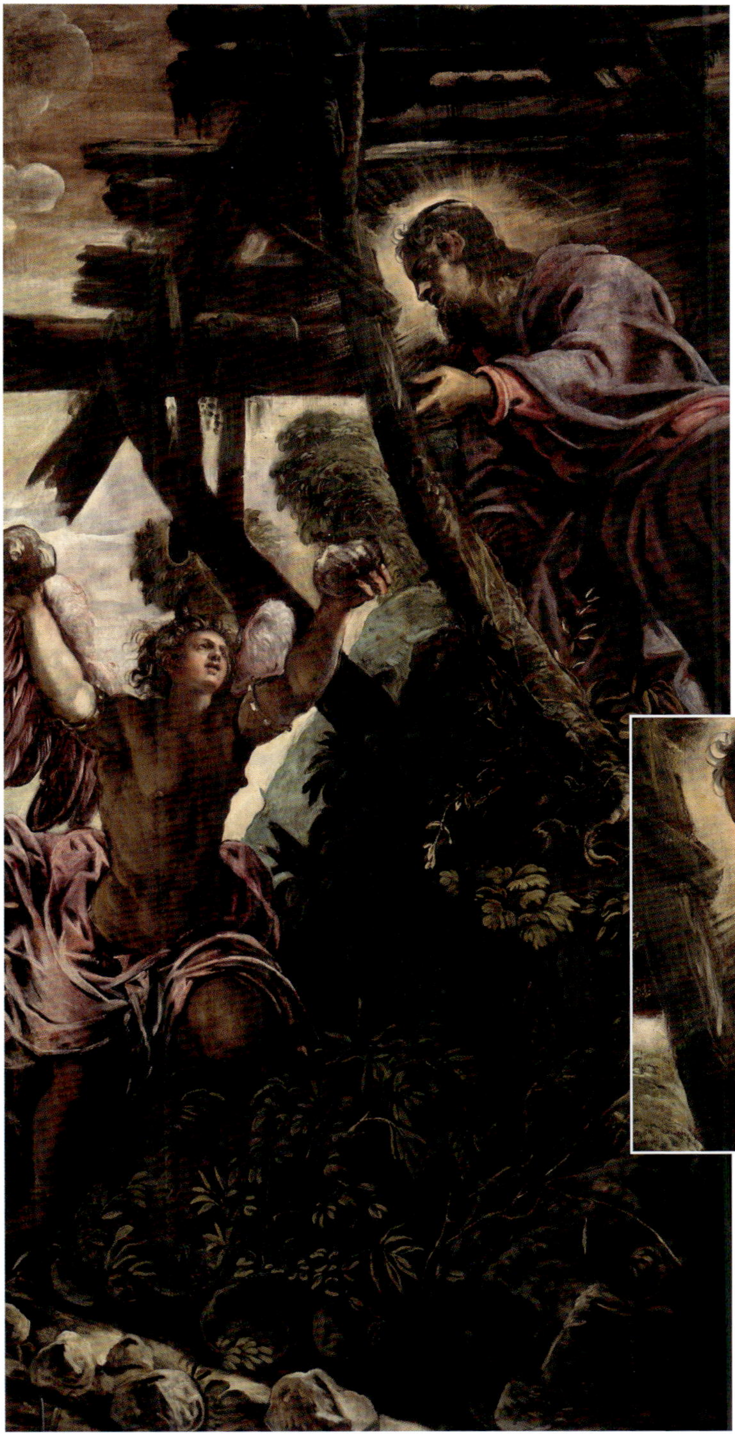

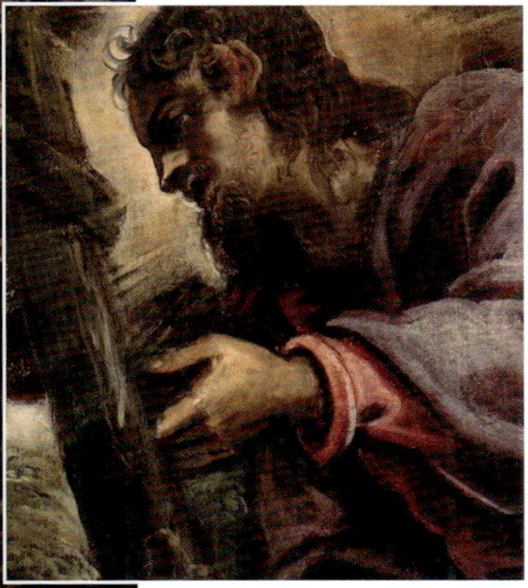

Fig. 37 - Jesus is indicating the wood, or rather the cross: contrary to the false and inutile bread that the devil wants from him, Jesus responds by symbolically indicating the place where his sacrifice will occur, the sacrifice that will make him Eucharistic bread for the life of man

Fig. 36 - Temptation of Christ

16. ADORATION OF THE SHEPHERDS [51]

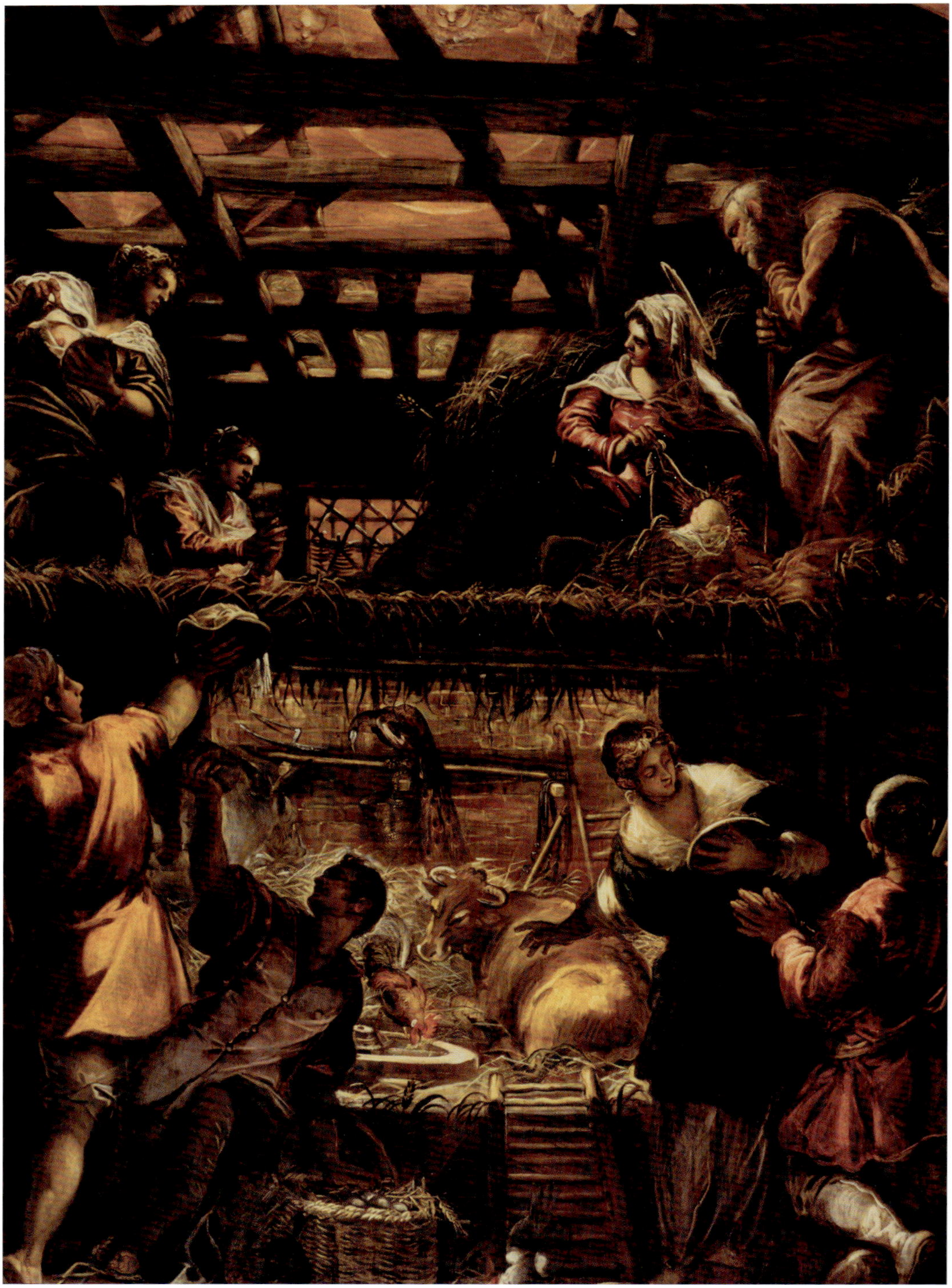

Adoration of the Shepherds

So it was, when the angels had gone away from them into heaven, that the shepherds said to one another, "Let us now go to Bethlehem and see this thing that has come to pass, which the Lord has made known to us." And they came with haste and found Mary and Joseph, and the Baby lying in a manger. Now when they had seen Him, they made widely known the saying which was told them concerning this Child. And all those who heard it marveled at those things which were told them by the shepherds. But Mary kept all these things and pondered them in her heart. Then the shepherds returned, glorifying and praising God for all the things that they had heard and seen, as it was told them. *(Luke 2:15-20)*

The *teleri* of the **Adoration of the Shepherds,** the first painting on the east wall, and of **The Eternal Father appears to Moses [32]** to the side of **Moses drawing water from the rock [29]** ***(note 12)*** mark two beginnings. The liberation of Israel begins with a call from the Lord; it is the episode of the burning bush, the moment of God's Revelation and the commanding of Moses to lead his people out of Egypt (see Exodus 3). The *telero* is therefore a necessary premise to the three big central paintings on the ceiling depicting the promised liberation through the Exodus. The *Biblia pauperum* (see box p. 44) typologically relates the episode of God commanding Moses to the Nativity, because they are both God's Revelations and the beginnings of a radical salvation. In both cases God descends to earth to elevate man. In fact, God tells Moses: *So I have come down to deliver them out of the hand of the Egyptians, and to bring them up from that land to a good and large land* (Exodus 3:8); and it is by *coming into the world* (Hebrews 10:5), or rather receiving from the Virgin a body and being born man among men, that Christ lifts man to the state of children of God. The Nativity brings about what pope Leo the Great called a *marvelous exchange* between sky and earth, an expression used in Roman liturgy.

The painting's theme is precisely the adoration of the Child Jesus by the shepherds, who give him gifts as they kneel before him. The scene is divided into two overlapping planes: the Holy Family occupies the right area of the upper plane, while to the left we see two women, inspired by the midwives Salome and Zelomi, who, according to the apocryphal Gospels (see box p. 123), were present during the miraculous birth. One of them has bared her chest, offering the child the first nourishment. The baby, representing the new Charity, commences the virtuous circle of good works since, by becoming man, he puts himself in the fragile condition of need: it is this act of putting himself in the hands of man, a prelude to the sacrifice, that is the great act of love that Tintoretto expresses in the mystery of Christmas. It is with this first cry that Christ inaugurates the life dedicated to the total offering of the self (see Hebrews 10:24). The theme was certainly dear to the brothers of San Rocco, who considered helping the needy the main mission of the Scuola.

In the lower area of the painting, while the two shepherds perform works of charity, a young woman draws the others' attention to what is happening in the barn crowded by symbolic animals. A chicken is descending the steps leading to the lower area ***(fig. 38)***: it is the Son who, according to St. Augustine (*Expositions on the Psalms*, 58 II:10), inspired by the Gospel According to Matthew (see Matthew 23:37), is coming down to earth assuming the fragility of flesh, in the same way that a mother hen imitates her chicks in order to take care of them. As in the prophecy of Isaac 1:3, we see the donkey about to eat because *he knows his master's manger*; while the ox, *who knows his owner*, is looking at a rooster, symbol of the sun-Jesus who drives away the darkness ***(fig. 39)***. Finally, the *Gallicinium,* the "hour of the rooster", has arrived: the birth of the new day defeats the death of night in expectance of the final resurrection. The peacock that Tintoretto paints behind the other animals has the same function; it is alone on a shelf, an old Christian symbol of Christ's victory over death.

Easter symbols accompany this Nativity, but on the other hand, the Lord's death and resurrection are central in the Gospels of the infancy and the liturgy. We see that Mary is literally *unveiling* Jesus' shinning body to the eyes of everyone present: with the left hand she lowers to the ground a heavy cloth, while with the right raises a transparent veil. She seems to be saying, alluding to the concepts expressed in the *Letters to the Hebrews*, that Christ is the new way of reaching the sanctuary, which, according to an ancient Hebrew cult, could be entered only by the supreme priest for expiatory sacrifices. Now, instead, it is the flesh of Christ, offered *once and for all* on the cross and then glorified, that is substituting the two curtains separating the temple (Hebrews 9:3; 10:20), here symbolized by the cloth and the veil. His sacrifice helps believers enter the reality of redemption and resurrection.

The beautiful spike that we see coming out of the shapeless mass behind Mary ***(fig. 40)*** alludes to these fruits of passion, because only *unless a grain of wheat falls into the ground and dies, it produces much fruit* (John 12:24); the planks resembling crosses on the ceiling allude to the way in which this grain will die.

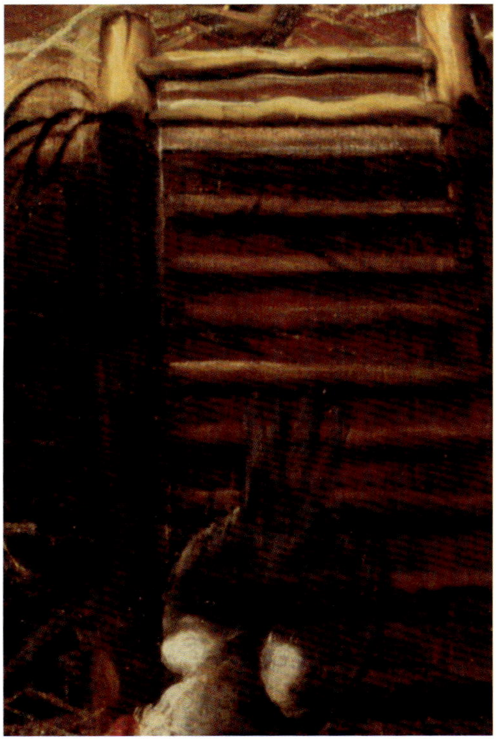

Fig. 38 - The Word becomes flesh: St. Augustine, referring to Matthew 23:37, compares him to a mother hen in which everything, from the sloppy and unkempt plumage to the harsh cackle, shows such incredible maternal care for her little ones, that even its untidiness should be imitated

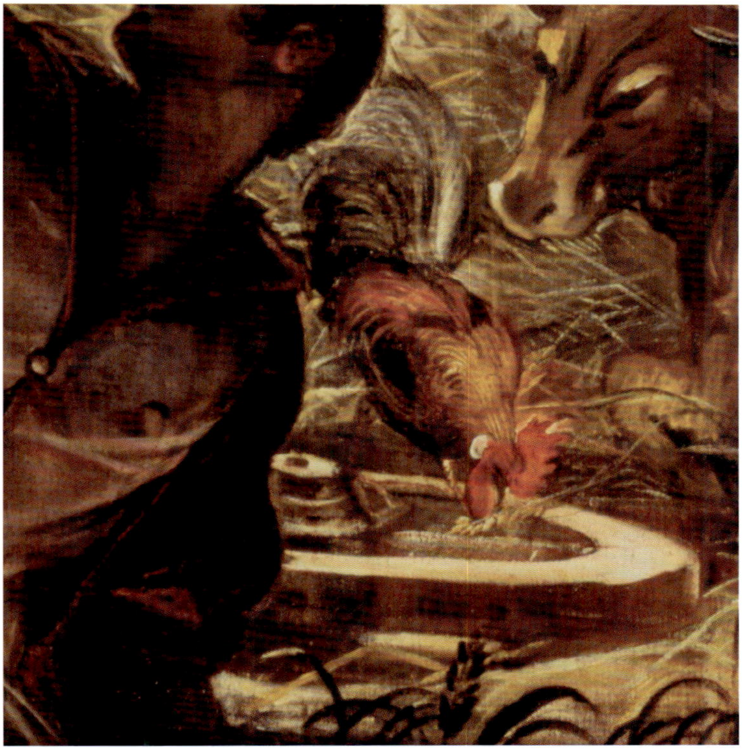

Fig. 39 - The rooster is another symbol of Christ and represents the sun that chases away the darkness

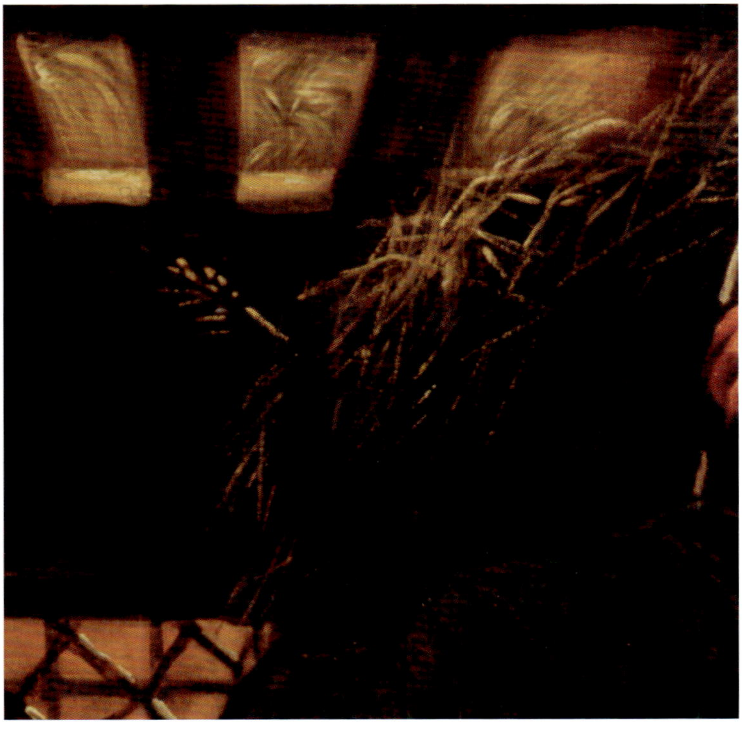

Fig. 40 - The spike, alluding to a passage from the Gospel According to John, means that only through death will the grain of wheat, that is Christ, produce lots of fruit

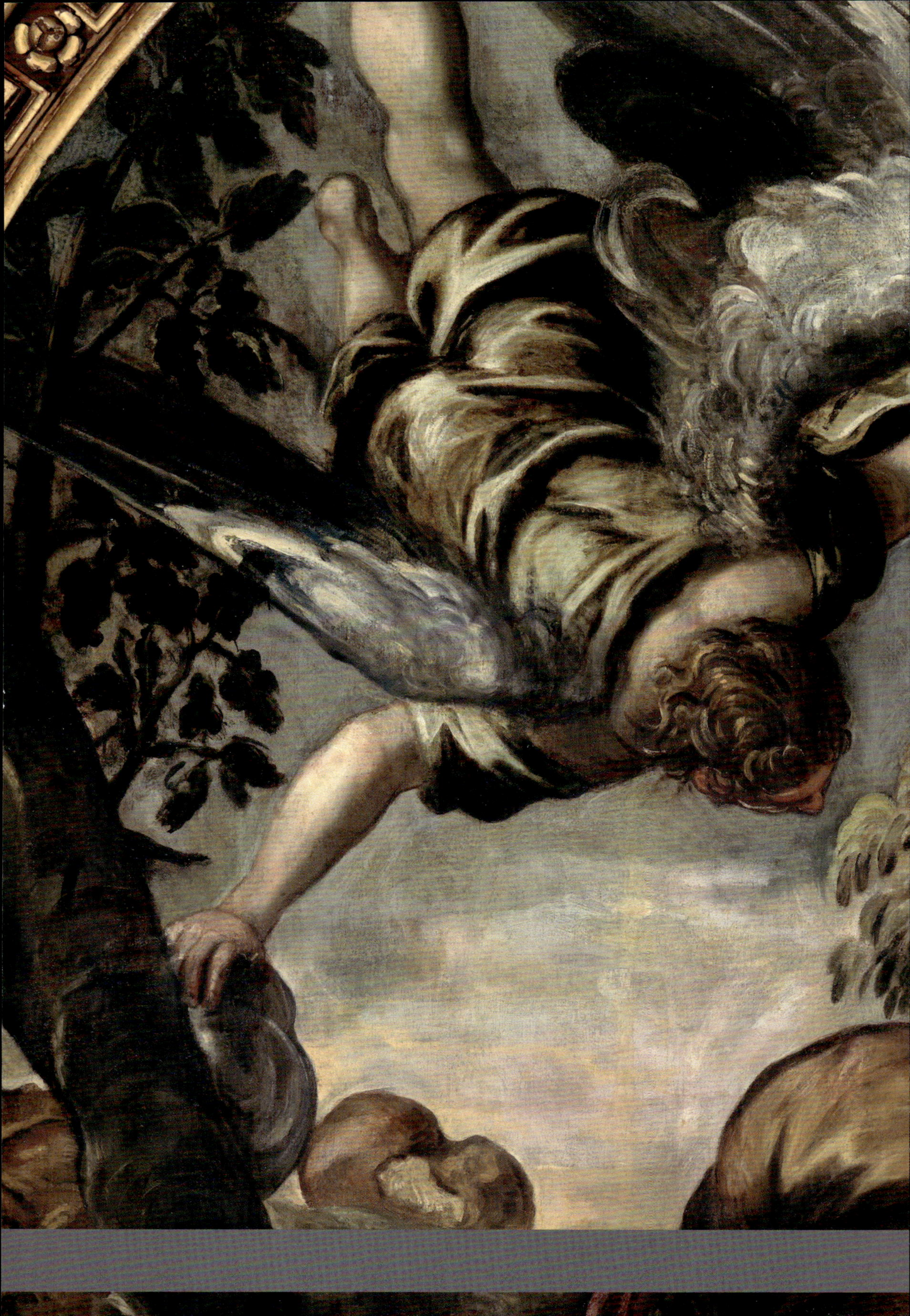

The Eucharist

The **Miracle of the Manna [30]** prefigures the **Last Supper [55],** which is the moment in which Jesus institutes the Eucharist. **Elisha multiplies the bread [38]** is the prefiguration of the **Miracle of the Loaves and Fishes [56]**, located in the back on the western wall. Another Eucharistic type and variant of the theme of salvational bread coming down from the sky is **Elijah fed by the Angel [39]**. Completing the thematic group dedicated to the Eucharist is the **Passover [40]**, located above the Hall's altar, and the **Agony in the Garden [54]**.

17. SACRIFICE OF ISAAC [37]

Now it came to pass after these things that God tested Abraham, and said to him, "Abraham!" And he said, "Here I am." Then He said, "Take now your son, your only son Isaac, whom you love, and go to the land of Moriah, and offer him there as a burnt offering on one of the mountains of which I shall tell you." So Abraham rose early in the morning and saddled his donkey, and took two of his young men with him, and Isaac his son; and he split the wood for the burnt offering, and arose and went to the place of which God had told him (...). Then they came to the place of which God had told him. And Abraham built an altar there and placed the wood in order; and he bound Isaac his son and laid him on the altar, upon the wood. And Abraham stretched out his hand and took the knife to slay his son. But the Angel of the Lord called to him from heaven and said, "Abraham, Abraham!" So he said, "Here I am." And He said, "Do not lay your hand on the lad, or do anything to him; for now I know that you fear God, since you have not withheld your son, your only son, from Me." Then Abraham lifted his eyes and looked, and there behind him was a ram caught in a thicket by its horns. So Abraham went and took the ram, and offered it up for a burnt offering instead of his son. *(Genesis 22,1-13)*

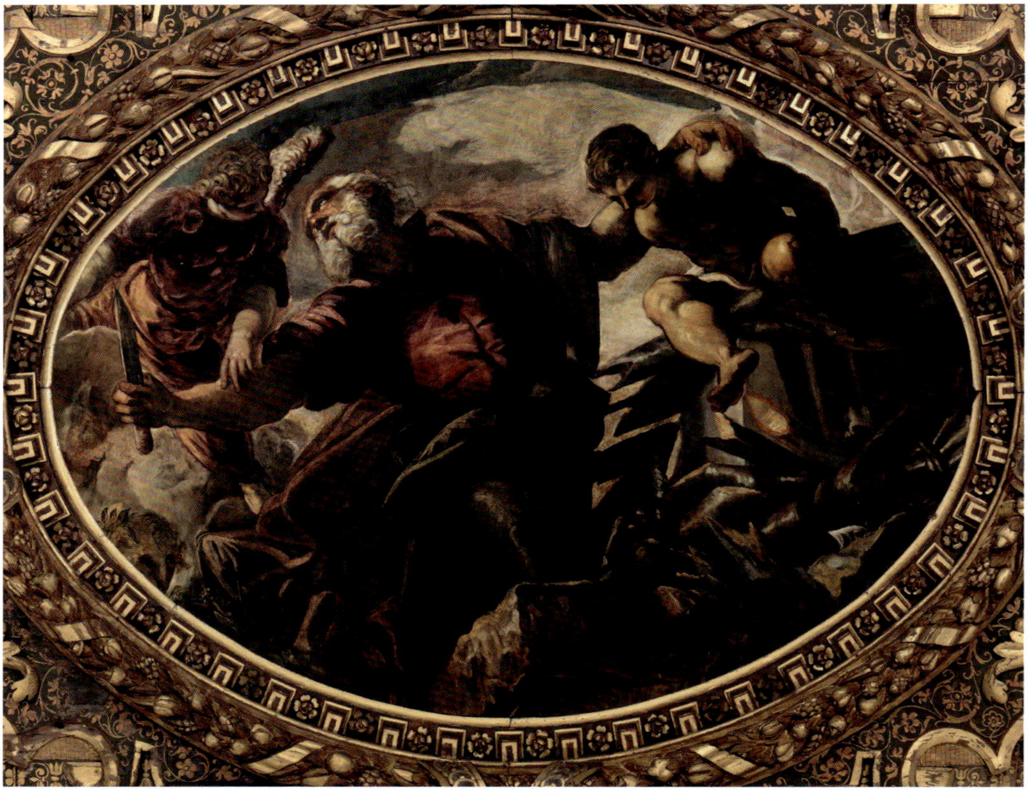

Sacrifice of Isaac

Just like **Jonah leaves the whale's belly [34]** ***(note 11)***, the **Sacrifice of Isaac** is also a pivotal painting: it prefigures the Lord's Easter depicted on the central paintings and introduces the southern section as a type of Eucharistic sacrifice.
The Catholic tradition sees in this Old Testament episode a clear prefiguration of Christ's sacrifice on the cross, something that is always repeated through Mass. According to the *Epistle to the Hebrews*, Christ is simultaneously victim and supreme priest: obedient to the Father to the very end, he sacrifices himself to God. On Golgotha he brings about a new *Yom Kippur*, the day of Expiation in the Jewish tradition: Christ is simultaneously the supreme priest, who enters the sanctuary by himself to make the offer, and the holocaust that is offered for the sins of mankind. Deducing from this interpretation, we understand that the figure of Christ is not Isaac but rather Abraham. The latter in fact obeys God up to the most extreme of trials: agonized, with the knife about to cut into his son, he could easily be saying, as Christ will say in Gethsemane, *"Father, if it is Your will, take this cup away from Me; nevertheless not My will, but Yours, be done"* (Luke 22:42). Sacrificing flesh from his own flesh, in a certain sense Abraham, like Isaac, is a holocaust. The sacrificed and the sacrificing are interpenetrating: Abraham, the figure of the new priesthood introduced by Christ, is practically immolating himself. Tintoretto subtly conveys this idea with the crosswise depiction of the patriarch's arms and with the blood-red color of the robe covering his chest, cut up into furrows resembling wounds.

The Mass as sacrifice. According to Protestantism, Mass cannot be considered a sacrifice; otherwise it would fall into the category of good works, performed by man in order to win God's grace, which according to Luther create the illusion of "earning" eternal life. Thus the Mass can only be the "memory" of the one and unrepeatable sacrifice of Christ on the cross. As emphasized in the documents of the Council of Trent, for Catholics the Mass is also memory, but with the more substantial meaning of "memorial": God's salvational action makes itself efficaciously present in the accomplishment of the rite. During Mass men can sacrifice to God precisely because Christ is continually sacrificed in the rite. In fact, the priest says, "This is my body": it is Christ, not man, who is speaking. The Mass and the cross for Catholics are one and the same sacrifice. Thus the Tridentine text defines Mass not only as commemoration, but also as a real "re-presentation" (*re-praesentatio*) of the cross.

18. MIRACLE OF MANNA [30]

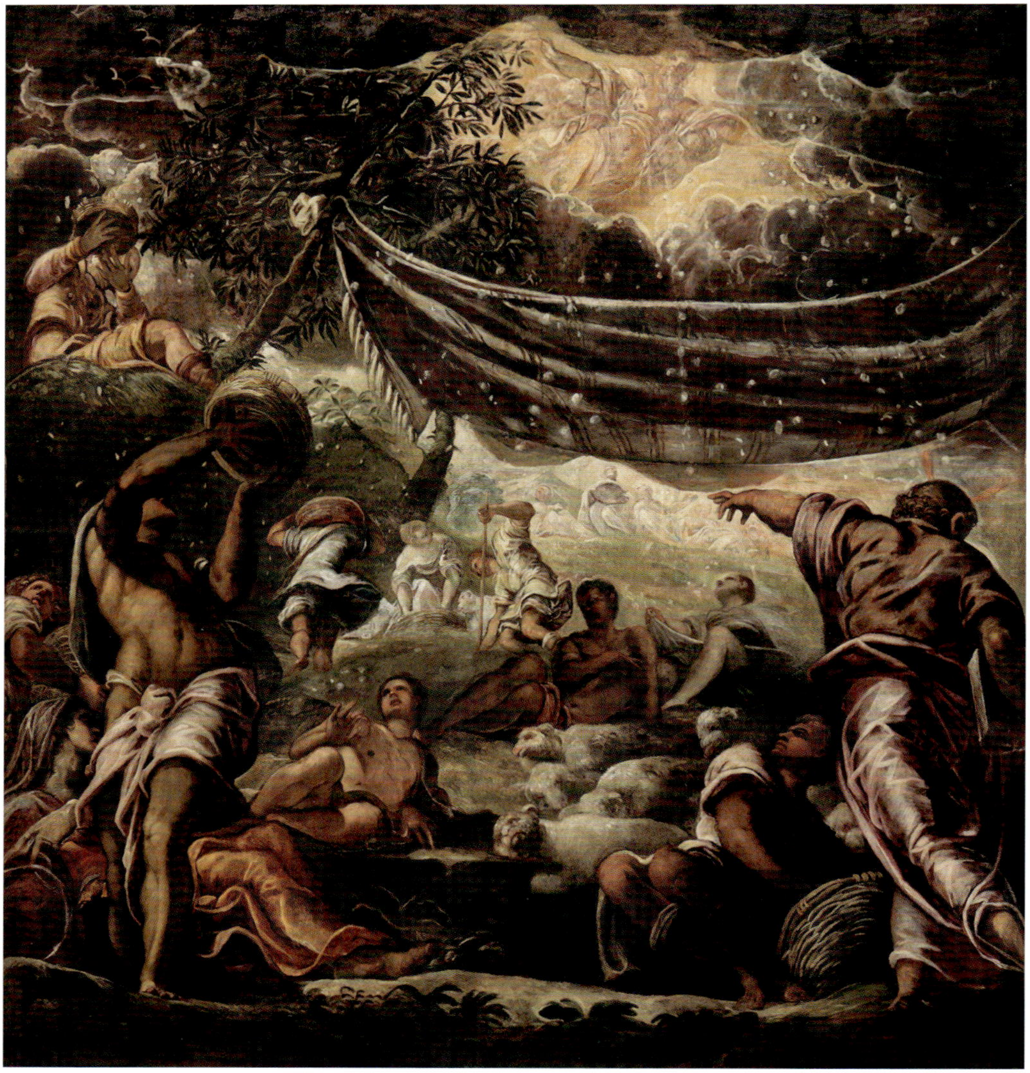

Miracle of Manna

And the Lord spoke to Moses, saying, "I have heard the complaints of the children of Israel. Speak to them, saying, 'At twilight you shall eat meat, and in the morning you shall be filled with bread. And you shall know that I am the Lord your God.'" So it was that quails came up at evening and covered the camp, and in the morning the dew lay all around the camp. And when the layer of dew lifted, there, on the surface of the wilderness, was a small round substance, as fine as frost on the ground. So when the children of Israel saw it, they said to one another, "What is it?" For they did not know what it was. And Moses said to them, "This is the bread which the Lord has given you to eat. This is the thing which the Lord has commanded: 'Let every man gather it according to each one's need, one omer for each person, according to the number of persons; let every man take for those who are in his tent.'" Then the children of Israel did so. *(Exodus 16:11-17)*

The **Miracle of Manna** is the prefiguration par excellence of the Eucharist. We find it in the *Biblia pauperum* (see box p. 44) as a type of Last Supper; Christian literature and Eucharistic prayers refer to it as a key moment since it foresees many aspects of the Christian Eucharist. As the Gospel According to John reminds us, Jesus, while speaking to the crowd, in continuity with the Old Testament, compares himself to the manna, simultaneously underlining the great novelty that he represents in relation to God's extraordinary salvational intervention in the history of Israel: *"I am the bread of life. Your fathers ate the manna in the wilderness, and are dead. This is the bread which comes down from heaven, that one may eat of it and not die. I am the living bread which came down from heaven. If anyone eats of this bread, he will live forever; and the bread that I shall give is My flesh, which I shall give for the life of the world"* (John 6:48-51). The manna, bread from the sky, is personified by Jesus, and especially by his flesh given for the life of the world. At the same time Jesus, as bread of life, is much more than just manna, which in the desert helped save the fathers but did not give them eternal life.

In this sense, the **Miracle of Manna**, along with **Elijah fed by the Angel [39]** ***(fig. 41)*** on one of the side ovals, is the representation of the Eucharist in its particular meaning as God's gift of eternal life. It thus emphasizes the salvational efficacy of the sacrament. The prophet Elijah, fleeing from his enemies, also falls, just like the Israelites in the desert, into a profound state of dejection: weak and hopeless, he asks God to take his life. Tintoretto depicts the moment in which an angel sent by God comes down from the sky bringing him bread and water; reinvigorated, the prophet continues his journey (see 1 Kings 19). Besides this particular Eucharistic meaning, Tintoretto also depicts the **Miracle of Manna** as a prefiguration of the Mass as sacrifice, returning to the theme developed in the **Adoration of the Shepherds [51]** ***(see note 16)***. The large curtain that the Israelites spread out to protect themselves from the sun is more than evident; with this prominent position it certainly has a symbolic meaning. It ideally separates two worlds: above, God immersed in

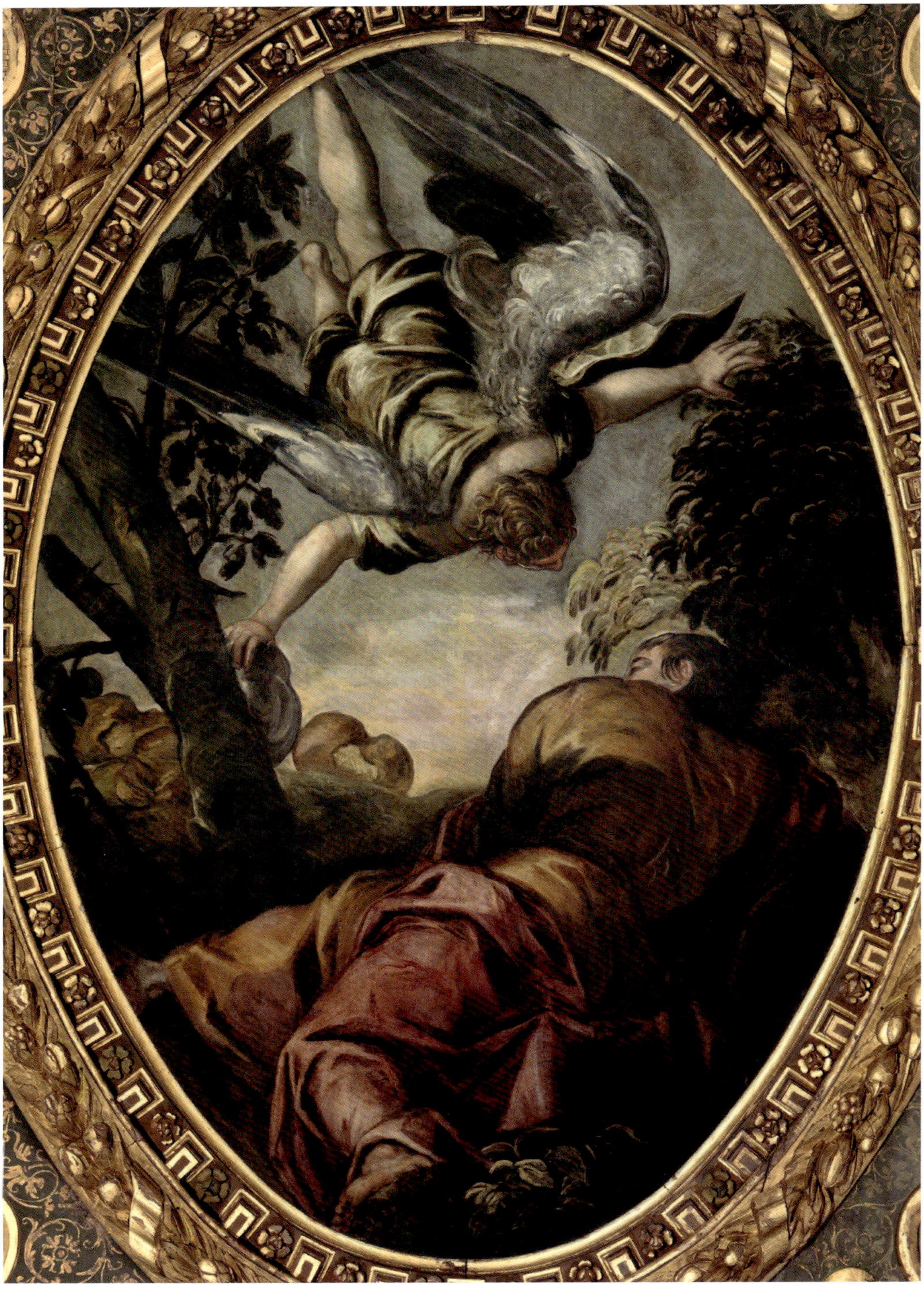

Fig. 41 - Elijah fed by the Angel

light is a hidden reality to man of the Old Testament; though active in the world, he is never seen. The impossibility to see the sacred in the cult is represented by the curtain of the temple, which prevents everyone from entering the sanctuary (the most sacred area), except the supreme priest.

However, the incarnation of the Son of God introduces a new way of reaching the Father: *No one has seen God at any time. The only begotten Son, who is in the bosom of the Father, He has declared Him* (John 1:18). It is his passion that opens this way for man; in fact, the Gospels specify that at the death of Christ *the veil of the temple was torn in two from top to bottom* (Mark 15:38). In the *Epistle to the Hebrews* Christ is indeed identified as the veil of the temple: his flesh immolated on the cross represents the new and definitive sacrifice for eternal redemption, which goes beyond the temporary purification obtained through the sacrifices in Judaic Law. Tintoretto depicts these sacrifices with the agonized flocks on the declivity of the hill ***(fig. 42)***. The curtain therefore bears witness to the fathers' situation and prophecies the novelty of the sacrifice of Christ, which always takes place in the Mass. It is the curtain of separation, but it also collects the manna-Eucharist. It is through the immolation of Christ's body that the canvas is no longer an obstacle but rather a way of access, welcoming the manna-Host as if it was the cloth of a new sacrificial altar.

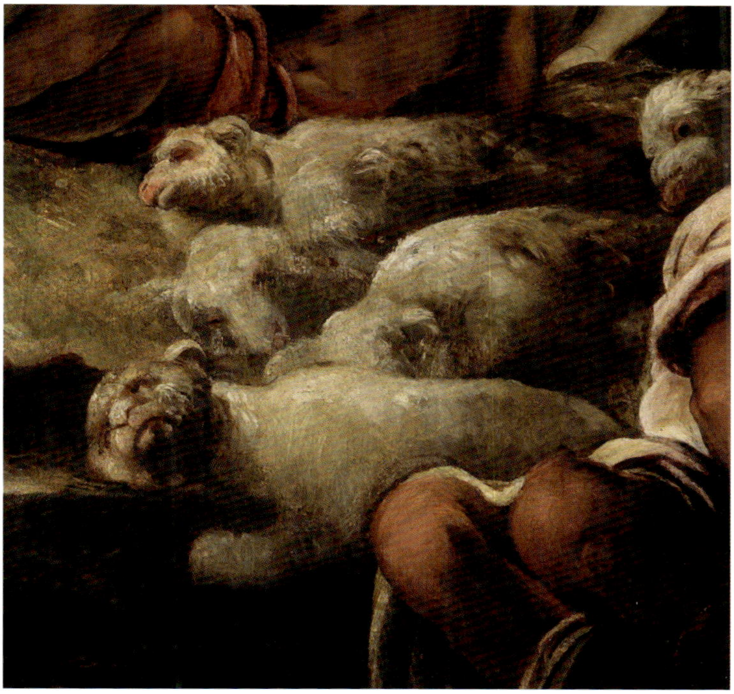

Fig. 42 - The bloody sacrifices of the Old Covenant, which the redemptory sacrifice of Christ has made useless, are here represented by agonized, dying herds

19. Agony in the Garden [54]

Coming out, Jesus went to the Mount of Olives, as He was accustomed, and His disciples also followed Him. When He came to the place, He said to them, "Pray that you may not enter into temptation." And He was withdrawn from them about a stone's throw, and He knelt down and prayed, saying, "Father, if it is Your will, take this cup away from Me; nevertheless not My will, but Yours, be done." Then an angel appeared to Him from heaven, strengthening Him. And being in agony, He prayed more earnestly. Then His sweat became like great drops of blood falling down to the ground. When He rose up from prayer, and had come to His disciples, He found them sleeping from sorrow. Then He said to them, "Why do you sleep? Rise and pray, lest you enter into temptation." *(Luke 22:39-46)*

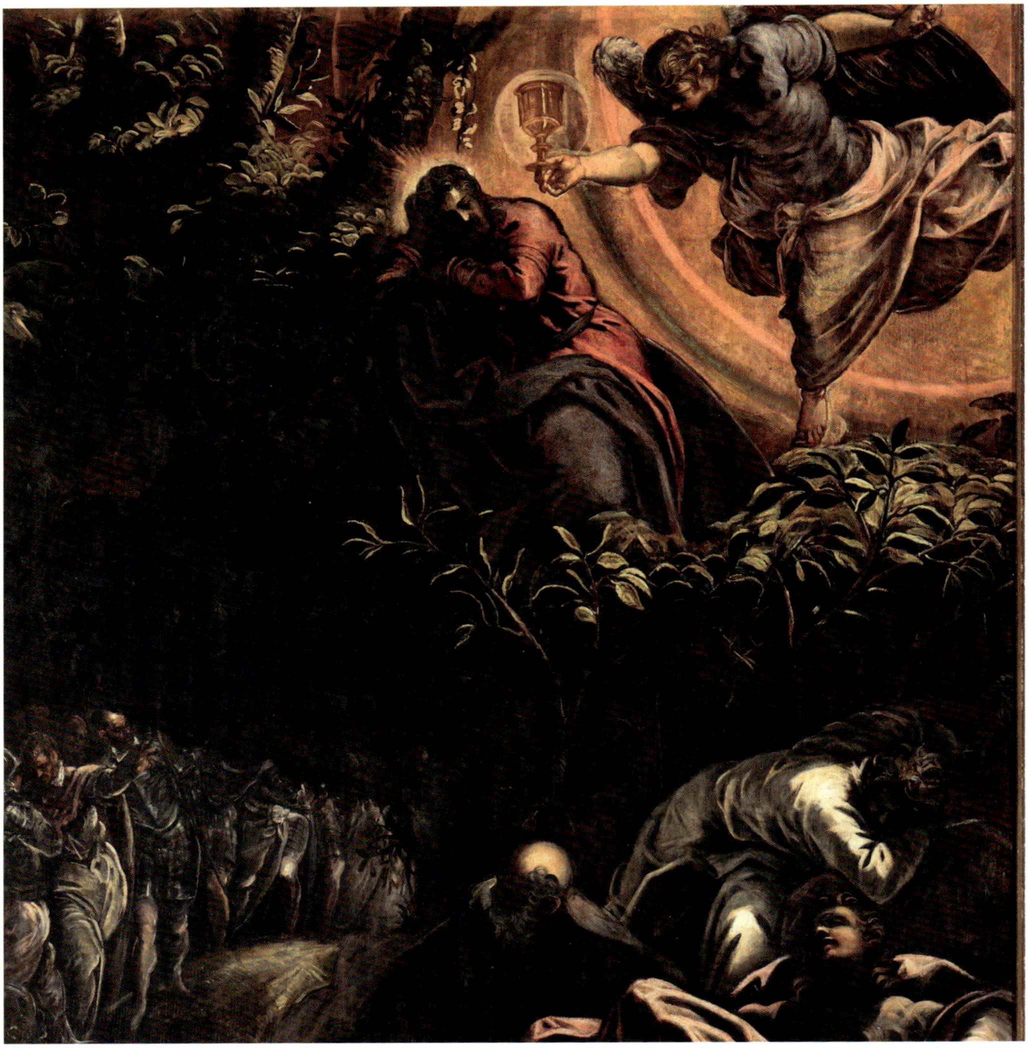

Agony in the Garden

Tintoretto depicts Jesus in the dramatic hour in Gethsemane in a meditative mood, veiled by a composed sadness. He already knows what will happen to him and is reflecting upon his destiny, in full awareness of his solitude. The angel's sympathy does not distract him from his introspection. Although John does not describe the scene, his Gospel is the one that best portrays the Master's self-control (see John 18:4) in the moment of the intense interior struggle between the rejection of pain and death, as is expected of his human nature, and the determination to obey the Father *to the point of death, even death on a cross* (Philippians 2:8).

Thanks to the Gospel According to John, we understand the theological meaning that Tintoretto gives to the light, which in this painting is particularly evident. Judas, *he who was night* (Augustine, *Tractates on the Gospel of John*, 62:6), as symbolized in this Gospel, is depicted as the head of the powers of darkness (see John 18:3): in fact, Tintoretto shows him at the bottom on the left as he is coming out of a rocky mass with the soldiers and the servants of the supreme priests, completely surrounded by darkness. Christ, instead, is the light: we are on the eve of an unforgettable clash – that of the light of Christ and the darkness of Judas.

The light coming from the angel in concentric circles also has the aim of highlighting the chalice that is offered to Jesus. Encircled by a shining nimbus, which makes it stand out all the more, the chalice is the pivot of the composition, having a precise Eucharistic meaning. It has been correctly noted that the chalice is not present in the **Last Supper [55]** ***(note 20)***, the *telero* that immediately follows on the wall. That which was prefigured by the Old Testament in the **Sacrifice of Isaac [37]** ***(note 17)*** is fulfilled in Gethsemane through Christ, who, drinking the bitter cup of passion, is both priest and victim of his own sacrifice. As priest, only he can drink from the chalice with his blood – which is oozing out copiously from his forehead ***(fig. 43)*** – while in the **Last Supper** the apostles, who represent the believers, receive only the Host. This was controversial with the Reformation's theologians, who thought that Christians have to receive Communion in the form of both the bread and the wine.

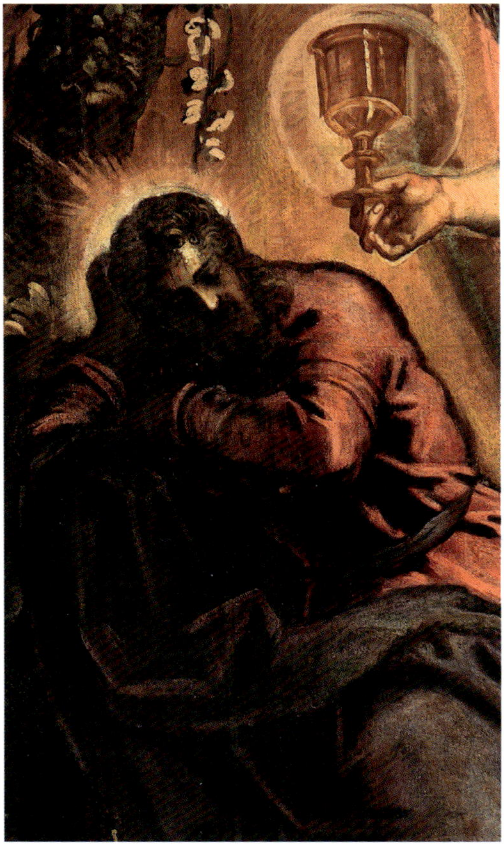

Fig. 43 - An angel is offering Christ, who is bleeding in agony, the bitter chalice of sacrifice, referring to the Eucharistic chalice

20. LAST SUPPER [55]

When the hour had come, [Jesus] sat down, and the twelve apostles with Him. Then He said to them, "With fervent desire I have desired to eat this Passover with you before I suffer; for I say to you, I will no longer eat of it until it is fulfilled in the kingdom of God." (...) And He took bread, gave thanks and broke it, and gave it to them, saying, "This is My body which is given for you; do this in remembrance of Me." Likewise He also took the cup after supper, saying, "This cup is the new covenant in My blood, which is shed for you. But behold, the hand of My betrayer is with Me on the table. And truly the Son of Man goes as it has been determined, but woe to that man by whom He is betrayed!" Then they began to question among themselves, which of them it was who would do this thing. *(Luke 22:14-23)*

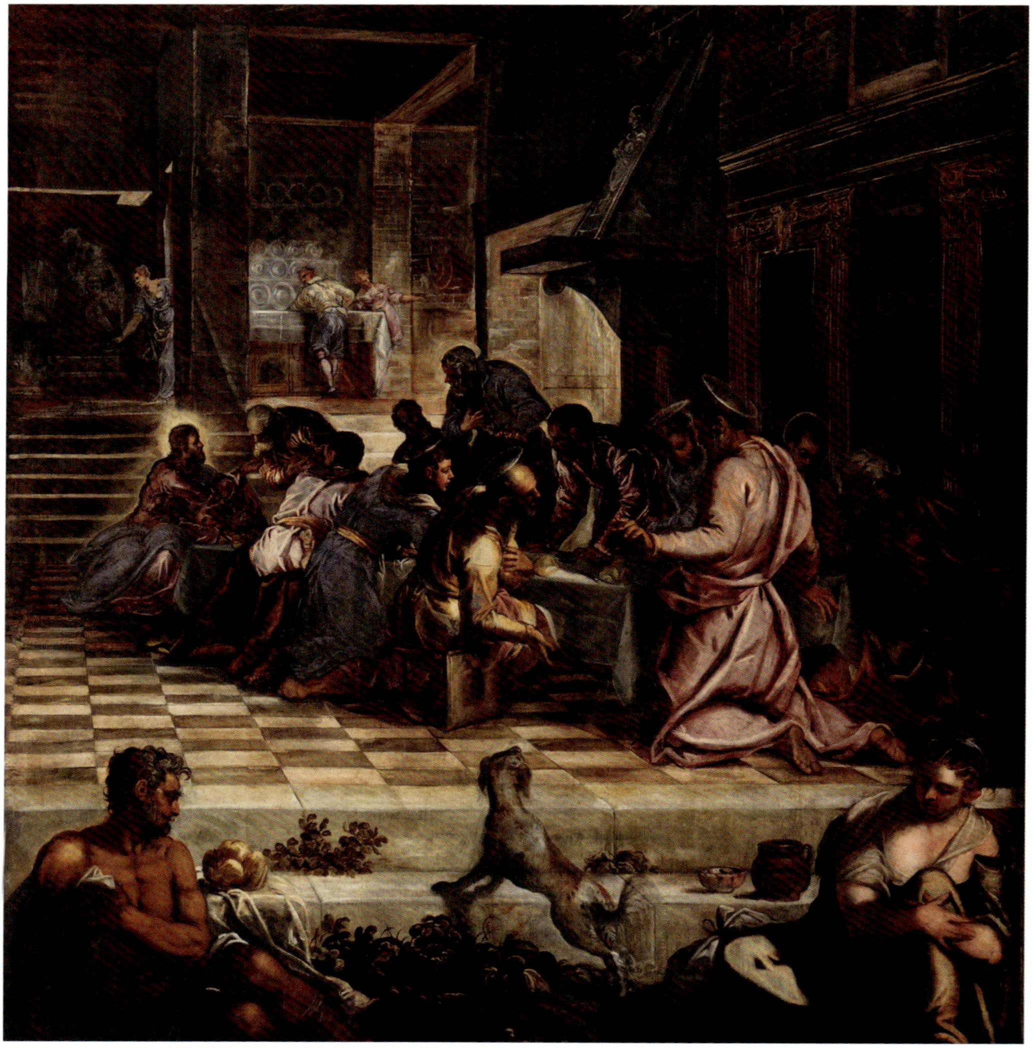

Last Supper

The space that Tintoretto allots to the **Last Supper** is divided into three levels: in the background is the kitchen, separated by the hall; in the foreground there are some steps under which we see two figures. If we imagine that the table can be prolonged towards the outside, it will lead directly to the altar of the Sala Superiore. Tintoretto is saying that the table and the altar are one and the same: the Last Supper represents the moment of instituting the Mass. The atmosphere, still turbulent due to the announcement of the betrayal, becomes less intense as we approach Jesus. The painter here is depicting the apostles' communion. Jesus sits at the head of the table, administering the Eucharist to Peter. The piece of bread that he is giving to the apostle is already in the form of the Host ***(fig. 44)***. Meanwhile, John is sleeping with his head on the Master's chest; he is nestled in his embrace, so much that we can hardly see him. The combination of the two actions (embracing John and giving Peter the Eucharist) has a precise meaning: in the communion Christians become one single entity in the body of Christ (see 1 Cor 10:14-17). But also Judas is sitting near Jesus. We see his back, recognizing him by the purse with the thirty pieces of silver tied to his belt ***(fig. 45)***. While everyone is distracted, he, drawn to what is happening, is the only one looking at the Master. Just like Judas, *whoever eats this bread or drinks this cup of the Lord in an unworthy manner will be guilty of the body and blood of the Lord* (1 Cor 11:27). Tintoretto seems to be telling us that within the Church, as within the group of apostles, appeared the new enemies of Christ who now wish to practice the sacrament giving it a meaning that is not in conformity with the Catholic doctrine.

The Eucharistic symbols of the bread and the pitcher of wine are present on the entrance steps ***(fig. 46)***. Nearby is a small white dog, a symbol of fidelity, while to the sides we see two mendicants. The figures of the poor present at the Lord's Supper are typical of Venetian painting from this period, alluding to a faith that, if true, cannot but transform into works of char-

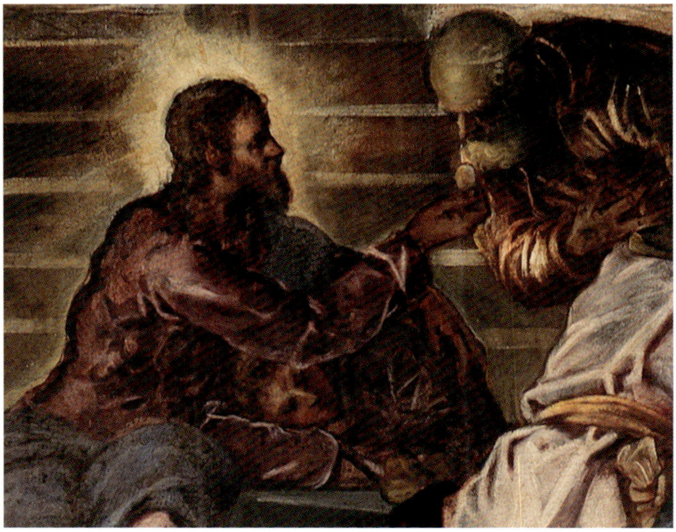

Fig. 44 - Christ administers the piece of bread, in the form of the Host, to Peter

ity. Here the two poor people turn their backs to what is happening behind them, yet not to distance themselves, but to become the connecting element between the two halls: the one depicted in the painting and the real one in which the brothers used to meet. According to the Tridentine Catechism, the Eucharist is in fact the *sacrament of Charity:* Christ's love generates love; his sacrifice, the supreme act of Charity, is the source of human charity; his willingness to help his neighbor is an example of charitable activity practiced by the Scuole such as San Rocco. Here, as in the other Scuole, among the charitable deeds canonically instituted was an annual banquet offered to the brothers of discipline (not those from the chapter) and to the poor coming from outside the Scuola, which not by chance was called *pastum* or *caritas*. Therefore, there exists a profound continuity between the painting and reality, between the biblical past and the period in which the painting was painted.

The supper that Christ has with the apostles is the Jewish Passover: *With fervent desire I have desired to eat this Passover with you,* says Christ to his disciples in Luke's recollection. The **Passover [40]** ***(fig. 47)***, celebrated annually in memory of the Exodus from Egypt, is the theme in the oval located above the Hall's altar. Here the people are united around a table: obeying the Lord's command, they are equipped with a walking stick, ready to embark upon the long journey awaiting them. God has meticulously described to Moses and Aaron the food that his people will have to eat on the occasion of the *Lord's Passover* (see Exodus 12). Yet here no one is eating. A blinding light shines from the table and illuminates everyone standing around it, highlighting that a loaf of bread at the edge of the counter top is missing a piece. It has been hypothesized that this piece is the piece that Christ is giving Peter in the **Last Supper**. In this way the supper clearly presents itself as the fulfillment of the Passover in the Old Covenant.

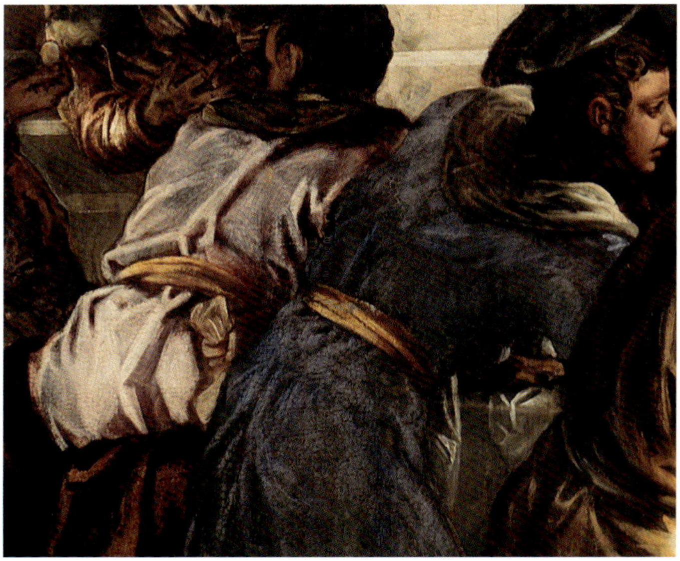

Fig. 45 - Judas is recognizable thanks to the purse that he has tied to his belt

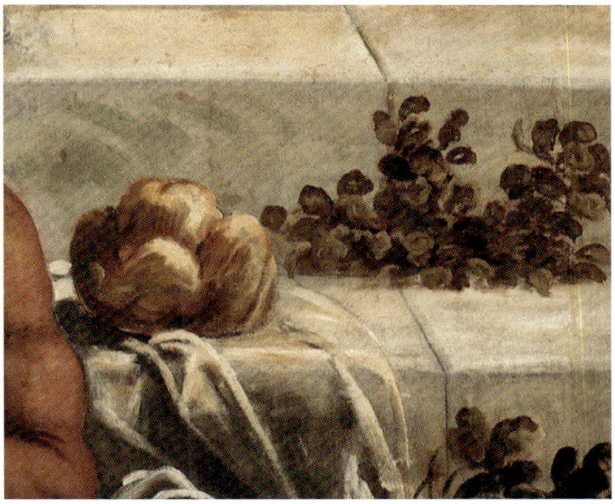

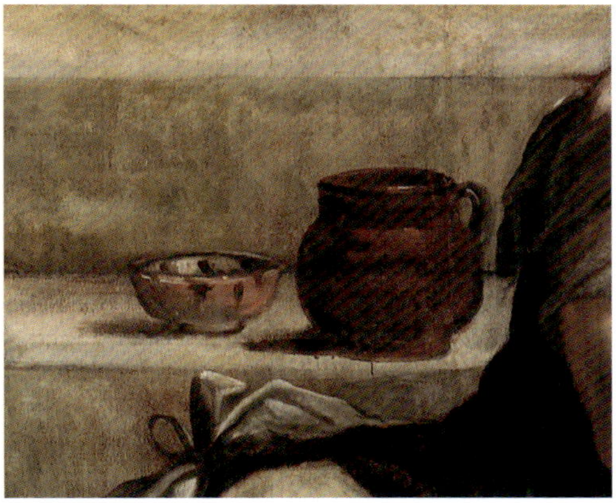

Fig. 46 - Here, as in the *Resurrection*, the bread and the pitcher are Eucharistic symbols

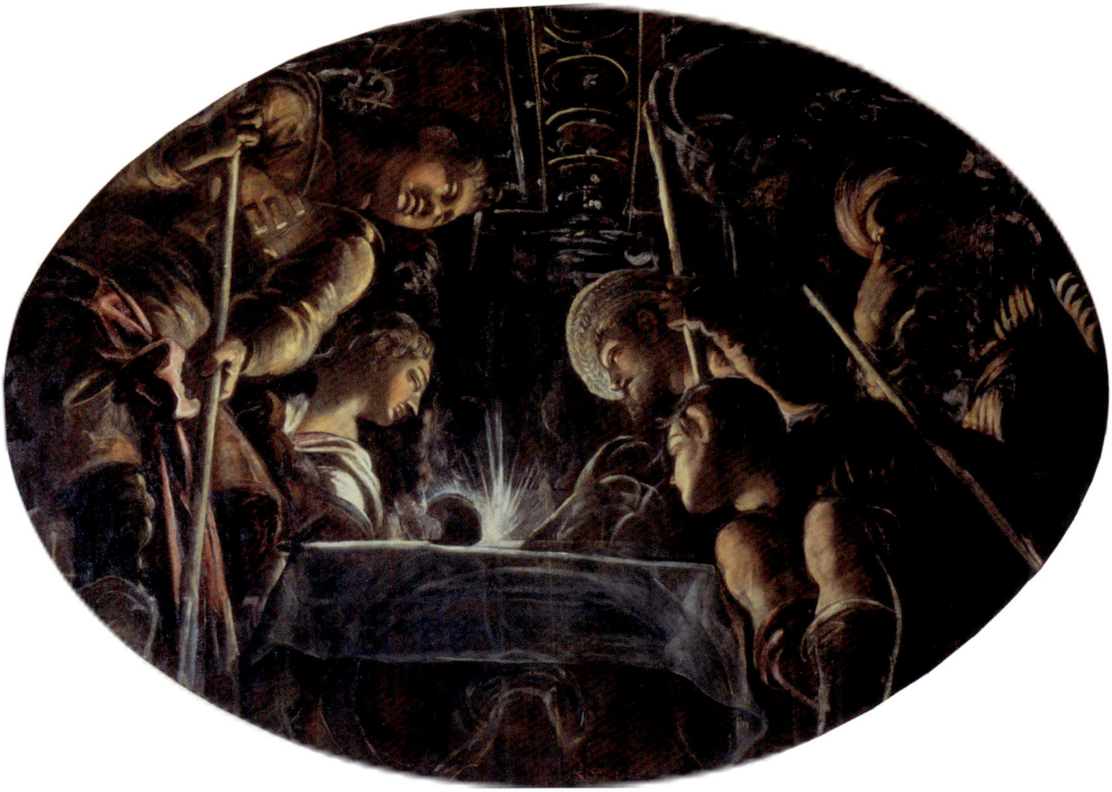

Fig. 47 - Passover

21. ELISHA MULTIPLIES THE BREAD [38]

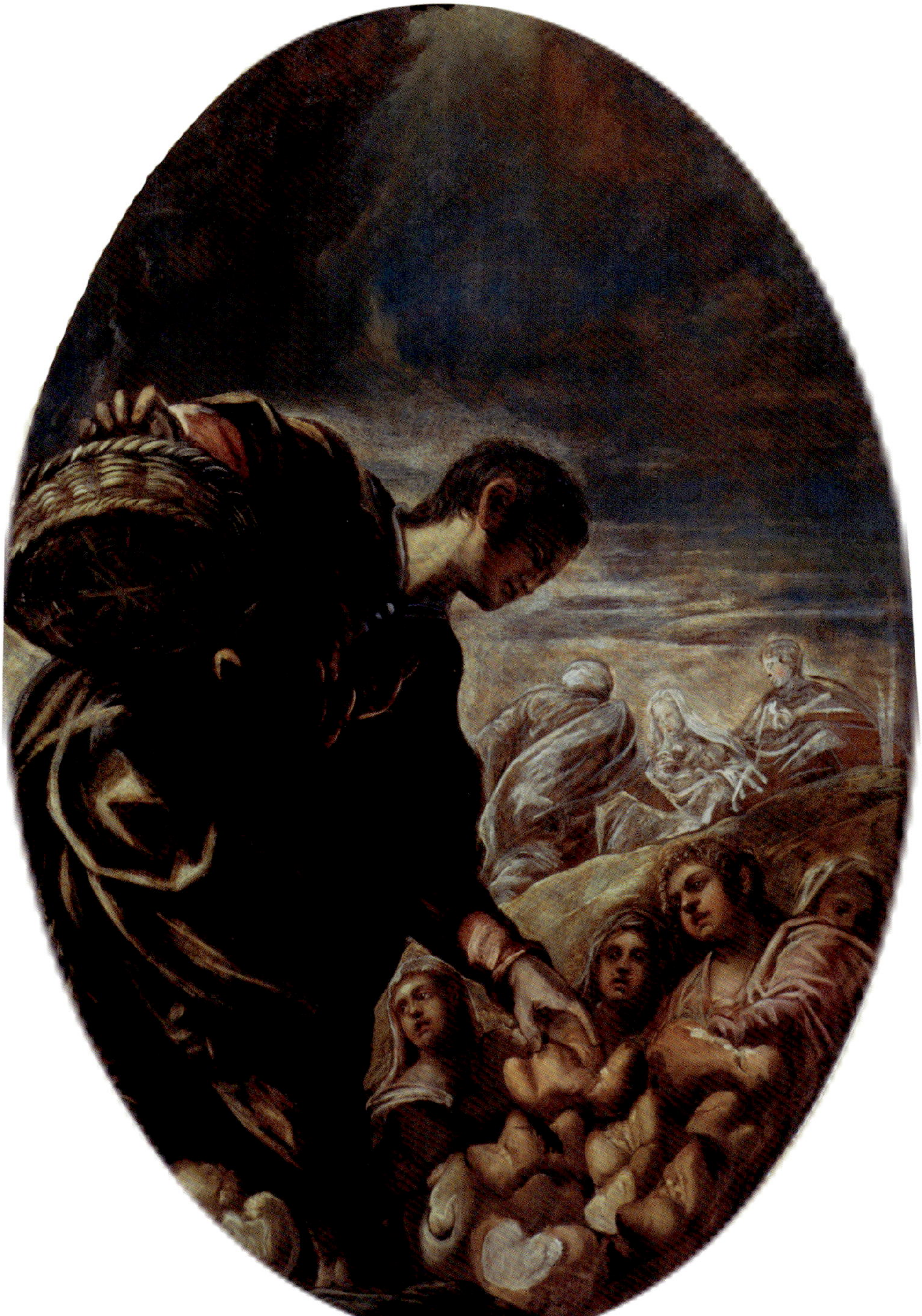

Elisha multiplies the bread

Then a man came from Baal Shalisha, and brought the man of God bread of the first fruits, twenty loaves of barley bread, and newly ripened grain in his knapsack. And he said, "Give it to the people, that they may eat." But his servant said, "What? Shall I set this before one hundred men?" He said again, "Give it to the people, that they may eat; for thus says the Lord: 'They shall eat and have some left over.'" So he set it before them; and they ate and had some left over, according to the word of the Lord. *(2 Kings 4:42-44)*

Here the Prophet Elisha, whose name means "God is salvation", is performing one of his many miracles, almost all to the benefit of the ill and the needy. It is clear that the episode is inserted in the Hall's scheme as the prefiguration of the **Miracle of the Loaves and Fishes [56]** ***(fig. 48)***, the painting that we find in the background on the west wall. But the subject of helping the needy, which we have seen intimately connected to the institution of the Eucharist in the **Last Supper [55]** ***(note 20)***, is fundamental in the activity of this man of God who places his extraordinary powers at the service of others, multiplying food, curing the sick, literally reviving them (see 2 Kings 4:1-7, 5:1-27, 13:21); these are the themes that are close to the relief mission of the Scuola Grande.

The **Miracle of the Loaves and Fishes** is read as the fulfillment of this particular prophetic conception. To the left of Christ Andrew the Apostle, with open arms, seems to be absorbing the needs of those present (John 6:9 *"There is a lad here who has five barley loaves and two small fish, but what are they among so many?")* and also indicating one of the many personifications of Charity on the painting's right border ***(fig. 49)***. In this sense the miracle of the multiplication, with which the Gospels associate the gestures of breaking and distributing the bread of the Last Supper, is the promise of the Eucharistic bread, or rather Christ's body that in Charity is broken as a gift and – although remaining a single whole – is "multiplied."

It has been noticed that, while Andrew is caring for the material needy in the crowd, Christ is indicating beyond the painting, beyond those present. If the painting is observed from a certain angle, we can see that Christ is indicating in the direction of the altar of the Sala Superiore. His preoccupation is different from that of the apostle, as John relates later in the narration: *Jesus answered them: (...) "You seek Me, not because you saw the signs, but because you ate of the loaves and were filled. Do not labor for the food which perishes, but for the food which endures to everlasting life, which the Son of Man will give you"* (John 6:26-27). Jesus says not to stop at the material aspect of the miracle, but to interpret it as a sign of a greater spiritual reality, which is the new and definitive Eucharistic food given to those who believe in him in order to have eternal life.

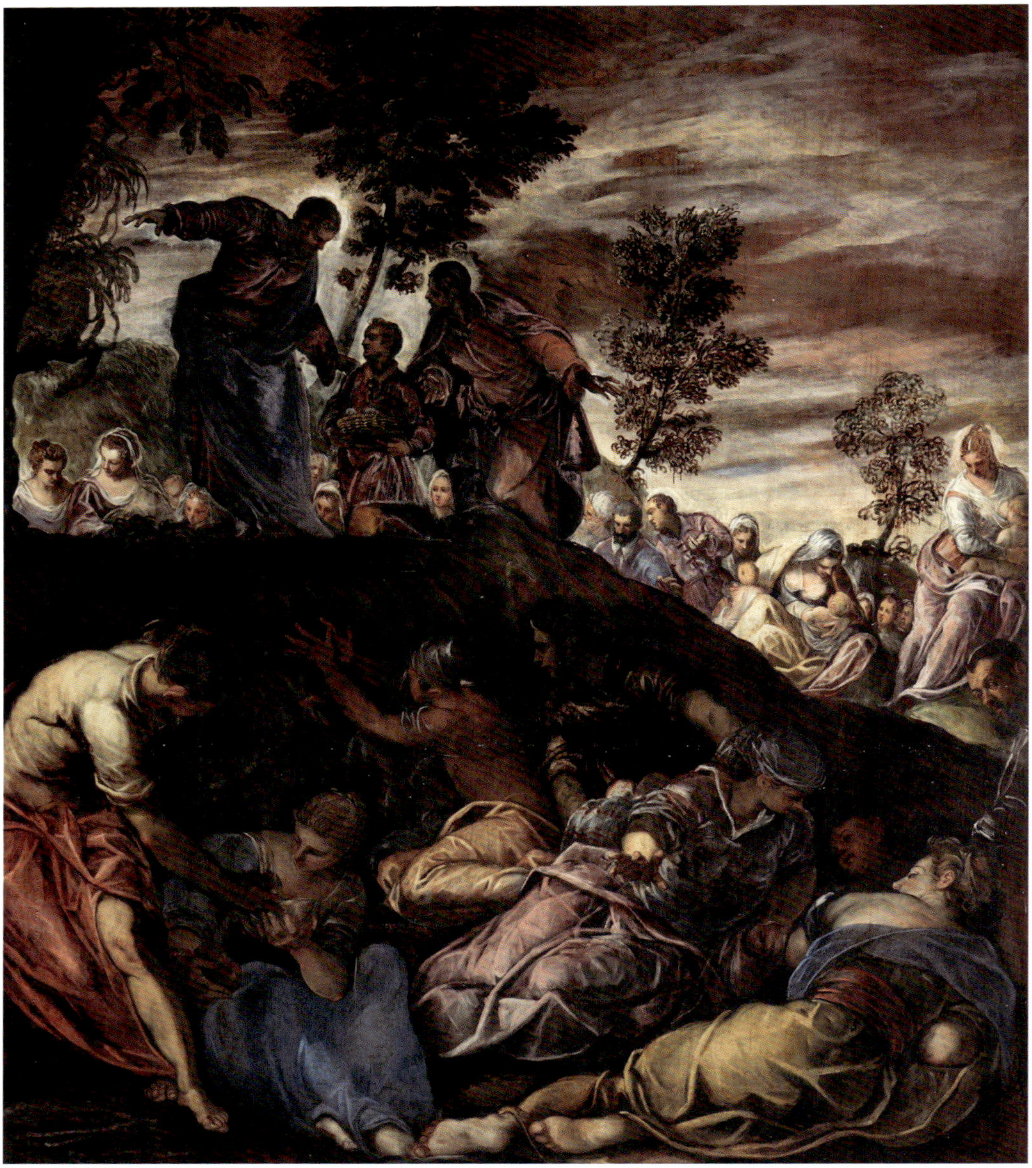

Fig. 48 - Miracle of the Loaves and Fishes

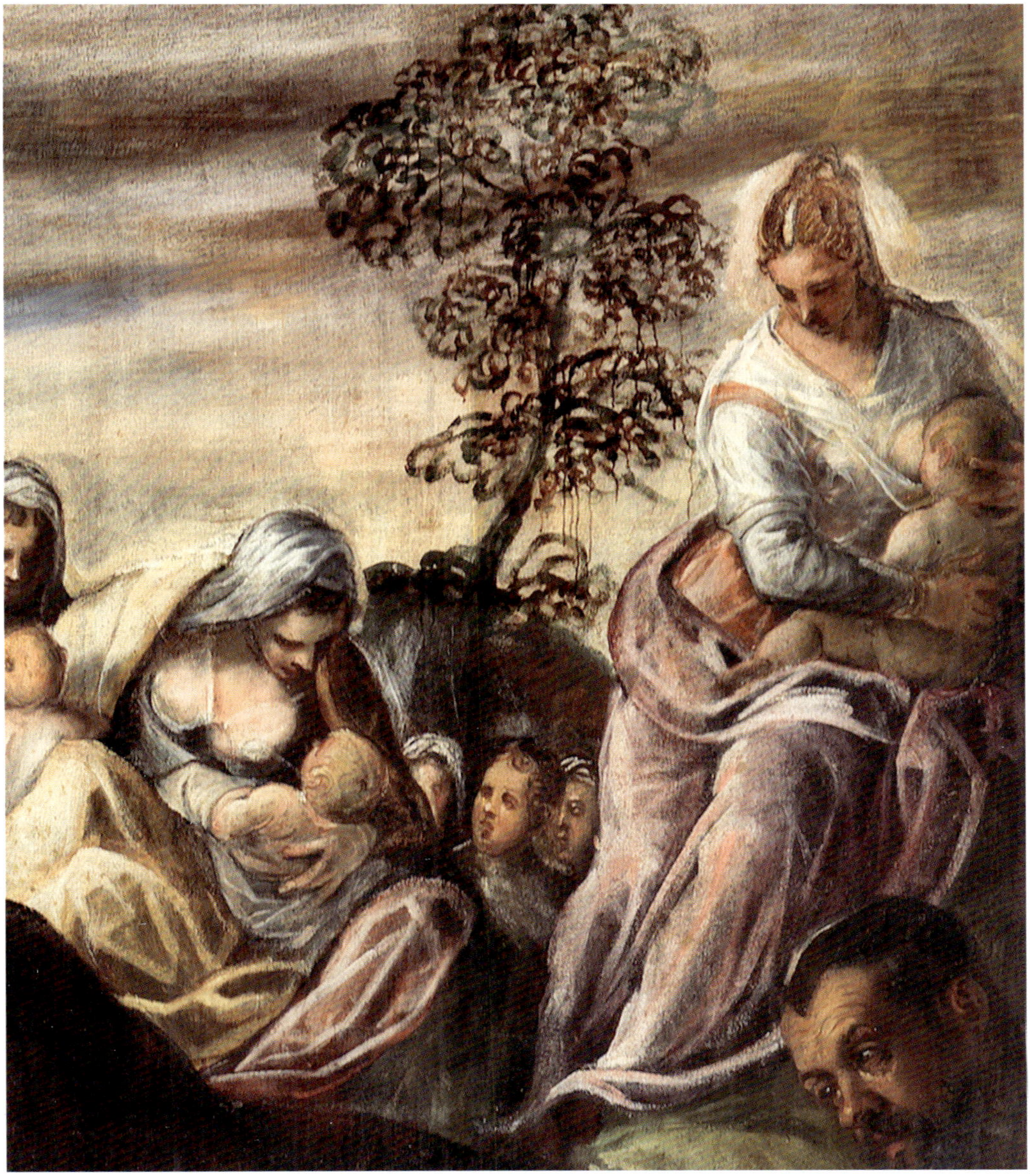

Fig. 49 - The women nursing in the background – here, as elsewhere, personifying Christian Charity – refer to the promise of Eucharistic bread, or rather to the body of Christ that in Charity breaks into pieces, to give itself by "multiplying itself"

The Sala Terrena

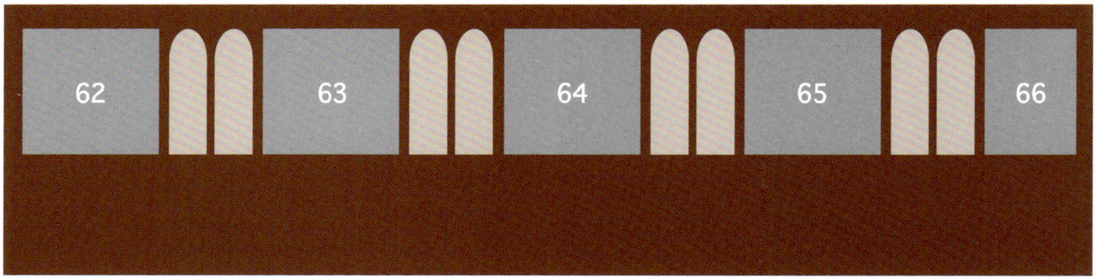

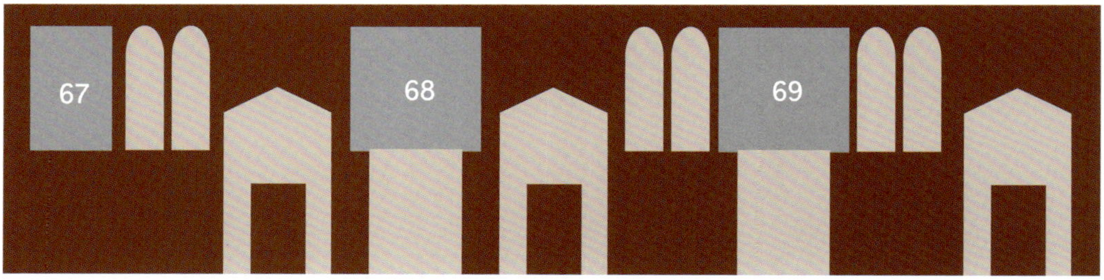

East wall

62. Annunciation
63. Adoration of the Magi
64. Flight into Egypt
65. Slaughter of the Innocents
66. Female figure reading

West wall

67. Female figure in meditation
68. Circumcision
69. Assumption of the Virgin

Contrary to other Scuole Grandi, the Sala Terrena in San Rocco was not a simple entrance hall used as a storehouse or as a mandatory passage through which one reached the upper floors. Although there are few documents that can today demonstrate its function, the altar in the Hall implies that the space occasionally served for liturgical purposes. It is known that the Hall was particularly used for musical performances and that all visitors coming to San Rocco one way or another passed through it. Therefore Tintoretto, helped by his son Domenico, decorated it with a series of *teleri* that are much richer in comparison to those in the other Scuole Grandi.

According to a recent hypothesis based on certain documentation, the paintings of the Sala Terrena were completed between

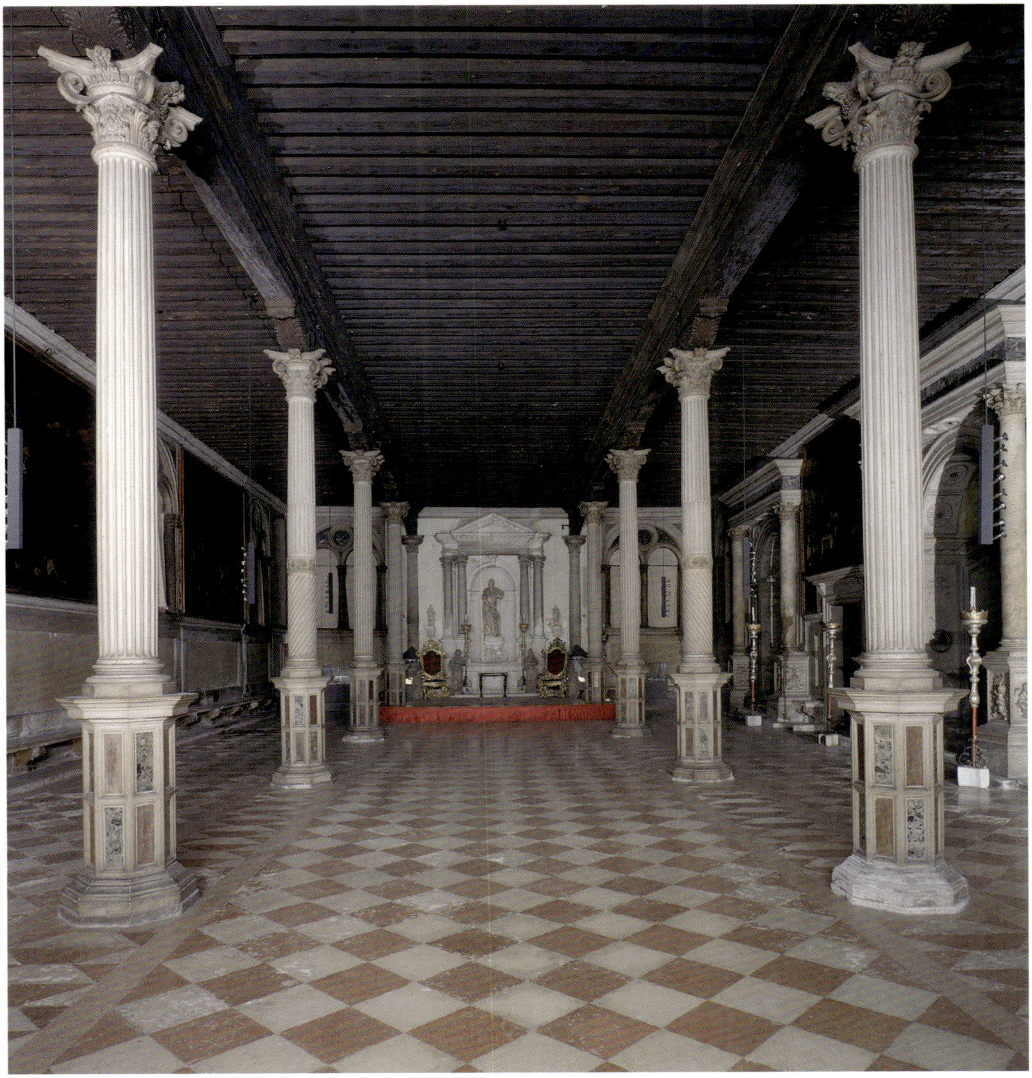

Fig. 50 - View of the Sala Terrena

1582 and 1584. It is a cycle dedicated to Mary: starting from the **Annunciation [62]** ***(note 22)***, the event in which Mary gives human life to the Son of God, the cycle continues with episodes in which the protagonists are Christ and the Virgin: the **Adoration of the Magi [63]**, the **Flight into Egypt [64]** ***(note 23)***, the **Slaughter of the Innocents [65]** and the **Circumcision [68]** ***(note 25)***. After the big staircase leading to the upper floor, the sequence ends with the **Assumption [69]**, which, according to some authors, shows a strong break with the previous themes, all related to Jesus' infancy. In reality, as was correctly noticed, the opening of the staircase expresses an ideal opening also to the paintings in the other halls, which depict Jesus' mission; the assumption, which occurs after the last events narrated on the first floor (the death, resurrection and ascension of Christ), is therefore considered an epilogue that concludes the life of the Mother of God.

Besides presenting some political aspects (such as the role that Venetian institutions played in dealing with poverty), theologically the cycle seems to be hinged on some central themes. The incarnation marks the beginning of the Son's historical mission; he is a real God and a real man. The episodes regarding Jesus' infancy allude to a historical event that from the start is connected to a "before" (the prophecies of the Old Testament) and to an "after" (Jesus' public mission and the Easter). In this sense Jesus' infancy is a mystery *(mysterion):* it is not closed in itself, but rather finds its profoundest meaning within a larger divine scheme, in a story of salvation that begins with the creation of the world, which Tintoretto has already illustrated in the typological relationships between the Old and the New Testaments of the Sala Superiore. Nevertheless, it is the story unfolding in this Hall, more than the typology, which better evokes the incarnation as a historical event: unique, unrepeatable, chronologically determined. It is in the opening to a "before" and an "after" that we can interpret the frequent references to the passion disseminated in the *teleri*, as well as the insistence on the theme of passing, which is set in the wonderful background landscapes of a fairytale Thebaid.

And it is in this context that we also understand Mary's role, which is, to use a common metaphor from medieval mysticism, simultaneously *reading* and *open book:* reading of the prophecies, which announce Jesus, and reading of Jesus, fulfillment of the prophecies; and at the same time book, which the Church must read. The entire cycle alludes to this role, especially with the two **female figures [66, 67]** in the last paintings on the walls, traditionally identified as St. Mary of Egypt and St. Mary Magdalene ***(note 24)***. Yet, these images can instead be depicting the Virgin Mary immersed in contemplative reading of the Scriptures; and Tintoretto invites the visitors to do the same, in order to understand the events told by the paintings in their historical and current meaning.

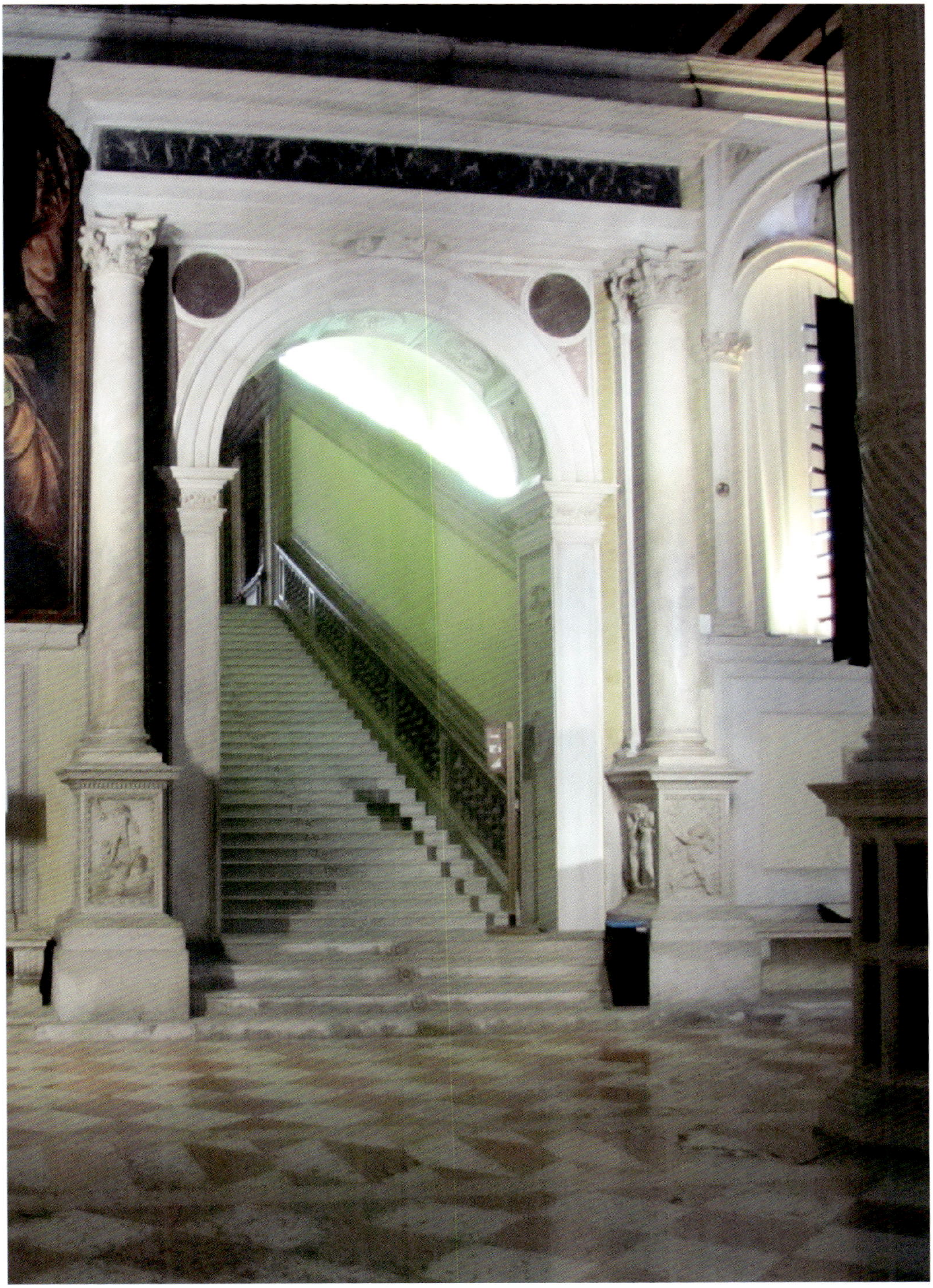

Fig. 51 - Sala Terrena, staircase leading to the Sala Superiore

22. ANNUNCIATION [62]

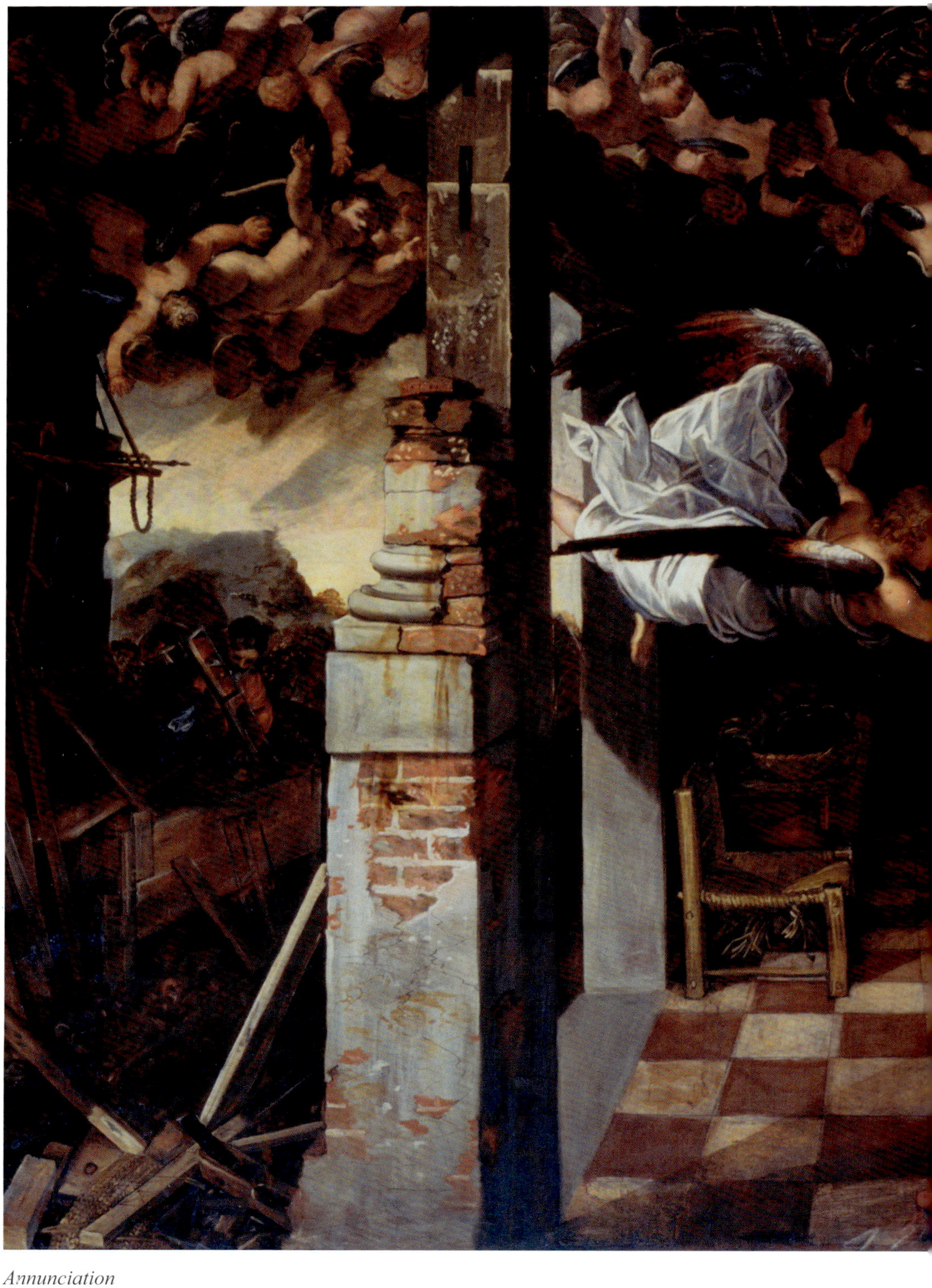

Annunciation

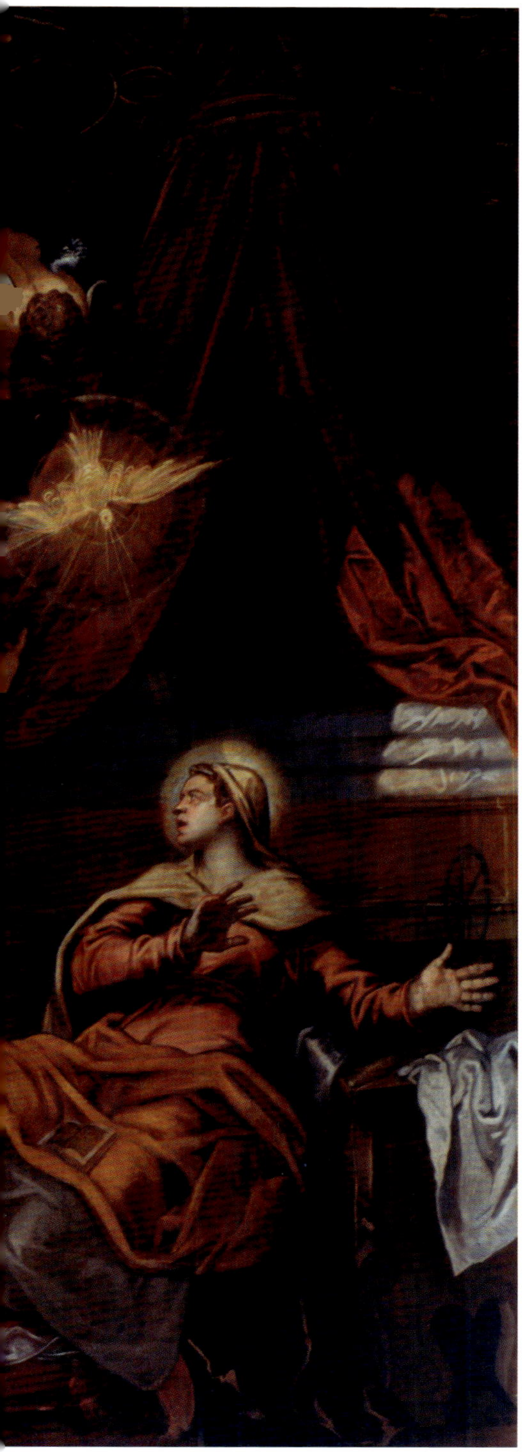

Now in the sixth month the angel Gabriel was sent by God to a city of Galilee named Nazareth, to a virgin betrothed to a man whose name was Joseph, of the house of David. The virgin's name was Mary. And having come in, the angel said to her, "Rejoice, highly favored one, the Lord is with you; blessed are you among women!" But when she saw him, she was troubled at his saying, and considered what manner of greeting this was. Then the angel said to her, "Do not be afraid, Mary, for you have found favor with God. And behold, you will conceive in your womb and bring forth a Son, and shall call His name Jesus. He will be great, and will be called the Son of the Highest; and the Lord God will give Him the throne of His father David. And He will reign over the house of Jacob forever, and of His kingdom there will be no end." Then Mary said to the angel, "How can this be, since I do not know a man?" And the angel answered and said to her, "The Holy Spirit will come upon you, and the power of the Highest will overshadow you; therefore, also, that Holy One who is to be born will be called the Son of God. (...) Then Mary said, "Behold the maidservant of the Lord! Let it be to me according to your word." And the angel departed from her. *(Luke 1:26-38)*

The Annunciation for Christians is the historical event that sanctions the Incarnation of the Word. Tintoretto presents the episode in a hall that, with a wooden ceiling and a two-tone floor, interacted with the original appearance of the space where the painting was collocated. This interaction is meant to create an analogy between

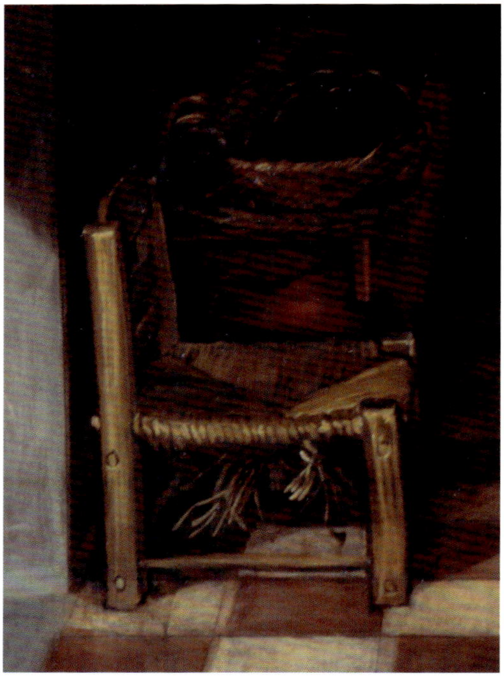

Fig. 52 - The chair with the ripped straw in a luxurious but collapsing room represents not only the Holy Family's humility, but also the passage between the two ages, from the Law of Moses to the Grace of Christ, Word Incarnate that takes the form of a servant

the Hall and that of the painting, an analogy that is needed to interpret the event. In fact, in this manner, more than just creating an illusion of continuity between pictorial and architectural space, Tintoretto wants to render the idea of *passage* more credible: in the same way that the visitor has just crossed the threshold of the Scuola, passing quickly from the open to the closed, the painting also clearly divides, by means of the mighty pillar located in the foreground, an open environment flooded by natural light and filled with daily activities from a closed environment, on which falls the solar light – but only slightly, not to cover the supernatural splendor that emanates from the Spirit's dove. It is a place of activity, not only material but also spiritual, where Mary is reading or praying with the help of a little book. In Mary prophecy and its fulfillment converge: the angel cites the prophecies that she is reading and precisely at that moment the prophecies are fulfilled in her.

The passage here is the one from the Age of the Law to the Age of Grace, which marks a radical renewal and overthrowing of all values. Mary herself, after the Annunciation, declares in the *Magnificat*: *"The Lord has shown strength with His arm; He has scattered the proud in the imagination of their hearts. He has put down the mighty from their thrones, and exalted the lowly. He has filled the hungry*

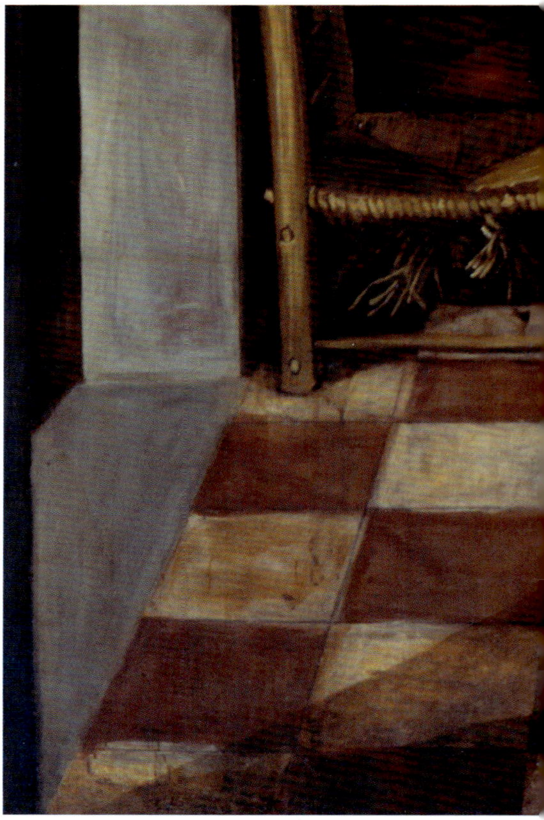

with good things, and the rich He has sent away empty" (Luke 1:51-53). The crumbling pillar, the remains of a once sumptuous building and the rickety chair with the ripped straw bottom ***(fig. 52)*** clearly show the transition between the two epochs, the dethroning of the powerful and the elevation of the humble.
Tintoretto depicts the moment in which Mary, astonished, is asking Gabriel how it is possible for her to conceive a child since she is still a virgin. *"The Holy Spirit will come upon you,"* responds the angel: the Spirit is in fact descending upon her from above, illuminating her head. *"And the power of the Highest will overshadow you,"* continues Gabriel. This image doubtlessly alludes to the divine cloud that in Exodus 33:7-11 casts its shadow over the sanctuary, indicating the presence of God. In the painting there is also a shadow that from the doorframe touches Mary's lap ***(fig. 53)***: the Virgin appears to be the holy tent upon which the hidden presence of God begins to act.

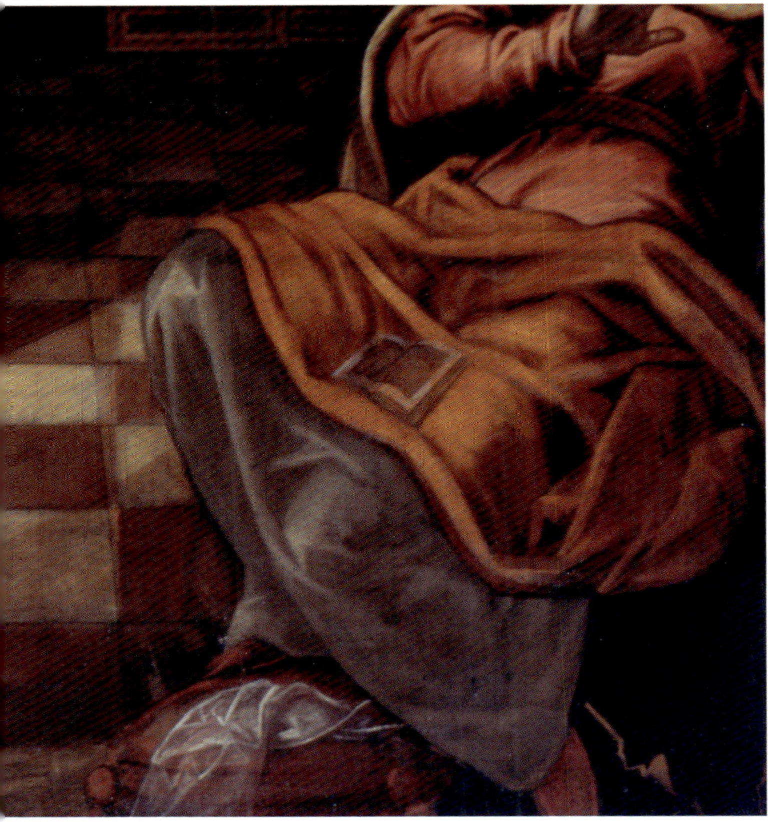

Fig. 53 - The pillar's shadow touching the Virgin's womb literally refers to Angel Gabriel's words: "And the power of the Highest will overshadow *(ubumbrabit)* you"

23. Flight into Egypt [64]

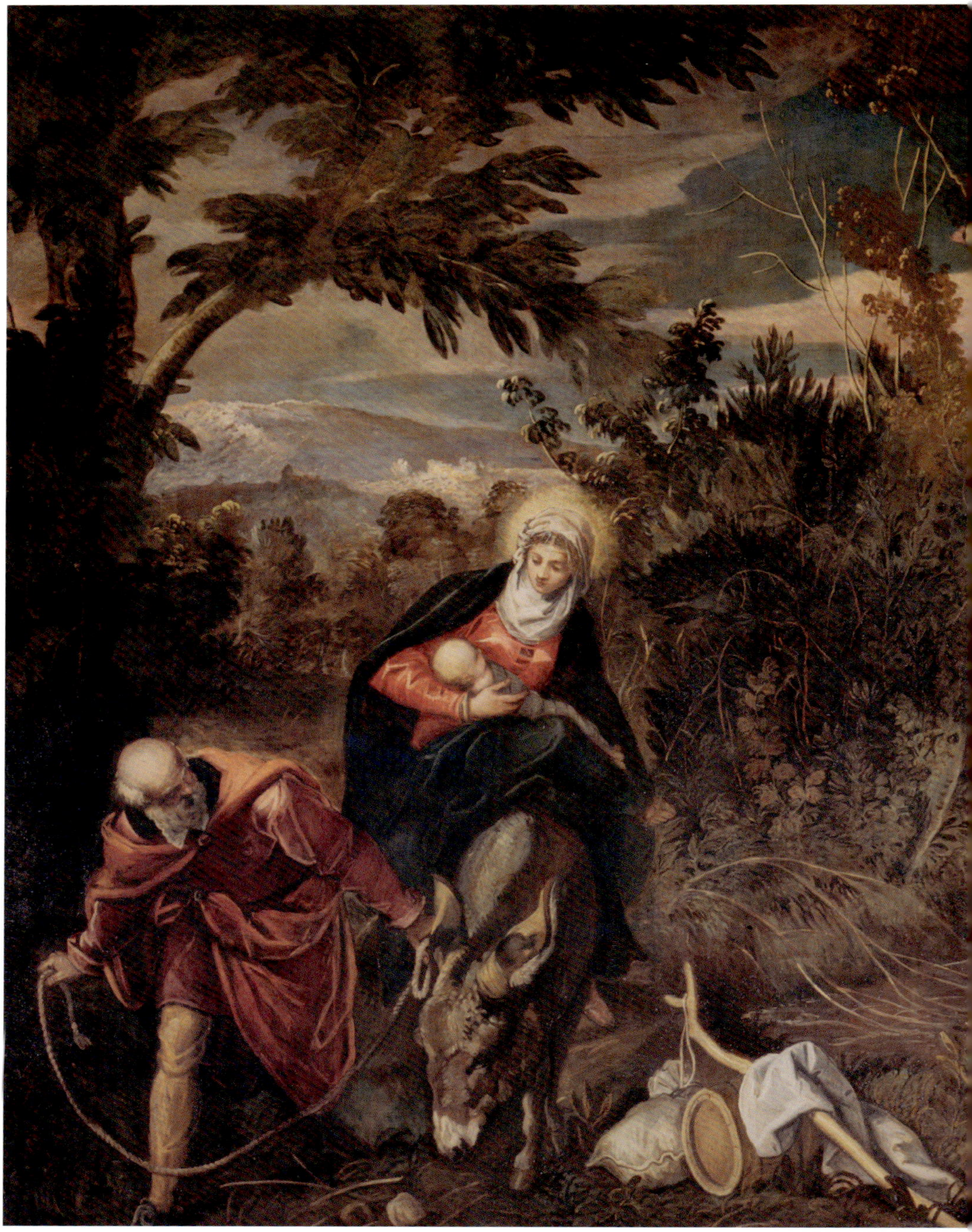

Flight into Egypt

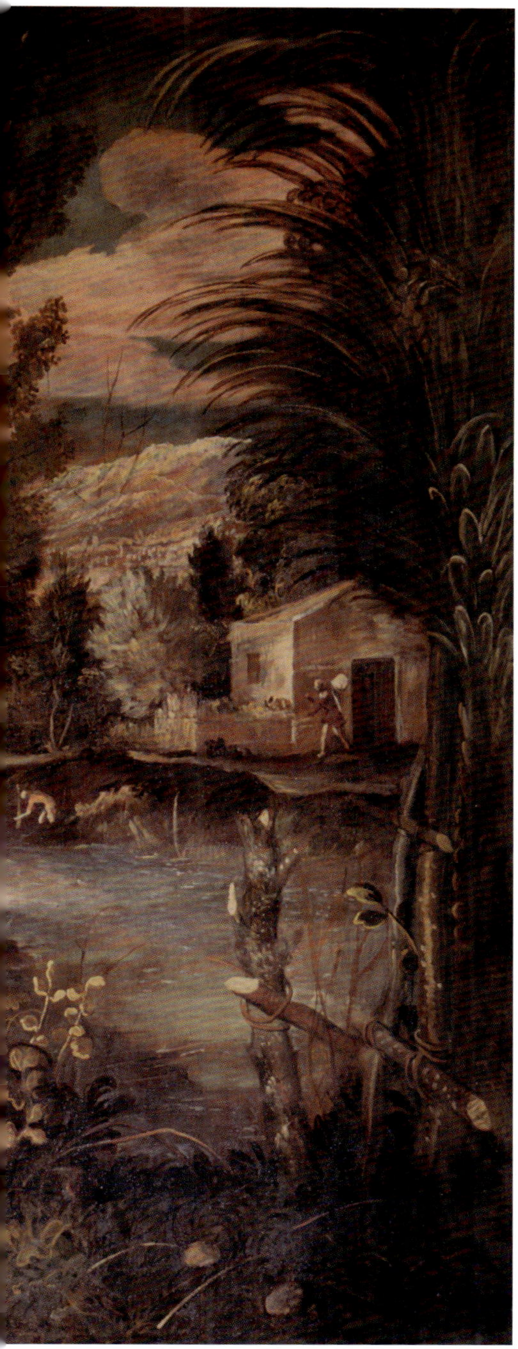

Now when they had departed, behold, an angel of the Lord appeared to Joseph in a dream, saying, "Arise, take the young Child and His mother, flee to Egypt, and stay there until I bring you word; for Herod will seek the young Child to destroy Him." When he arose, he took the young Child and His mother by night and departed for Egypt, and was there until the death of Herod, that it might be fulfilled which was spoken by the Lord through the prophet, saying, *Out of Egypt I called My Son. (Matthew 2:13-15)*

Matthew, in his Gospel, is the only one to remember the flight into Egypt, which in the apocryphal gospels (see box p. 123), along with many other events from the Lord's infancy, is instead described in great detail. In this painting Tintoretto is referring to the passage in the *Gospel of Pseudo Matthew.* Here the Virgin, exhausted from the heat, asks Joseph to stop and rest in the shade of a palm tree; seeing the tree full of dates, she would like to eat some but Joseph tells her it is impossible, for the tree is too high. Then Jesus, sitting on his mother's lap, commands the palm tree to bend over and give its fruits to Mary, which it does. The palm remains bent over until the Child orders it to rise. Jesus also tells it to make a spring pour out of the ground, from which the tree draws water with its roots, permitting Joseph, who is worried about the lack of reserves, to fill the water bags and refresh the mares. The Holy Family of the Scuola di San Rocco is captured in the moment in which Joseph, acting upon Mary's request, is stopping the donkey in order to let her get down. The palm tree hovers on the right, full of fruit. In the foreground and in central position a wayfarer's stick, a sack of provisions and a little barrel are lying on the ground, revealing their owners' intention to have a break. It has been noticed that the painter, although capturing a precise moment, is also depicting the episode in its entirety, inserting elements that advance the story: we see that both the tree's lowest branches on the left and the shrub behind Mary ***(fig. 54)*** are bent towards the ground, alluding to what the palm will do a bit later.

For the Evangelists Jesus' entire infancy is a fulfillment of old prophecies; the Church will root Jesus' childhood and adolescence in the prefigurative aspects of the Easter. Thus the references to the passion are present here as in many other *teleri* of the cycle. Joseph's worried look and sudden turn to the right reveal that he has noticed the three crosses at the foot of the palm tree, an obvious allusion to Golgotha ***(fig. 55)***. The palm that fructifies above the cross refers to the sacrifice of the seed that has to die in order to bear lots of fruit (John 12:24); and it is also the tree of Paradise, the one that Child Jesus mentions in the *Gospel of Pseudo Matthew*: *"Raise thyself, O palm tree, and be strong, and be the companion of my trees, which are in the paradise of my Father."* Also in the preceding paint-

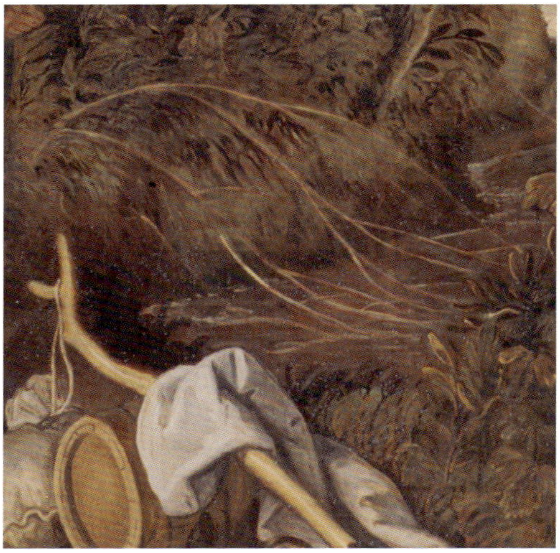

Fig. 54 - The shrub behind Mary is completely bent to the ground in expectance of the events about to occur; in fact, according to the apocryphal gospel of Pseudo-Matthew, the palm tree full of dates on the right of the painting will soon bend miraculously over Mary to give her some fruit

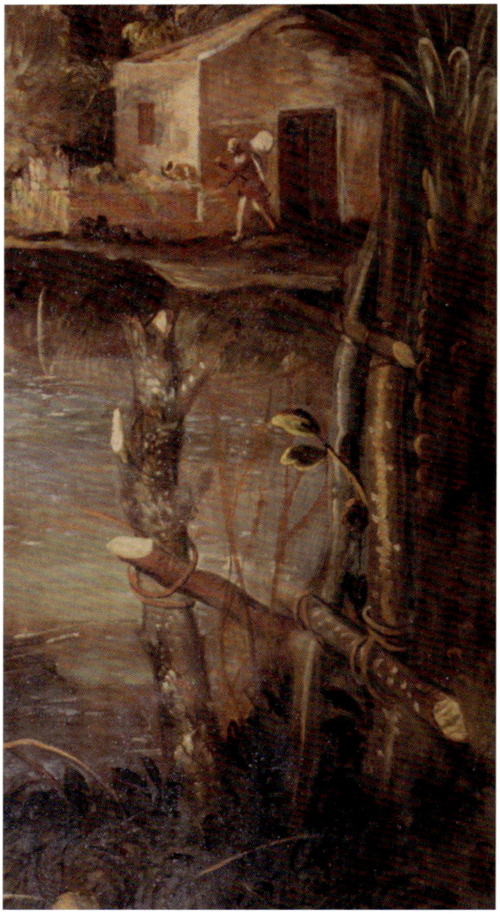

Fig. 55 - Three crosses, composed of what seems to be an old fence, refer to the Golgotha, prefiguring future events

ing, the **Adoration of the Magi [63]** ***(fig. 56)***, the cup and the golden vase in the form of a chalice, representing precious liturgical objects, allude to the Mass, and therefore to Christ's sacrifice; while in the **Annunciation [62]** ***(note 22)*** a young Joseph (or perhaps even, as hypothesized, adolescent Christ himself, if in this scene, as in others, Tintoretto is referring to the future with the aim of better defining the meaning of the work as a whole) intends to construct crosslike beams, above which we can spot a noose and a lance, instruments of the passion.

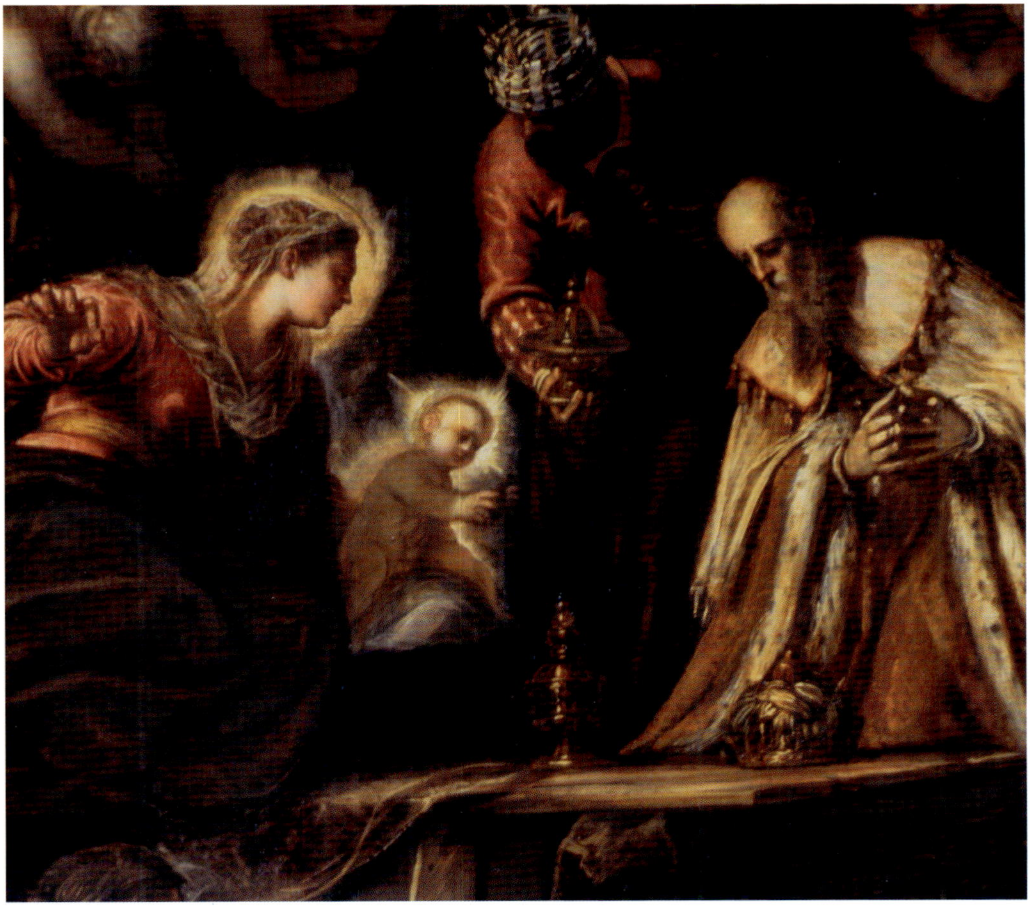

Fig. 56 - Adoration of the Magi, detail

24. Female figures reading and in meditation [66,67]

The two paintings ending the long walls of the Hall are different, in genre and format, from the cycle dedicated to Christ's infancy. In fact, they seem estranged from the course of the narration: no event is related here. The two female figures, immersed in a landscape that from up close resembles the one in the **Flight into Egypt [64]** ***(note 23)***, are captured near a stream, one while reading and the other while meditating. 19th century artistic literature interpreted them as Mary of Egypt and Mary Magdalene, both penitent saints whom 16th century painting often set amid wonderful landscapes. But their identity is not definite, with other theories also emerging about the women being Mary and her cousin Elizabeth, who the apocryphal gospels say fled into the desert after the **Slaughter of the Innocents [65]**. There are also theories about them personifying the Church and the Synagogue, about them being Mary and the Magdalene, but also about them being Mary captured in two different moments, in different times of day (sunrise and sunset).

Indeed the particular context in which the two paintings are positioned would inspire a purely Marian interpretation of the scene. The events related to Jesus' infancy are presented on the one hand as a realization of the prophecies contained in the Scriptures and on the other as a pre-

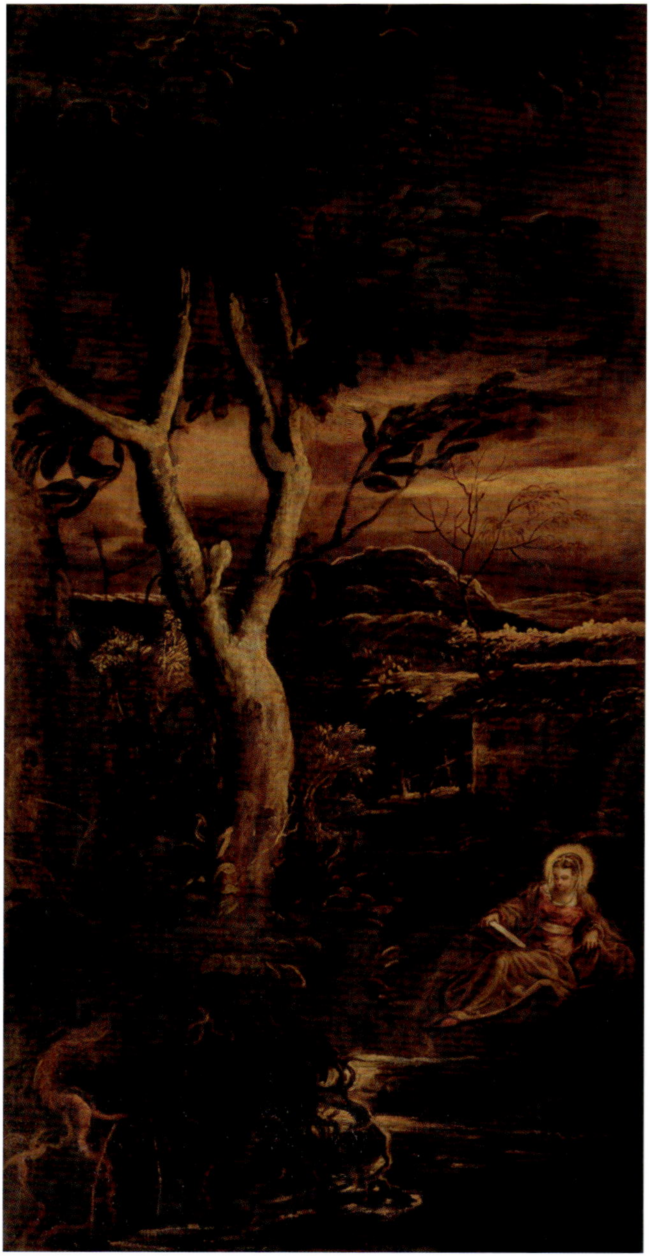

Female figure reading

vision of future events, above all of the passion. Mary here seems to be reflecting upon this continuously regenerated chain of prefigurations and realizations, contemplating past events and foreseeing the future ones. Starting with two passages from the Gospel According to Luke *(Mary kept all these things and pondered them in her heart,* 2:19; and *His mother kept all these things in her heart,* 2:51), a long series of medieval texts, above all monastic, clearly individuated the way in which the Mother of God was brought up in the faith, reading and profoundly understanding the Scriptures. According to this tradition, with the Scriptures having announced the reality to which Mary would bear witness, she is continuously comparing what she hears or reads (the prophets' sayings) with that which she sees (the facts of Jesus' life). Mary sees and reads, remembers and compares, in silent, incessant meditation. She thus becomes a model of meditative reading, which was particularly developed by monastic tradition that read the text in order to absorb it with the heart in an atmosphere of contemplative calm. This is the inseparable pair of actions, that of reading/listening and meditating, which Mary, starting from the Annunciation, is continuously performing. This is what the two paintings seem to be expressing.

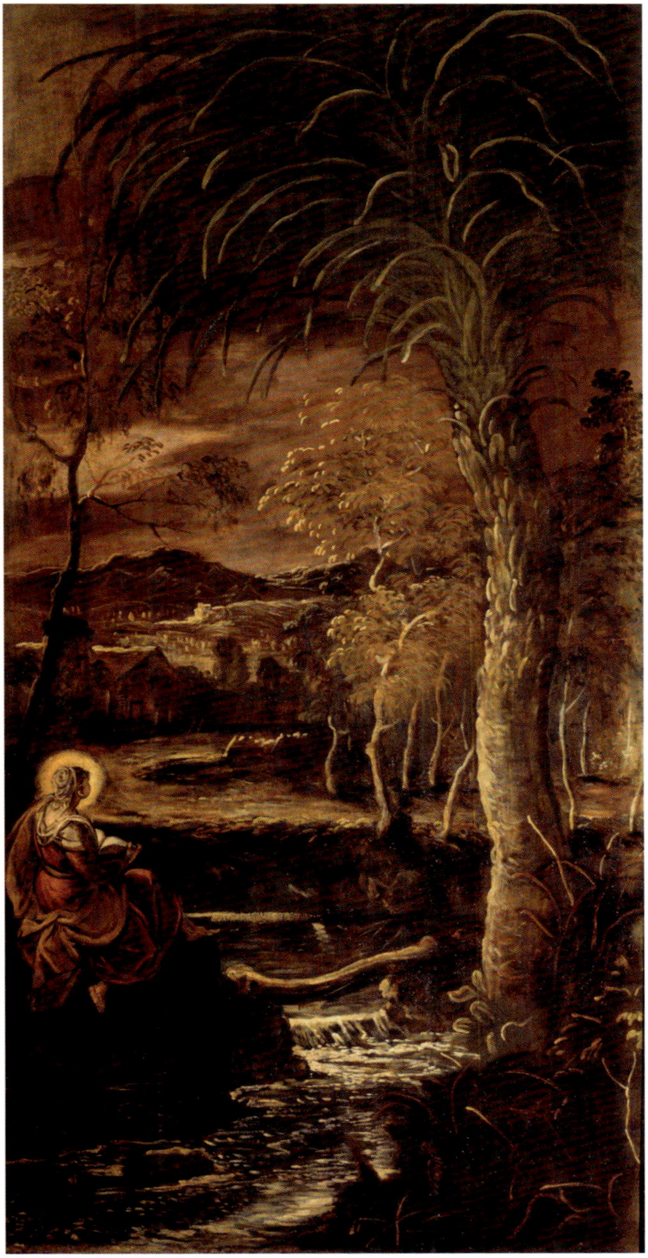

Female figure in meditation

25. Circumcision [68]

And when eight days were completed for the circumcision of the Child, His name was called Jesus, the name given by the angel before He was conceived in the womb. Now when the days of her purification according to the law of Moses were completed, they brought Him to Jerusalem to present Him to the Lord (as it is written in the law of the Lord, *Every male who opens the womb shall be called holy to the Lord)*, and to offer a sacrifice according to what is said in the law of the Lord, *A pair of turtledoves or two young pigeons. (Luke 2:21-24)*

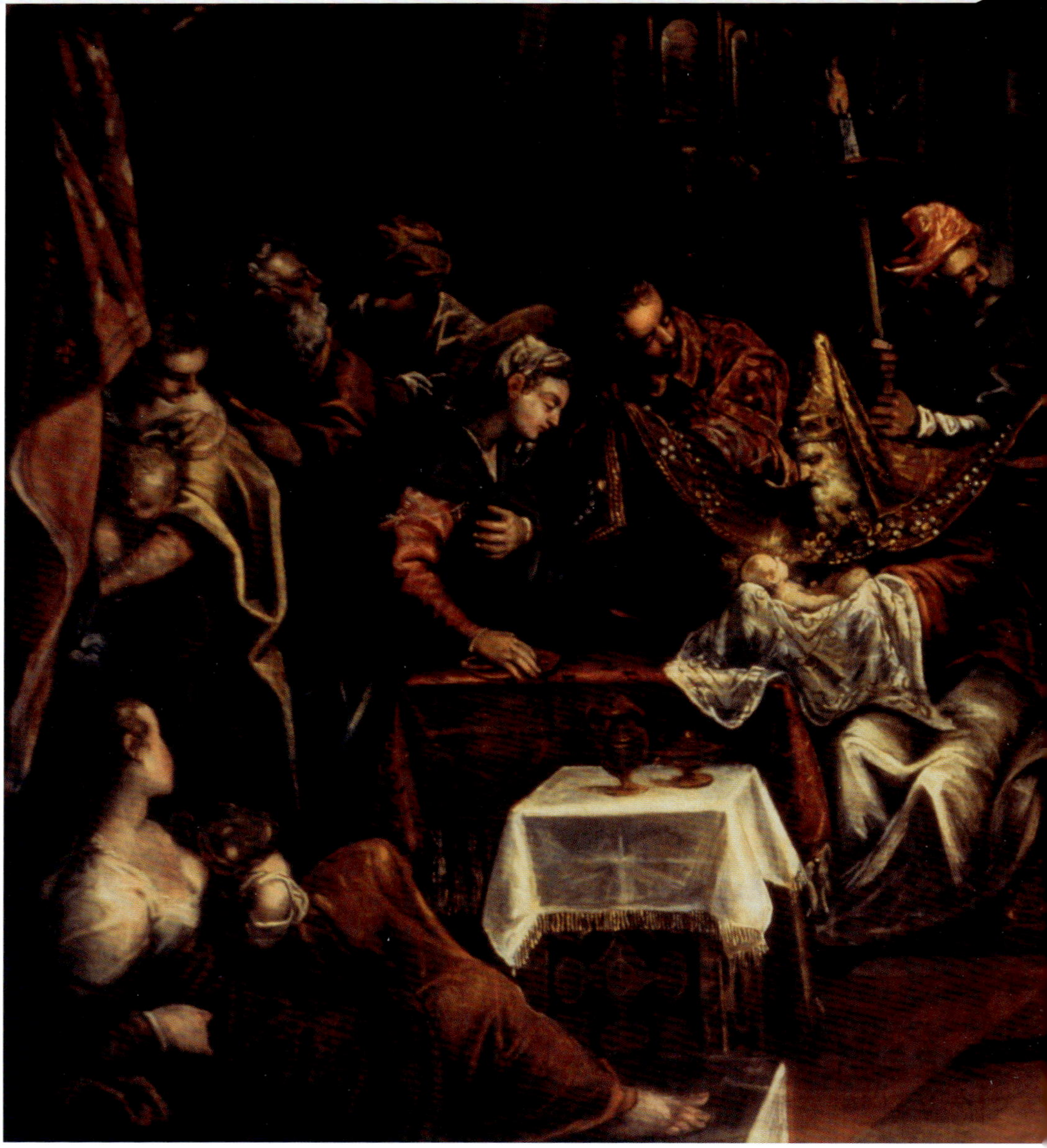

Circumcision

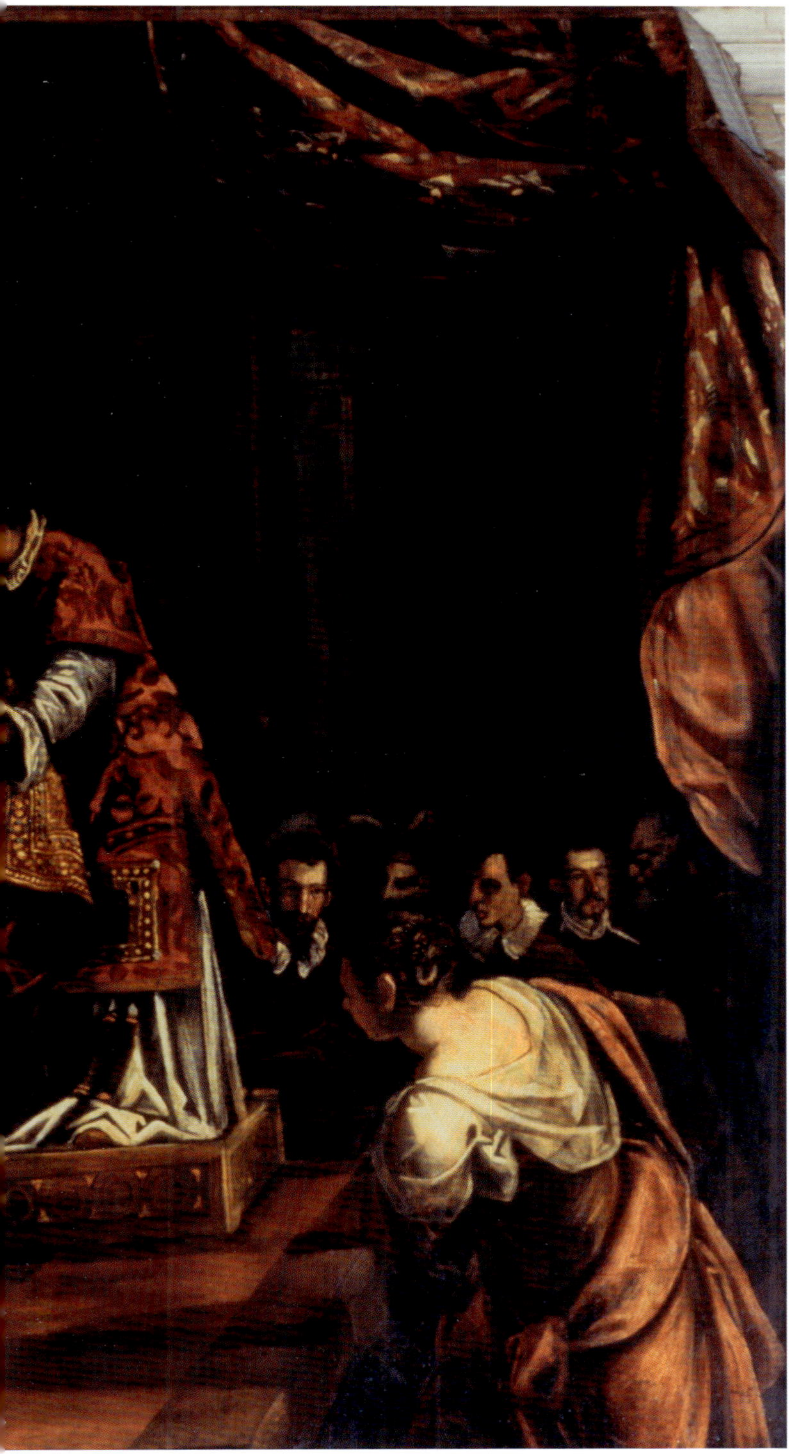

After the tumultuous **Slaughter of the Innocents [65]** ***(fig. 57)***, which concludes the series of narrative paintings on the eastern wall, the stories of Jesus' infancy continue with the **Circumcision.** Only Luke recollects the tale of the circumcision. Behind the high priest a cult attendant bears the cup with the blood that the Child has lost during the removal of the foreskin. The circumcision-passion link is evident and is sanctioned by the effusion of blood. As in the **Adoration of the Magi [63],** the liturgical vases placed apart on a little table ***(fig. 58)*** allude to the Eucharist, of which the circumcision is one of the first symbols.

To the right of the young priest a man is holding a candelabrum. The candle, which is entrancing Joseph, and the big hanging lamp perhaps evoke the liturgical celebration of the event that immediately follows, in the Gospel According to Luke, the circumcision, that is, the Presentation of Jesus in the Temple. It is the feast of the *Candelora* (February 2), in which all the church lamps were lit and the candles blessed in remembrance of the canticle with which Simeon – the just man to whom the Spirit had announced the vision of the Savior (Luke 2:25-35) – blesses God, defining Jesus as the *light to bring revelation to the Gentiles, and the glory of Your people Israel.* The feast also commemorates the Purification of Mary; in conformity with the Law of Moses, the mothers of firstborns presented themselves to the temple in order to be purified after the birth and to redeem their children with an offer. If this is how it was, the archpriest would here coincide with the figure of Simeon. The *Proto-Gospel of James* (see box p.123), in fact, says that he is the successor to the archpriest Zackary (chapter XXIV) and therefore in many works that illustrate the Presentation in the Temple we see him wearing the sacerdotal robe. Indirectly alluding to the Purification of Mary, Tintoretto's **Circumcision** in this way obtains more of a Marian connotation, in line with the Hall's cycle, which not by chance concludes with the **Assumption [69].**

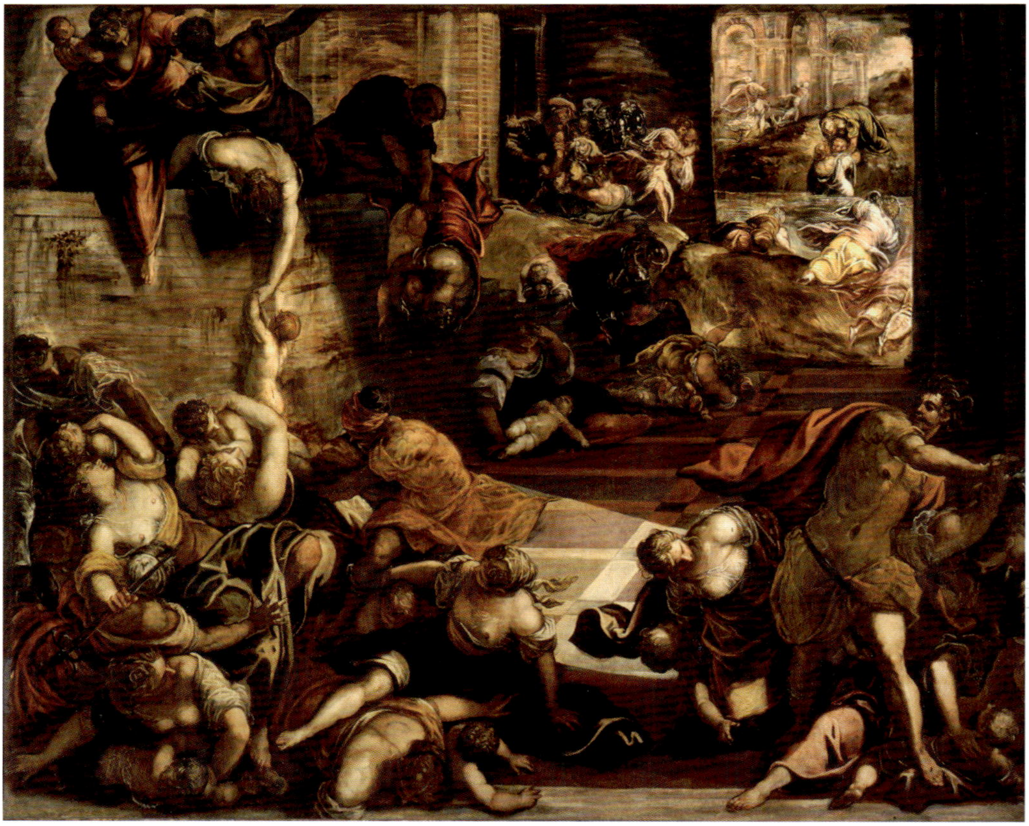

Fig. 57 - Slaughter of the Innocents

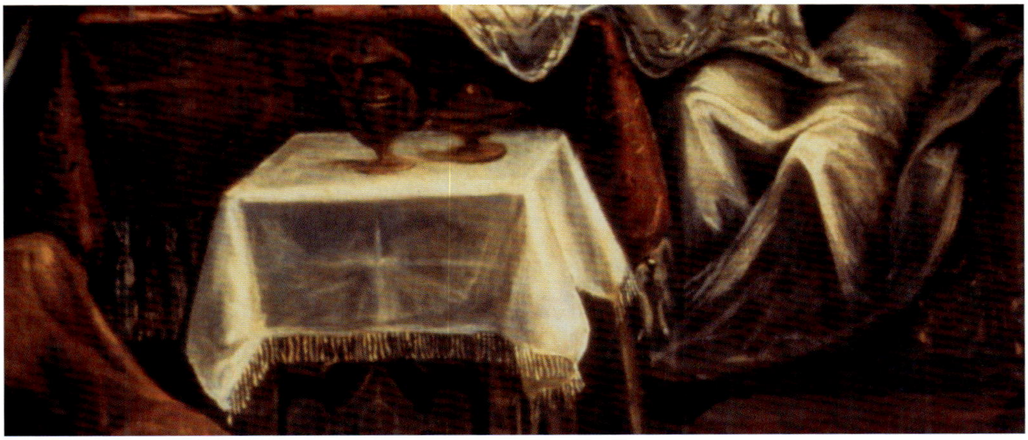

Fig. 58 - The liturgical vases on the table with the white tablecloth allude to the Eucharistic sacrifice, of which the blood of Jesus' circumcision is a prefiguration

The apocryphal gospels. One of the main art sources for illustrating the life of Mary and her son before the Baptism are the so-called apocryphal gospels of infancy. The apocryphal writings, which imitate the literary forms of the New Testament, were not welcomed by the Church in the Canon of Scripture because of their resemblance to legends and associations with heretical doctrine. The term apocrypha (hidden) often indicates not so much their secrecy, as esoteric writings reserved for initiates, but the fact that their exclusion from the canon made them remote, irrelevant, segregated. It can also refer to their origin, which is obscure and therefore unverifiable. Among the most important apocrypha of the infancy, besides the Pseudo-Matthew, are the so-called *Gospel of Pseudo-Thomas* and the *Proto-Gospel of James*. The latter work, which inspired Tintoretto to paint the cycle, and above all the **Adoration of the Magi [63]**, had been translated earlier from Greek to Latin by Guillaume Postel, an intellectual who was very controversial for his heterodox writings and who is considered to be present in the **Adoration** (perhaps he is the character kneeling down at the right in the foreground). His theories on mankind's need for purification and redemption from its guilt by means of a female figure, just like his exhortation to humble and assiduous acts of charity, could have influenced – provided they did not have any heterodox implication – some iconographic details of the Sala Terrena and the more general imposition of the Marian theme.

Essential Bibliography

Having been devised as a guide for easy consultation, the text does not present notes that make punctual references to literature written previously on the subject.
This editorial choice was obviously not made to appropriate in any manner the exegetic work that has been done, above all in the last twenty years, on religious themes present in the Tintoretto cycles at San Rocco, to which this guide is in great debt. The following are texts that the author considered fundamental sources for this book and are recommended for further study. As will be noticed, a great part of the texts cited comes from the journal *Venezia Cinquecento*, a formidable forge of iconographical studies; essential were also the studies carried out by Andrea Gallo, Giandomenico Romanelli, Astrid Zenkert, as well as some valuable theses and dissertations by young experts on modern art from the Università Ca' Foscari di Venezia.

BELLO, N., *Sotto le sue ali troverai rifugio. La Passione di Gesù Cristo di Jacopo Tintoretto nell'Albergo della Scuola Grande di San Rocco*, Graduation thesis for a degree in History of Modern Art from the Università Ca' Foscari, Venezia (tutor prof. A. Gentili), 2003-2004.

BRUNET, E., *«Aliter ulla salutis spes reliqua». Cristologia soteriologica nei dipinti di Jacopo Tintoretto nella Sala Superiore della Scuola Grande di San Rocco*, in *Marcianum* 6 (2010), 65-100.

CASELLATO, L., *Agonia e apologia. L'"Orazione nell'orto" nella cultura figurativa veneziana del Cinquecento,* in *Venezia Cinquecento* 25 (2003), 5-98.

DE TOLNAY, CH., *L'interpretazione dei cicli pittorici del Tintoretto nella Scuola di San Rocco*, in *Critica d'Arte* 7 (1960), 341-376.

GALLO, A., *Retorica tintorettiana*, in *Venezia Cinquecento* 9 (1995), 171-251.
- , *Scuola Grande di San Rocco. Le "Allegorie" di Iacopo Tintoretto nella Sala dell'Albergo*, (lecture notes from the course "Christian Iconography and Iconology", ISSR S. Lorenzo Giustiniani, Venezia, 2009-2010).

GENTILI, A., *Tempi della narrazione e tempo dell'allegoria. Tintoretto alla Madonna dell'Orto, a San Cassiano, alla Scuola Grande di San Rocco,* in ID., *La bilancia dell'arcangelo. Vedere i dettagli nella pittura veneziana del Cinquecento*, Bulzoni, Roma 2009, 215-243.

HÜTTINGER, E., *Die Bilderzyklen Tintorettos in der Scuola di S. Rocco zu Venedig*, Univ., Diss., Zürich 1962.

La Scuola Grande di San Rocco a Venezia. Testi, a cura di F. POSOCCO – S. SETTIS, («Mirabilia Italiae» 15), Franco Cosimo Panini, Modena, 2008.

MOZZETTI, F., *Educare per immagini: gesti di carità e attivismo caritatevole,* in *Venezia Cinquecento* 16 (1998), 53-80.

PERIA, B., *Tintoretto e l'Ultima cena*, in *Venezia Cinquecento* 13 (1997), 79-139.

ROMANELLI, G., *Temi biblici nel ciclo dei "teleri" di Tintoretto a San Rocco*, in *L'arte e la Bibbia. Immagine come esegesi biblica*, Atti del Convegno Internazionale di Studi «L'arte e la Bibbia», Venezia 1988, a cura di T. VERDON, Biblia, Settimello (FI) 1992, 191-217.
- , *Tintoretto a San Rocco. Pittura, teologia, narrazione,* in *Tintoretto. La Scuola Grande di San Rocco*, a cura di G. ROMANELLI, Electa, Milano 1994, 7-50.
- , *Tintoretto a San Rocco: committenza, teologia, iconografia,* in *Jacopo Tintoretto nel quarto centenario della morte*, Atti del Convegno Internazionale di Studi organizzato dal Dipartimento di Storia e Critica delle Arti "Giuseppe Mazzariol" dell'Università Ca' Foscari di Venezia, Venezia, 24 - 26 novembre 1994, a cura di P. ROSSI – L. PUPPI, Il Poligrafo, Padova 1996, 91-95.
- , *La luce e le tenebre. Tintoretto alla Scuola Grande di San Rocco*, Marsilio, Venezia 2011.

TAMBURIN, P., *Simbologia cristologica alla Scuola Grande di San Rocco. La sala superiore come anno liturgico*, Graduation thesis for a degree in History of Modern Art from the Università Ca' Foscari, Venezia (tutor prof. A. Gentili), 2005-2006.

THODE, H., *Tintoretto. Kritische Studien über des Meisters Werke,* in *Repertorium für Kunstwissenschaft* 27 (1904), 24-45.

Venezia e la peste, 1348-1797, exhibition catalogue, ed. by O. PUGLIESE, Marsilio, Venezia 1979.

ZENKERT, A., *Tintoretto in der Scuola di San Rocco: Ensemble und Wirkung*, Wasmuth, Tübingen 2003.

MARCIANUM PRESS S.r.l.
Dorsoduro, 1 - 30123 Venezia
Tel. +39-041-29.60.608 - Fax +39-041-24.19.658
marcianumpress@marcianum.it
www.marcianumpress.it

Published in June 2012
Stampa: GRAFICHE VENEZIANE (Venezia)